# Women's Work and Wages in the Soviet Union

*for*
*Tom and Alexander*

# Women's Work and Wages in the Soviet Union

ALASTAIR McAULEY
*University of Essex*

London
GEORGE ALLEN & UNWIN
Boston          Sydney

First published in 1981

GEORGE ALLEN & UNWIN LTD
40 Museum Street, London WC1A 1LU

© Alastair McAuley 1981

**British Library Cataloguing in Publication Data**

McAuley, Alastair
    Women's work and wages in the Soviet Union.
    1. Women – Employment – Russia
    I. Title
    331.4′0947      HD6166


ISBN 0-04-339020-X

Set in 10 on 11 point Press Roman by Katerprint Co. Ltd., Oxford
and printed in Great Britain
by Mackays of Chatham

# Contents

# List of Figures

# List of Tables

# Preface

This study is concerned with the extent to which the goal of sexual equality in employment, as set out, for example, in the Soviet constitutions of 1936 or 1977, has been realised in the USSR. I came to this topic as a logical extension of earlier work on the nature and extent of economic inequality in the Soviet Union and this remains my main focus; the subject has wider implications, however, not only for our understanding of the USSR but also for our perceptions of the way that labour markets operate in a more general setting. I hope, therefore, that this book will be of interest to feminists and labour economists as well as to those with a professional interest in the Soviet Union.

The research on which it is based was started in the summer of 1977; I am grateful to Norton Dodge, the Cremona Foundation and the Kennan Institute for providing surroundings and facilities that made the work so enjoyable. Facilities and materials have also been provided by the British Library of Economic and Political Science and the Alexander Baykov Library at Birmingham University; I would like to offer my thanks to the staff at both these institutions. But, above all, I am conscious of how much I owe to Stuart Rees at the Essex University Library; his tact and consideration and the extent of the collection that he has charge of make research at Essex a positive pleasure.

I should also like to acknowledge the receipt of a grant from the Nuffield Foundation. This, too, contributed to the ease with which the research was completed by facilitating the acquisition of materials.

I am grateful to those scholars who have read and commented on various versions of the manuscript. In particular, I should like to single out the following: Elisabeth Garnsey was discussant at a NASEES session in 1978 at which an early version of Chapters 2, 4 and 5 was read. Her comments have, I believe, substantially improved the cogency of the argument in the early part of the book. More recently, Gina Sapiro, Maxine Molyneux and Joy Townsend all read the manuscript in its entirety as did Gail Lapidus and an anonymous referee. Their comments and criticisms have saved me from gratuitous error and have forced me to reconsider my opinions on a number of topics. Such too has been the contribution of my wife, Mary McAuley; her insistence on clarity and logical argument have made this book much more readable than it would otherwise have been. I value her opinions most highly when she seems to care the least for mine. But, of course, I alone accept responsibility for the views expressed in this volume.

Finally, I would like to thank Neil Lewis for drawing the figures and Sheila Ogden for typing the most boring parts of the manuscript with accuracy, good humour and dispatch.

# Glossary

*babushka* literally grandmother, granny; used affectionately and familiarly to refer to any elderly woman.

*feldsher* feldscher, doctor's or surgeon's assistant; a medical auxiliary with secondary medical education, usually consisting of a three-year course at a medical training college.

*ITR (inzhenirno-tekhnicheskie rabotniki)* literally engineering-technical employees; used to describe the bulk of managerial and supervisory personnel in industrial and other enterprises, including foremen and technicians but excluding accounts department staff and secretaries.

*kolkhoznik* member of a *kolkhoz* or collective farm.

*kolkhoznitsa* feminine form of *kolkhoznik*.

*komandirovka* sending on business or a mission; usually involves the employee in spending one or more nights away from home – for which expenses will be paid.

*Narkom trud (Narodnyi komissariat truda)* People's Commissariat of Labour, the title of the organisation that functioned as a ministry of labour in the 1920s and early 1930s.

*PTU (professionalno-tekhnicheskoye uchilishche)* occupational-technical training establishment; trade school or vocational school; an establishment providing training for those wishing to acquire industrial skills.

*razryad* literally category, but here used to denote skill category, a component of the Soviet wages system. Virtually all manual workers are assigned to a *razryad* that depends upon the skills they have acquired and the degree of responsibility they are called upon to exercise.

*shturmovshchina* (pejorative) literally attacking by storm; used to describe the practice of using any and every method to fulfil plans at the last moment followed by relaxation at the beginning of the next period.

*sovkhoznik* a worker on a *sovkhoz* or state farm.

*sovkhoznitsa* feminine form of *sovkhoznik*.

*stavka* wage rate, basic wage.

*stazh* term or length of service, employment record.

*tarifnaya setka* wage scale; set of wage rates, differentiated by skill, payable to manual workers employed in a plant or industry.

*uravnitelnost (uravnilovka)* egalitarianism; a policy of (excessive) reductions in wage differentials, criticised by Stalin in the early 1930s and frequently still held to be undesirable today.

*VUZ (vysshee uchebnoye zavedenie)* higher educational establishment; a university or other educational institution that provides courses leading to a degree.

*Chapter 1*

# Sexual Equality in Socialist and Soviet Theory

*Der gesellschaftsliche Fortschritt lässt sich exakt messen an
der gessellschaftslichen Stellung des schönen Geschlechts
(die Hässlichen eingeschlossen).* [1]
    (Karl Marx to Ludwig Kugelmann, 12 December 1868)

Writers critical of the subordinate status of women in Western Europe and
North America have, for a long time, held up the USSR as a model of what
could be achieved, both in the economy and in society at large. (See, for
example, Smith, 1927, or Halle, 1934; for a recent example of this genre, see
Mandel, 1975.) But, too often I believe, such books have confused Soviet
aspirations with Soviet reality, have taken the exception for the rule, have
failed to consider the full range of available evidence; they do not explore
the shortcomings of Soviet policies along with their successes.

The first substantial Western analysis of the position of women in the
Soviet economy was published in 1966. In a seminal work, Dodge examined
the contribution that female employment had made to Soviet economic,
technical and scientific development. Subsequent papers by the same author
have explored the position of women in Soviet agriculture and in the
professions (Dodge and Feshbach, 1967; Dodge, 1971, 1977). Although he
was primarily concerned to chart the scale of female employment and assess
the contribution that women had made to various branches of the economy,
Dodge was obliged to raise wider issues: the nature and extent of educational
opportunities for women, the conflict between employment and motherhood,
Soviet policies towards the family and the provision of consumer services. In
all of these areas, the analysis given below echoes his in many important
respects. Its justification lies in the fact that it is organised according to a
different perspective (the contribution of various measures to the attainment
of sexual equality in the labour market) and also because it draws upon the
fruits of the renaissance of empirical sociology in the USSR - a process that
had barely got under way when *Women in the Soviet Economy* was written.

The position of women in Soviet society has been the subject of a number
of other recent studies, both Soviet and Western. The findings of Soviet
sociologists and economists are discussed in detail in the chapters that follow.
Here I concentrate on the work of Western scholars whose analysis has

influenced my thinking. Lapidus's study *Women in Soviet Society* was published in 1978 but was preceded by a number of papers that deal with particular aspects of her thesis. (See Lapidus, 1975a, 1975b, 1976.) In these papers Lapidus charts the expansion of female participation in polity, economy and society but argues that 'the terms on which it occurred both sustained and reinforced a pervasive asymmetry of male and female roles' (Lapidus, 1978, p. 335). This asymmetry she ascribes not only (and certainly not mainly) to the social and political circumstances in the USSR during the period of modernisation. The failure of Soviet women to achieve equality cannot be attributed to the cultural backwardness of the country in 1917 or 1928; it cannot be attributed to the exigencies of war, civil war and revolution; it cannot even be attributed to the distortions in social priorities implicit in 'forced draft' industrialisation under Stalin, although all of these factors contributed to the peculiar position of women in Soviet society in the 1960s and 1970s. Lapidus argues that the analysis of sexual equality by Marx, Engels and Lenin is both limited and contradictory. Despite a formal adherence to the desirability of sexual equality, all three tended to regard the sexual division of labour as natural and all three displayed 'an unwillingness to confront a set of issues that was potentially disruptive to class solidarity' (Lapidus, 1978, p. 338). The shortcomings of socialist ideology have been accentuated in the process of their adaptation to the Soviet environment. Russian traditional concepts of service and 'common cause' served to transform a concern for equality into an acceptance of equal liability for mobilisation. Thus, although Lapidus does not question the commitment to sexual equality in socialist theory or even Soviet ideology, she does cast doubt on the adequacy of the analysis that underlies that commitment. She is also doubtful about the priority that has been ascribed to the goal of equality in the past half-century and about the primary objectives of the policies that have been adopted. Rather, she suggests that the changes in female roles that have occurred in the USSR since 1928, if not 1917, have been the product of a modernisation drive whose focus was mobilisation and not equality.

Lapidus's work is but one example of a recent resurgence of interest in the position of women in the USSR. Although the explosive growth of women's studies in the USA has not yet affected the Soviet field (a recent catalogue of doctoral dissertations on feminism and women's studies listed only two out of 680 concerned with the position of women in the USSR and Eastern Europe – but this may reflect the idiosyncracies of its compilers rather than the state of affairs on American campuses), a number of sociologists and historians have turned their attention to this question. There are detailed studies of the position of women in the pre-revolutionary economy and society either under way or in publication; the role of women in the early post-revolutionary years has also received attention. Further, scholars have turned their attention to early Soviet policies on education, on the family and family law, on the development of the social services. All of these have implications for the evolution of Soviet attitudes towards sexual equality. (For a sample of recent work on these questions, see Atkinson, Dallin and Lapidus, 1977, and further references cited therein; see also Massell, 1974,

Sacks, 1976, and Heitlinger, 1979.) These studies afford us a clearer idea of the complexities involved in attempts to chart the evolution of women's roles in the USSR, allow us to distinguish more precisely, perhaps, between the impact of modernisation, urbanisation and industrialisation on the one hand and that of socialist ideology on the other. They also permit an assessment of the contribution that Russian history and Russian cultural traditions have made to the position of Soviet women today.

Another thought-provoking book is Hilda Scott's *Women and Socialism* (2nd edn, London, 1976). Although the empirical material in it is drawn from Eastern Europe, primarily Czechoslovakia, it does raise many of the issues that are of concern in this field. And, in fact, its emphasis on other socialist countries adds a comparative dimension. Like Lapidus, Scott concludes that women in Eastern Europe have not yet attained equality in the economy or in society at large. But her analysis of the sources of this failure contains different emphases. She would argue that both the founding fathers of scientific socialism and the governments of socialist countries in Eastern Europe have a more honest commitment to sexual equality than Lapidus suggests. But sexual equality has only been one among a number of social objectives; often, its attainment has been surrendered in the interests of other goals. Also, there are shortcomings in the socialist analysis of the sources of sexual inequality. These have led to the adoption of inappropriate policies.

My own conclusions are probably closer to those of Hilda Scott than Gail Lapidus. But taking sides in this dispute (if dispute there be) has not been a primary concern. Rather, I have attempted to collate available evidence on the scale of female employment, on the jobs done by men and women, on differences in their earnings. Secondly, I have tried to ascertain why a legal framework that precludes wage discrimination and, in many respects, guarantees equality of opportunity has apparently failed to bring about equality in earnings and, indeed, despite certain notable successes, has not inhibited the growth of occupational segregation. The material presented here should contribute to our understanding of the position of women in the Soviet economy. This, in turn, may affect assessments of the scale and character of sexual inequality in Soviet society. Also, I hope, an analysis of Soviet policies towards the employment of women will have some relevance for the formulation of policies designed to achieve greater equality for women in Britain and other market economies.

As Scott and Lapidus suggest, Soviet attitudes towards sexual equality and Soviet policies towards female employment have been conditioned, if not determined, by the analysis of these questions to be found in the works of Marx and Engels (although this assertion has been challenged). Consequently, the rest of this chapter is devoted to a brief statement of their views and of the way that these have been incorporated into the framework of Soviet policy.

## The Soviet Theory of Sexual Inequality

The Marxist analysis of sexual inequality can be paraphrased as follows: women's inferior status under capitalism is a consequence of their dependence upon men within the context of the bourgeois family. This, in turn, derives its *raison d'être* from the existence of private property. The implication is thus clear. The abolition of private property will lead to far-reaching changes in the nature of the family; it will lead to the emergence of women from the confines of the domestic hearth, to their assumption of the full range of political, economic and social roles. The socialist revolution, then, will result in the eradication of sexual inequality and the exploitation of women by men, just as it will result in the elimination of class inequality and the exploitation of workers by the owners of property.

This analysis was based upon a realisation that the family, the structure of family relationships, far from being immutable, from being determined by biological necessity, was a social institution. Like other social institutions it was susceptible to change in response to changes in economic relationships. With the development of capitalism, if not with the decay of primitive communism, the family became a social vehicle for the accumulation, preservation and inter-generational transmission of property. This, in turn, involved the introduction of monogamy; it implied the subjection of women to men. The development of machine-based industry had two further consequences for the nature of family relationships. The enormous expansion in productive capital and its concentration in the hands of a few families emphasised the property aspects of marriage among the bourgeoisie. It underlined the loveless nature of bourgeois marriage and condemned the wives and daughters of the middle class to a life of circumscribed and sterile idleness. On the other hand, by simplifying the tasks involved in productive labour, by reducing the demands they made upon the physical strength of the operative, a whole range of new employments was opened up to women and even children. Industrialisation had the effect of destroying family life for the vast majority of the population, of emasculating men and dehumanising women.

This view of the family and its role in the propagation of sexual inequality is to be found in the Communist Manifesto of 1848; it is articulated at greater length, with a wealth of supporting material, in Engels's *The Origin of the Family* in 1884. Both works contain, I believe, a certain ambivalence towards the employment of women. In the Manifesto, for example, Marx and Engels write:

> On what foundation is the present family, the bourgeois family based? On capital, on private gain. In its completely developed form this family exists only among the bourgeoisie. But this state of things finds its complement in the practical absence of the family among the proletarians, and in public prostitution.
> The bourgeois family will vanish as a matter of course when its complement vanishes and both will vanish with the vanishing of capital. (Communist Manifesto, Moscow, 1955, p. 86)

That is, the vanishing of capital, after the revolution, will lead to the emergence (or re-emergence) of family relations among the working class. Certainly the socialist family is consistent with, indeed is predicated upon, the widespread participation of women in production. But there is a sense in which outside employment is less important for women than for men. Both Engels and Marx were affronted by examples of role-reversal (in which men stayed at home while women went out to work) occasioned by the industrial revolution in England; both give the impression that they think it right that a man should come home to his wife and children. Their abhorrence of the conditions in which women were frequently employed in early factories led them to support the introduction of special legislation regulating the terms and conditions of women's employment – an element that has remained part of the socialist programme to this day.

By the early years of the twentieth century, this Marxist analysis had crystallised into a distinctively socialist perception of the sources of sexual inequality and a socialist programme for its eradication. This was formulated succinctly, if not persuasively, at the Third Comintern Congress in Moscow in 1921. Among the theses of a report on Methods and Forms of Work among Communist Party Women it was stated:

> Women should understand firmly: the enslavement of women in all its forms grows out of bourgeois society. In order to eradicate female slavery it is necessary to go over to a communist structure of society. (*Kommunisticheskii* . . . , 1933, p. 245)

From this proposition two consequences follow: women, particularly working-class women, can gain nothing from collaboration with bourgeois feminist organisations. At best, these are concerned with superficial manifestations of the subordination of women, with the right to vote, with equality of opportunity in education, and so forth. At worst, they are concerned with irrelevancies. Collaboration can only dissipate revolutionary energies and may strengthen bourgeois social institutions. Secondly, since the attainment of sexual equality is predicated upon the attainment of social equality (and since, implicitly at least, it follows almost automatically from the eradication of class relationships based on private property), there can be no justification for a separate women's organisation.

At the same time, the communist parties, meeting in Moscow, adopted the following programme, pledging themselves to work for the following measures that would alleviate if not eliminate sexual inequality:

> The social equalisation of women and men in law and everyday life, the radical restructuring of marriage and family law, the acknowledgement of motherhood as a social function, protection for motherhood and childhood. A beginning to the provision by society of care for children and young people and their training, *vospitanie* (day-nurseries, kindergartens, homes, etc.). The construction of institutions for the gradual elimination of domestic work (public kitchens and laundries), a conscious, *planomernaya*, cultural campaign against the ideology and traditions that result in the enslavement of women. Prohibition, as a rule, of nightwork and work in exceptionally harmful industries of all persons of the female sex. Prohibition of child labour. Prohibition of overtime work. (*Kommunisticheskii* . . . , 1933, p. 22)

For most of the signatories, these remained no more than objectives; only the CPSU was in power and only in the RSFSR[2] was a start made at implementing them.

As I show below (see Chapter 9), many of these provisions were included in the labour legislation of the 1920s and in various social security regulations. Some effort was also made to encourage the development of pre-school child care facilities and consumer services. But the Soviet economy remained backward; added to which, the disruptions of war and civil war, of urban unemployment and rampant inflation, meant that few resources were devoted to these social programmes. It remains a moot question how far the protection built into the law was operational, even for the urban population, in the 1920s. It was never intended to apply to the peasantry, who continued to form four-fifths or more of the population.

Among the urban intelligentsia, and possibly among certain members of the working class, the 1920s witnessed a measure of intellectual ferment, a preoccupation with new forms of family arrangement, even with sexual liberation. A number of more or less utopian visions of the communist future were produced in which the state assumed the parents' responsibilities for the care and upbringing of children and in which men and women were free to form liaisons guided only by infatuation, romantic love, or the transitory urgings of sexual desire. Although some of the advocates of the new 'communist' family urged that a start should be made immediately in the transformation of personal relationships and social responsibilities, there is little to suggest that these calls for action evoked any widespread response among the population at large. At least, I believe that the substantial growth in the number of homeless orphans, of one-parent families and the persistence of certain forms of prostitution can as plausibly be attributed to the social dislocation attendant on war and revolution as they can to the decay of so-called moral standards.

But such was not, perhaps, the perception of some members of the Soviet government in the mid-1920s. As part of its attack on religion, the party had introduced changes in the Marriage Code as early as 1918. These had the effect of restricting recognition to marriages registered with the civil authorities and of restricting liability for support to recognised marriages. In 1925–6 the government proposed the introduction of a new marriage law that, *inter alia*, would extend recognition to *de facto* unions as well as extending liability for support. In spite of the date (it occurred during the period of conflict between Stalin and Trotsky) these proposals were the occasion of a good deal of controversy that, in the words of one recent study:

> ... emphasised the persistence of other perhaps more fundamental schisms within Party and society; the traditional division between the sexes and, to a lesser extent, the friction between the generations. These schisms transcended not only temporary political alignments but even, at times, the rural–urban cleavage. For the future of women and the family in Soviet Russia they were enormously significant.[3]

Even making allowances for a certain amount of special pleading on the part of a specialist, this conclusion underlines the existence of differing attitudes towards marriage and the family within Soviet society and, particularly, within its policy-making elite.

The adoption of central planning and the commitment to forced industrialisation resulted in changes in the nature of the Soviet conception of sexual equality. The role of the family was strengthened in two respects. It, rather than the state's social security system, became the 'provider of last resort' in law as well as in practice. It also became the locus for the care and upbringing of children and the provision of consumer services. For the forseeable future, the state's role was reduced to one of providing assistance. Again this was a formal change. The family had continued to provide these services for the vast majority of Soviet citizens in the 1920s as it had before the revolution.

This conception of the family has so completely permeated Soviet consciousness that the following vision of the communist future (published in 1964 by a man who was active in the 1920s) evokes little support; it even gives rise to a *frisson* of horror among some official spokesmen (and myself, I may add):

> Recognising that social forms of child care are undoubtedly superior to all others, we must continue to expand these facilities at such a rate that, in fifteen or twenty years time, they will be freely available to the population of the country – from the cradle to the age of majority. Each Soviet citizen, on leaving the maternity home, will be sent to a day-nursery; from there he will go on to a children's home or a kindergarten with twenty-four hour attendance; afterwards, he will go on to boarding-school from which he will set out upon his independent life – either in production or in further study of his chosen speciality. (Strumilin, 1964, in Urlanis, 1976, p. 74)

Although in recent years there has been a revival of interest in schemes for the socialisation of housework (as opposed to the production of durables like washing-machines that would reduce the time and effort spent on household chores), this proposal for the socialisation of child care has largely failed to strike an echo among modern sociologists or, as far as I can tell, among the population at large.

Secondly, the importance of female employment was underlined. Both the right and, implicitly, the obligation of women to find gainful employment were written into the 1936 Constitution and this was made the primary source of sexual equality:

> A woman in the USSR is afforded equal rights with a man in all areas of economic, civil, cultural and socio-political life.
>
> The possibility of realising these women's rights is guaranteed by offering to the woman, on the same terms as to a man, *ravnogo s muzhchinoi*, the right to work, to payment for labour, to rest, social insurance and education, [by offering] state protection of the interests of mother and child, state assistance to single mothers and those with many children, by providing for women maternity leave with financial support,

[by the maintenance of] and extensive network of maternity homes, day-nurseries and kindergartens. (Constitution of the USSR, 1936, Article 122)

The 1936 Constitution, then, envisages a society in which both men and women work but one in which legal responsibility for the care and upbringing of children is still vested in the parents, the family. In practice, this has meant that women bear the brunt of the work involved in looking after children. And, consequently, they have been the primary recipients of government support. This has taken three forms. First, women are given legal guarantees of equal pay for equal work; they are also offered some protection from unsuitable conditions of employment. Secondly, through access to education they are offered the opportunity of developing their potential (and, incidentally, of becoming more valued members of the labour force). Finally, through the provision of financial assistance and (subsidised) child care facilities, it is made easier for women to reconcile the conflicting demands of job and home.

The actual policies pursued by the Soviet government, especially under Stalin, the exigencies of war and of the demographic imbalance experienced by the USSR in the last fifty years, and the distortions introduced by Soviet industrialisation priorities, mean that Soviet reality has often diverged substantially from the perception set out above. But the ideal has retained a hold on the official mind and, I believe, in the popular consciousness.[4] It is against this standard that Soviet policies should, in the first instance, be judged.

The plan of the book is as follows. In Chapter 2 the available evidence on the earnings of men and women is reviewed. Although the statistics are woefully inadequate, they suggest that gross differentials in the USSR are substantial, on a par with those to be found in Western Europe. They also indicate that recent reductions in intra-sectoral earnings differentials have had little effect on the overall disparity between men and women.

Since these differences in earnings cannot be attributed to what I call *rate discrimination*, the payment of different rates for the same job, they must be the result of differences in participation or of occupational segregation. They also constitute *prima facie* evidence of persisting sexual inequality in the Soviet labour market. Evidence about changes in the level of female participation is reviewed in Chapter 3; the question of occupational segregation is explored in Chapters 4 and 5. Taken together, these chapters show that the Soviet authorities have been successful in their primary aim of expanding female employment. According to one calculation, in 1975 as many as 83 per cent of women of working age were gainfully occupied. This is probably an overestimate, but there can be no doubt that, by international standards, Soviet participation rates are extremely high. But high and rising rates of female employment have not led to the breaking down of occupational distinctions. The material in Chapters 4 and 5 suggests that, if anything, occupational differentiation between men and women has increased since 1939. This is most clear among those engaged in manual non-agricultural occupations. Expanded employment here has led to changes in the boundaries of what is conventionally regarded as 'women's work' rather than to the development of sexually integrated occupations. Further, despite a notable expansion in professional female employment, women tend to be over-represented at the bottom of status hierarchies.

Chapter 6 is devoted to an analysis of the position of women in agriculture. Here, too, the same pattern is to be found. Women earn less than men. But, in addition to being confined to low-skilled, largely manual occupations, it appears that they are more frequently laid off. Their attachment to the public labour force is intermittent.

The next four chapters are concerned with an analysis of the reasons for the persistence of sexual segregation in the Soviet labour market and the inequality it generates. First, I review recent Soviet analyses of the problem. These identify three areas for further study: education, protective legislation and the burdens of motherhood and domestic responsibility. They also suggest that social attitudes continue to exert a constraining role on girls' choice of careers.

The educational attainments of men and women are dealt with in Chapter 8. The material presented there shows that by 1970, if not by 1959, the formal educational attainments of girls at the completion of full-time education were as great as, if not greater than, those of boys. But fewer women than men go on to intensive vocational training and women are less likely than men to acquire new skills or further education in the first twenty years of active life. Thus, to some extent, the persistence of occupational segregation can be explained in terms of differences in human capital.

The failure of the Soviet educational system to equip women for an active life can be attributed in part to the existence of protective legislation. This serves to preclude girls from enrolment in certain forms of vocational training. The avenues that remain lead, for the most part, to occupations that are less skilled and less highly paid. Of more importance, in my view, are shortcomings in the assistance provided by the state to enable women to reconcile the roles of worker and mother. Inadequate financial support, shortage of child care facilities, overcrowded housing and a rudimentary services sector put an enormous strain on working women. They limit women's opportunities for professional advancement and hence promotion, they result in interruptions in employment; on the other hand, they have surely contributed to a decline in birth rates that has adversely affected labour-force growth for the rest of the century.

Thus, I suggest, Soviet policies have failed to achieve their goals. Full employment for women does not automatically entail sexual equality in the labour market, in spite of rising levels of educational attainment. Nor does state provision of child care facilities, at least on the scale achieved in the USSR in the past four decades, mean that women can combine paid employment with motherhood. How far these failures can be attributed to specifically Soviet factors and how far they are a result of flaws in the underlying theory is taken up in the concluding chapter.

## Notes: Chapter 1

1   Social progress can be exactly measured by the social position of the fair sex (its plain members included).

2   The country now known as the USSR did not come into existence formally until 1922. For the first five years after the revolution the territory ruled by the Bolshevik Party was known as the RSFSR, the Russian Soviet Federated Socialist Republic. In 1922, a more explicitly federal formal structure was adopted and the RSFSR became one of the republics. In subsequent years, further republics were added until, today, there are fifteen union republics. But the RSFSR remains the largest, in terms of both area and population.

3   Farnsworth, 1977, p. 142; the same author provides an account of the more utopian proposals for the transformation of personal relationships referred to above. See also Scott, 1976, pp. 42–3.

4   Article 122 was replaced by Article 35 in the new (1977) Constitution which expressed similar objectives in almost identical words:

> Women in the USSR possess equal rights with men. The realisation of these rights is guaranteed by offering to women equal opportunities for obtaining education and occupational training, [equal opportunities] in employment and its remuneration, in promotion at work, in socio-political and cultural activities; [it is also secured] by special measures for the protection of women's health and work, by legal protection of and moral and material support for motherhood and childhood, including the provision of paid maternity leave and other concessions to pregnant women and mothers and state aid for single mothers. (cited from *Kommunist*, 1977, no. 8)

*Chapter 2*

# The Earnings of Men and Women, 1956-75

Throughout the world employed women earn less than men. This is the case in such mature market economies as Britain or the USA, it is the case in the agrarian economies of the Third World, it is the case in centrally planned (socialist) economies like Poland, Czechoslovakia and Hungary. Evidence produced below demonstrates that it is also true of the USSR. Further, although the statistics are inadequate in many respects, they suggest that the gross differential is substantial in all countries; in most, there is little indication that it has been reduced appreciably in the postwar period.

As argued in the last chapter, sexual equality is both an ideal espoused by the founders of socialism and a constitutional right embodied in Soviet law. The fact that the Soviet authorities appear to have not yet succeeded in achieving their aim suggests that they may have approached the problem in the wrong way, or that they have not pursued this objective as vigorously and as conscientiously as possible. As the experience of other countries shows, it may also be that the objective is rather more difficult to attain than at first thought.

The primary purpose of this chapter is to establish the scale of disparities in the earnings of men and women in the USSR and, in so far as the available statistics permit it, to trace their evolution through time. But two further topics are dealt with. In the next section I examine Soviet attitudes towards the differentiation of earnings and suggest that it is based on principles that may be inconsistent with sexual equality in earnings. The third section takes up the question of the formal sources of earnings inequality and attempts to distinguish between those that may be called rational and those that are, at first glance, indicative of sex discrimination. The last two sections of the chapter contain the available empirical evidence.

## Earnings Differentials under Socialism

Recent Soviet discussions of inequality have been formulated within a Marxist analytical framework; because this may not be familiar and because the Soviet version may contain its own peculiar glosses, it is desirable to set this out briefly. Marx's own views on the distribution of income in a socialist society are set out clearly and succinctly in the *Critique of the Gotha Programme*. (References given here are to the International Publishers edition

New York, 1967.) In it, Marx distinguishes between two phases of post-revolutionary society; these are now commonly called socialism and communism, although Marx himself refers to them as the lower and higher phases of communism, a source of some confusion. The distinction between these two stages is important but it is often neglected in popular comment and criticism in the West.

Under communism, labour productivity is sufficiently great for there to be an abundance of material goods; also, labour itself confers utility or, in Marx's own words '. . . labour, from a mere means of life, has become the prime necessity of life' (p. 10). At this stage the problem of income distribution, and hence earnings differentials, will disappear, it will be possible for '. . . society to inscribe upon its banners: from each according to his ability, to each according to his needs' (p. 10). Socialism, on the other hand, is characterised by relatively low labour productivity; material goods are still scarce so that some form of rationing is required. Also, individuals still work to live rather than live to work - incentives and coercion are still needed to elicit the necessary supply of labour. At this stage '. . . the right of producers [should be] proportional to the labour they supply . . . this equal right is an unequal right for unequal labour' (p. 9). Soviet economists refer to this as the socialist principle of distribution: from each according to his ability, to each according to his labour. And since the USSR is still only a *socialist* society, only this second principle applies there.

Soviet economists, then, start from the proposition that under socialism as under capitalism individuals are unequal - they are unequal in their capacity for work, in their skills and abilities, in their needs, tastes and preferences; they should be unequal in their incomes. The sole gain from the revolution (but, they would argue, it is a crucial one) is that the elimination of private ownership of the means of production, and hence of exploitation, impose upon all an equal obligation to work, to be judged by their work (Rakitskii, 1967, p. 171). Any attempt to eliminate earnings differentials or even to reduce them prematurely would undermine the main objective of socialist society - the building of communism (Kulikov, 1972, pp. 58-9).

In the context of this view of socialism, what determines the extent of earnings differentials and what is the role of the state? According to the labour theory of value, all work, whatever its concrete form, whatever the skills involved, the conditions in which it is undertaken, and so on, can be 'reduced' to a greater or smaller amount of simple labour. It is this reducibility that permits labour to act as a rationing device under socialism. But it also implies that 'the sources of differentiation are to be found in the quantitative and qualitative inhomogeneity of labour . . . [that] the differentiation of earnings in its broadest sense is the result of the existing relationships between the quantity and quality of labour at the disposal of a socialist society. Its extent is at each moment objectively determined' (Rabkina and Rimashevskaya, 1972, pp. 18-19). The role of the state, of government wages policy, is to specify wage relativities that will encourage workers to acquire the relevant skills, that will encourage those with special abilities or training to exercise them (Kuprienko, 1976, p. 44). If the authorities select the 'right' set of differentials, the growth of productivity and the smooth operation of the economy is facilitated; if they choose a wrong set, bottlenecks in the supply of particular types of labour will occur, turnover will be high and wages policy will be contravened, leading to the possibility of inflation or other undesirable phenomena (Rabkina and Rimashevskaya, 1972, p. 17; see also Kulikov, 1972, p. 51).

At the same time, the socialist principle of distribution is taken to imply that Soviet wage and salary structures should be characterised by 'equal pay for equal work' – a principle of equity that appeals far beyond the specifically Marxist framework of analysis. The doctrine of the reducibility of labour, however, gives this principle a specific interpretation in the USSR. Since all jobs, all work, can be reduced to more or less simple labour, it implies more than that all doing the same job should receive the same pay; rather, it means that all jobs containing the same amount of labour should pay the same rates. This is seen to justify, if not to necessitate, the widespread use of job evaluation procedures (not only within particular plants or industries but on an economy-wide scale) and the introduction of centralised, bureaucratic wage determination procedures (McAuley, 1979, ch. 8; Sukharevskii, 1974, p. 216ff.).

This emphasis on the objective determinants of earnings differentials, on the limited scope for state intervention, on the dangers associated with ignorant or shortsighted actions, should be seen in large part, I think, as a reaction to the arbitrariness of the Stalinist period. It constitutes an affirmation of the need for information, for calculation, for theoretical understanding. It reflects a distaste for ill-conceived radical innovations. At the same time, it implies a particular view of an appropriate distribution of income and attempts to relate it to the wider objectives of government policy.

First, a majority of Soviet economists are opposed to formal equality, to too great an emphasis on the equalisation of consumption opportunities: '... all that bears the stamp of social security, that is not connected with production, should be separated from wages' (Rabkina and Rimashevskaya, 1972, p. 26). Or again 'in determining the wage rates of workers with various skills, office staff, technical and higher administrative personnel, all thought of egalitarianism, *uravnitelnost*, should be rejected'.[1] To quote one more judgement:

Any form of payment for labour is in no case compatible with egalitarianism, *uravnilovka*. All such tendencies are harmful, in conflict with the rapid development of productive forces and the creation of conditions necessary for the continuing growth in workers' welfare. Egalitarianism undermines material incentives and, in the last analysis, causes irreparable harm to the building of communism. (Kulikov, 1972, pp. 58-9)

That is, the state should not use its power over the wage determination process to pursue social objectives not directly connected with production. Wage differentials should be used primarily, if not solely, to ensure an efficient allocation of labour. The resultant distribution of income, if regarded as inappropriate, should subsequently be adjusted by other means (social security payments, taxes, subsidies, and so on).

Secondly, most Soviet economists appear to advocate what one might call a meritocratic structure of wages:

Labour has still not become a necessity of life for all members of society. It is possible to guarantee the participation of the majority in work only if the possibility of receiving a share of society's output is made conditional upon undertaking socially useful labour and if the size of this share depends upon the importance, *vesomostyu*, of the contribution made. (Maier, 1968, p. 19)

Or again:

Under socialism greater rewards are given to those workers who create more value, whose contribution to the fulfilment of plans and the development of production is larger. This is achieved by paying higher wages to skilled workers, to those requiring longer training. Work undertaken in dangerous or harmful conditions is also better paid. If this were not so, there would be no incentive to acquire education, to raise skills, to undertake more complex and responsible work. (Kulikov, 1972, pp. 53–4)

And the authority of Lenin is invoked in support of the assertion that such work does not constitute its own reward (Kulikov, 1972, p. 48).

For the purposes of this chapter, I think that three conclusions follow from this discussion of Soviet attitudes to wage determination and earnings inequality. It seems clear that the dominant view (and it should be pointed out that there are those who dissent from the opinions articulated here) is that wages policy should not be used to pursue social objectives other than those connected with production. Further, although this point may not have been brought out very clearly, other social goals, including the elimination of sexual differentiation in earnings, should be subordinated to the so-called socialist principle of distribution. Finally, Soviet analyses reveal an ambiguity about the determinants of differentials. On the one hand, they appear to suggest that these can (and in equity terms should) be determined by reference to the labour process itself; on the other, they also ascribe a significant role to the forces of supply and demand. Differentials should be as large as is necessary to attract workers to particular jobs. If it turns out that in equilibrium (or, rather, on the appropriate growth path) these involve paying more to men than to women, this is what should be done. It is in accordance with the socialist principle. And Soviet economists would deny that this constitutes sex discrimination.

### Earnings Inequality and Sex Discrimination

The principle of sexual equality is enshrined in the 1936 Constitution of the USSR (and the relevant clause has been repeated almost verbatim in the Brezhnev Constitution). But, as argued above, so far as earnings have been concerned this has been subordinated to the socialist principle of distribution, the differentiation of rewards according to 'merit'. It is the purpose of this section to inquire how far these two principles are compatible, how far, that is, sex-linked differences in earnings may be claimed to be rational (in the economist's sense of the word) and whether they should be condemned as inequitable.

Formally, the lower average earnings of women in the USSR can be ascribed to one (or more) of three causes. They must be due either to the fact that women are paid less than men for doing the same work, to *rate discrimination* as I shall call it. Or they must be due to the fact that women are more heavily concentrated in low-paying industries or in low-paying jobs within a given industry than men, to *occupational segregation* as I shall term it. Or, finally, they must be due to the fact that women work shorter hours than men, or in some other sense supply less labour. Tentatively, I propose to call this *differential participation*. This classification of causes is purely formal; one's attitude to the three sorts of phenomena will depend upon the social factors that lead to their emergence. Let us consider each of them in more detail.

Unless it can be shown that rate differences accurately reflect productivity differences, rate discrimination is both inefficient and inequitable. Soviet labour economists and policy-makers, both in the past and at present, believe that such a demonstration is impossible. And this view is shared by most of those who have considered the question in other countries. Certainly there are differences between the productivity of men and women in specific occupations; but there are also differences between men and between women. In most jobs, the productivity distributions of the two sexes overlap to a considerable extent. As a result, the Soviet Labour Code of 1922 and the Constitutions of 1936 and 1978 explicitly guaranteed women equal pay for equal work. But this guarantee only means that men and women doing identical jobs will receive the same pay; it does not necessarily imply equal pay for equal work in the sense of the previous section.

There are three features of the practice of wage imputation (the assignment of earnings to individual employees) in the USSR which might be thought to contravene the spirit of the law. First, while it is true that the centralised procedures for wage determination result in the specification of a single 'rate for the job', there is scope for some bias in the way in which these are applied. In discharging its responsibilities, the State Committee on Labour and Social Problems[2] has proceeded by specifying a number of general wage scales and then assigning individuals jobs and occupations to points on the scale on the basis of job evaluation procedures. Since many jobs can be filled at more than one level, this approach leaves some scope for local initiative. It is up to the management of individual enterprises, in consultation with the local trade union committee, to decide whether any particular job should be filled at Grade II level, say, or whether it should be classified as Grade III or IV. There are some reasons for supposing that the way in which this initiative has been used has resulted in systematic bias against women workers.

In addition to the differentials that are supposed to reflect differences in skill, the Soviet wage system contains provisions for higher wages to be paid to those who work in hot, heavy, or otherwise harmful conditions. But it appears that the premia built into the system for this purpose have, on the average, been insufficient to attract the necessary labour. Managements have responded by upgrading many of the jobs concerned (Kirsch, 1972, pp. 134–42). Since, due to the operation of protective legislation, a majority of those working in hot, heavy and harmful conditions are men, the operation of the system tends to result in the fact that work which is officially regarded as of equal skill and complexity is unequally rewarded. This phenomenon reflects the difficulty of divorcing evaluation procedures from supply and demand considerations. Whether it is inequitable or not depends upon whether or not one believes that value can be ascribed to work independently of market forces.

Secondly, the legal guarantee enshrined in Soviet labour law and the constitution applies only to wage rates. But in the USSR, as elsewhere, the earnings of manual workers particularly depend upon more than the rate for the job: they are also influenced by norms and bonuses. The influence of work norms is seen most clearly in the case of pieceworkers. Here, in order to earn his or her basic wage, the worker is required to complete a certain amount of work per shift. If more is done, earnings exceed the basic wage. In Soviet factories it has been common practice to pay a higher rate for above-norm output. Timeworkers are also expected to meet their output norms. Soviet workers also receive a variety of bonuses. Since 1965–7 these have depended in part upon the profitability of the enterprise in which the worker is employed, but they still depend much more upon individual performance.

Until 1970–1, output norms against which individual performance was judged were not differentiated by sex. Such is still the position throughout most of the Soviet economy.[3] Men and women doing the same jobs are expected to complete the same amount of work in a given period. In so far as manual jobs in Soviet industry (and other sectors like construction) often require physical strength as well as manual dexterity and in so far as tools and other equipment are usually more suited ergonomically to men than to women, it is to be expected that men will find it easier to fulfil their output norms than women. And this is what the evidence shows, such as it is. Kotlyar and Turchaninova cite results from two factories in the course of their recent study of female employment:

|  | *Average percentage Norm fulfilment* | |
|---|---|---|
|  | Men | Women |
| Factory 1 | 143·1 | 130·9 |
| Factory 2 | 154·2 | 146·4 |

(Kotlyar and Turchaninova, 1975, p. 10)

And, of course, in so far as bonuses depend upon individual performance, they will accentuate differences in earnings that derive from norm fulfilment factors. In periods when these components make up a substantial proportion of take-home pay, the earnings of men will be higher than those of women. Because wage rates are bureaucratically determined in the USSR, they are changed at infrequent intervals; therefore periods in which bonuses are a substantial proportion of earnings are relatively frequent. Also, in so far as norm fulfilment affects the worker's chances of promotion (and hence the possibility of a higher basic wage), men will be in an advantageous position.

The phenomenon described above cannot be called rate discrimination. Indeed, from the point of view of both enterprise and society it is 'rational'. After all, men have, on the average, produced more; therefore, in accordance with the socialist principle of distribution, they should receive the higher wages. But it does demonstrate a limitation to the legislative approach to equal pay. Equality of wage rates does not entail equality of earnings. As an economist, one might predict that the response to this situation will be a tendency for women to avoid those jobs and occupations in which there is a premium on physical strength (or any other attribute in which men have an advantage). That is, one would expect to see a measure of occupational segregation. How extensive this is will depend upon the importance of biologically determined differences in the work process. It will also depend upon the demand side of the labour market: upon whether the state's development programme results in the creation of sufficient jobs with attributes more suited to women's abilities. (The above argument presupposes that equality of opportunity in other respects is guaranteed; if social factors affect access to training and so forth, it will not only be biological differences that will lead to occupational segregation, but social pressures too.)

In this instance, too, there is a conflict between the socialist principle of distribution and sexual equality, in some interpretations at least. If wages are a reward for performing particular actions and if those actions require physical strength, then the failure to use differentiated norms means that women have been set the harder task. Relative to their abilities, they may have performed as well, but they still receive a lower reward. But this is inevitable unless one abandons the principle of 'from each according to his labour'.

The tendency towards occupational segregation that may result in part from the non-differentiation of norms facilitates the third feature of the wage imputation process giving rise to sexual inequality in earnings. If the jobs done by men differ from those done by women and if there are factors that inhibit the recruitment of one sex to occupations commonly done by the other, there will exist parallel but relatively independent labour markets for men and women. The earnings available in each may differ.

Now, according to the Marxist theory of value, labour content and hence wages can be determined independently of market forces. There is no reason, therefore, to suppose that the earnings in these parallel markets will be out of line with each other. That is, if typically women's jobs in the garment industry, say, involve as much training or whatever as typically male jobs in construction, they will be paid as well. But, as argued in the previous section, wage determination in the Soviet Union is not carried out in isolation from the market; supply and demand factors exert an influence. If, for example, as a result of 'overcrowding' or the operation of protective legislation, the supply of female labour is more elastic than that of male, equilibrium wages in women's jobs may be lower than those in men's. Whether one regards this as inequitable or not depends upon one's standards, but it is clear that a legal prohibition of rate discrimination is not sufficient to ensure that men's and women's earnings will be the same.

So much for rate discrimination; I turn now to a briefer discussion of the other two sources of earnings inequality. Whether one regards occupational segregation as inequitable or not depends upon one's assessment of its causes. If it is a consequence of the rational matching of jobs to abilities, it is unobjectionable. But one may question the procedure that assigns different values to the abilities of men and women. Equally, one may ask how far the abilities in question are innate? Or do they (even though they are correctly valued) result from differential access to training facilities? That is, if occupational segregation is a consequence of selective access to the acquisition of human capital (in amount or type) it too should be considered as evidence of sex discrimination.

To be more explicit: occupational segregation can serve as a source of earnings differentiation only if the jobs most commonly done by women are worse paid than those of men. Now it is possible to distinguish (conceptually if not empirically) three ways in which the jobs of men and women may differ. First, the jobs done by men may involve higher levels of skill and responsibility than those done by women. And in the Soviet Union, as in most other countries, skill and responsibility are rewarded by higher wages. But one must ask why it is that typically men have the greater skill or are called upon to exercise the greater responsibility.

Secondly, it might be that the jobs done by men are concentrated in industries or sectors to which the authorities (and society generally) ascribe particular importance. In Soviet practice, high-priority sectors tend to enjoy higher average earnings than low-priority sectors. This is to ensure that enterprises in these sectors are able to attract the labour they need to fulfil their plans. This is unexceptionable and analogous practices are true of economies organised on different lines. But, again, one may legitimately ask whether there are institutional or customary barriers that prevent women from taking up jobs in these high-priority fields.

Thirdly, the jobs done by men may be physically more arduous, more unpleasant, or may be undertaken in more difficult and dangerous surroundings than those done by women. Since wage supplements are paid for all these factors, this might lead to the higher average earnings of men. (Additionally, since regional supplements are paid to those working in enterprises located in climatically hostile regions, but until recently have not been payable in all sectors, this might explain part of the observed Soviet male–female differential.)

If any or all of these factors are to explain existing differentials, then, since the disparity in male–female earnings appears to have remained largely unchanged in the past twenty years, its causative factors must also have remained unchanged (that is, unless one is prepared to accept the somewhat implausible possibility of mutually offsetting changes in causes). Further, since observed disparities in the USSR do not differ greatly from those to be found in other industrial economies, one might expect the causes of this phenomenon to be relatively system-free. This must cast doubt upon any explanation that relies too heavily upon specific features of the Soviet wages structure.

Finally, it must be recognised that occupational segregation can only serve as a proximate explanation of disparities in earnings. If it is accepted, then one must ask why men and women tend to do different jobs; that is, one must inquire into those mechanisms in the labour market or in society more generally that operate so as to maintain differential occupational choices.

Turning now to what I have called differential participation: there are several different senses in which this may contribute to disparities in the gross earnings of men and women. First, in any particular occupation and at a given point in time, the greater domestic responsibilities of women may lead them to work less overtime than men; more generally, their domestic responsibilities may induce them to select preferentially occupations in which there is a lower probability of being asked to work overtime. (That is, they might be led to emphasise convenience rather than earnings opportunities or career prospects in the selection of jobs.) At the limit, it will be difficult to distinguish this from other sources of occupational segregation.

Again, domestic responsibilities may make women less willing than men to undertake secondary employment - either moonlighting in the public and private sectors or social-political activities in the more accepted sense. This too will result in lower gross earnings and, possibly, impaired promotion prospects. Similarly, domestic responsibilities may make women less likely than men to invest time in further education and the acquisition of skills. While this need not affect earnings at a point in time, it will clearly impair their chances of promotion - and hence, in the longer run, result in the emergence of sex-linked disparities in earnings.

Finally, interruptions in work experience (related to family formation) may reduce the speed at which women acquire skills, particularly in the early years of their careers, and this may result in slower rates of promotion. Since the Soviet social security system, in common with that of most other countries, makes provision for earlier retirement for women than for men, these two factors will interact to produce lower levels of skill on average among women than among men.

Of the factors enumerated above, only maternity and breast-feeding can be said to be biologically determined. And one's attitude to the equity of differential participation must be conditioned by that fact. If the greater involvement of women in domestic affairs is the outcome of free choices by equal individuals, it cannot be said to be inequitable. But if it is the consequence of wider social pressures, of differences in the allocation of domestic responsibilities, it will be a reflection of a more pervasive sexual inequality. It too must be thought of as a product of sex discrimination.

There are, then, three possible sources of inequality in the earnings of men and women: rate discrimination, occupational segregation and differential participation. All three might be consistent with a rational allocation of labour but it is more likely that all three reflect sex discrimination either in the labour market itself or in society at large. If this is the case, one may infer that labour is being allocated inefficiently and also, I believe, that the wage imputation process is inequitable.

In the remainder of this chapter the available statistics on the earnings of men and women in the USSR are examined and an attempt is made to determine the contribution of each of the three sources to existing disparities.

### Statistics on Male and Female Earnings, 1956–75

As pointed out above, both the Labour Code of 1922 and the Constitution of 1936 explicitly guarantee women equal pay for equal work in the sense of identical jobs. Further, there is no scope for the introduction of separate wage scales for the two sexes in the system of wage determination. It is therefore highly improbable that observed differences in the earnings of men and women in the 1950s and 1960s can be attributed in any direct way to rate discrimination or its aftermath. And since it is only rate discrimination that Soviet economists call sex discrimination in the labour market, they are able to deny the existence of the latter in the USSR in spite of the fact that male–female earnings disparities appear to be substantial.

I say that earnings disparities appear to be substantial, but the study of this question is made difficult by the fact that the Soviet authorities do not publish official data on wages and salaries classified by sex. This seems to be more a consequence of shortcomings in official data collection procedures than yet a further example of the government's obsessive secretiveness about economic statistics (or of official embarrassment about the size of such differentials). It appears that Soviet policy-makers and labour economists do not possess any extensive information about this question either since:

> established forms of reporting on the level of qualifications, the average earnings of workers, training and increases in skills on the shop floor, *neposredstvenno na proizvodstve*, do not envisage the differentiation of this information by sex. The only method [of obtaining the relevant data] is through sample surveys. (Mikhailyuk, 1970, p. 81)

There is nothing to suggest that there have been any material changes in the relevant statistical procedures since this passage was written. I assume that this situation is the result of the fact that male–female earnings differentials are not seen as a pressing political or economic problem in Moscow rather than being due to any nicety of feeling on the part of the authorities.

Since official figures on the gap between men's and women's earnings in the USSR are not available, the estimates given here are based on a variety of sample surveys. They have been compiled by means of an extensive (but not exhaustive) search of empirical sociological and economic studies published in the last fifteen or twenty years. The statistics are confined to non-agricultural state employees;[4] unfortunately, they are also confined to the European part of the USSR. More generally, relying on sample data for estimates of economy-wide relationships raises a number of problems. First, the surveys used were conducted on a relatively small scale, in particular areas and among specific groups. Any information they contain about earnings can be legitimately generalised only to the relevant parent populations (e.g. to workers in specified industrial areas, employees in a given industry, and so on) and these may not be typical of the Soviet population as a whole. Further, in general, the surveys were addressed to problems other than the elucidation of earnings differentials; hence, even if the samples were appropriately representative for the questions they were designed to answer, the sample selection procedures used might involve substantial bias with respect to earnings. There is little one can do to avoid these problems. Until Soviet social scientists publish their own studies of the nature and extent of sexual inequality in the USSR, or unless one can oneself collect primary data in the Soviet Union, one is forced to rely upon available material. One can only hope that the accumulation of instances will in some measure compensate for the inadequacies of any particular example. Still, it is as well to bear these reservations in mind and to treat the figures given below with due caution.

Table 2.1   *Gross Differentials in Male–Female Earnings: USSR, 1960–74 (multisectoral samples)*

| Date | Location and Labour Force Group | Male Earnings (R per month) | Female Earnings (R per month) | Female as % of Male Earnings |
|---|---|---|---|---|
| 1960–5 | Leningrad: workers | n.a. | n.a. | 69·3 |
| 1963 | Erevan: state employees | 114·59 | 74·29 | 64·8 |
| 1965–8 | S. Russian industrial town: workers | 131·00 | 84·00 | 64·1 |
| 1967 | Latvia: women who married in 1959* | 120·89 | 76·03 | 62·9 |
| 1968 | Kiev: divorce petitioners* | 134·00 | 88·00 | 65·7 |
| 1965–70 | Moldavia: industrial employees* | (145–155) | 90–100 | 58–69 |
| 1965–70 | unspecified | n.a. | n.a. | 66·7 |
| 1970 | Kiev: newly weds | 116·00 | 84·00 | 72·4 |
| 1972–4 | European Russia: urban workers | 160·30 | 96·50 | 60·2 |
| | urban white-collar | 188·90 | 113·10 | 59·9 |

*Sources:* Row (1) Pimenova, 1966, p. 40; Row (2) Swafford, 1977, Table 2; Row (3) Gordon and Klopov, 1970, p. 205; Row (4) Shlindman and Zvidrin'sh, 1973, pp. 54, 61. Rows (5) and (8) Chuiko, 1975, pp. 81, 145; Row (6) Shishkan, 1976, p. 54; Row (7) Ryurikov, 1977, p. 119; Rows (9) and (10) Ofer and Vinokur, 1979, p. 39.

*Note:* An asterisk indicates that the figures given in the table have been calculated from data given in the relevant Soviet source.

Table 2.1 contains ten estimates of the differences between male and female earnings in the USSR. With the exception of the survey by Ofer and Vinokur, all were completed between 1960 and 1970; the samples were all drawn from urban populations and, with the exception of that reported by Swafford, all relate to the European part of the USSR. There is also some tendency for workers (or even industrial workers) to be overrepresented. All the surveys quoted show that the earnings of women were between 60 and 70 per cent of those of men. There is little to suggest that the gap closed appreciably during the decade or that it was greater in the Transcaucasus than in the more developed areas like the RSFSR or Latvia. On the other hand, if one assumes that those marrying at the wedding palace will be younger than the employed population as a whole, Chuiko's figures suggest that disparities widen with age. (Alternatively, it might be that those indulging in a formal wedding are more affluent than most and that disparities are less in this group than in the population as a whole.)

It should be recognised, however, that sectors such as health or trade, both employing substantially more women than men and both characterised by relatively low earnings, are probably underrepresented in the samples on which the estimates of Table 2.1 are based. The same is probably true of such high-wage male-dominated sectors as transport and construction. This at least seems to be the implication that should be drawn from the Ofer-Vinokur figures which are derived from the reported earnings of Soviet emigrants to Israel combined using urban population weights for the various occupational groups. And, of course, agriculture is excluded as are most of the less developed non-Slav areas of the country. I would therefore infer that the estimates of Table 2.1 constitute a lower bound on the size of the gross differential in male–female earnings in the Soviet Union.

The formal estimates of Table 2.1 can be complemented by numerous references in the sociological literature to the fact that wives in general earn less than their husbands. Kharchev claims that in his 1961 sample of Leningrad workers, in 18 per cent of families the wife earned more than her husband; in a further 33 per cent of families the difference in earnings was less than 10 rubles a month (Kharchev, 1964, p. 223). On the basis of a sample drawn from the same area at about the same time, Pimenova suggests that in 73 per cent of families the husband earns more than the wife, in 20 per cent earnings are about the same and in only 7 per cent do wives earn more than their husbands (Pimenova, 1966, p. 40). Rabkina and Rimashevskaya report that in their sample (drawn from an industrial centre in the RSFSR in 1967) some 15 per cent of wives earned more than their husbands, and in a further 17 per cent of families the earnings of both were about the same. They also claim that the category 'low-paid workers' consists primarily of women doing unskilled or semi-skilled work and suggest that when account is taken of differences in ages, in education and qualifications, the sample results imply 'equal opportunities unequally realised by men and women' (Rabkina and Rimashevskaya, 1972, p. 47). There is little discussion about why this might be the case, apart from a passing reference to the conflict between the roles of worker and mother.

Slesarev and Yankova simply state that few of the married women in their sample (drawn from factories in Moscow and Penza and an apartment block in Leningrad in the mid-1960s) earned as much as their husbands although they claim that in most cases the differential did not exceed 25 rubles a month (Slesarev and Kankova, 1969, p. 431). A more recent sample, drawn this time from the Ukraine, gives the same proportions as those reported by Pimenova (Mikhailyuk, 1970, p. 126). Sakharova, on the other hand, drawing upon a sample of 650 families from four industrial enterprises in Kiev, suggests that between 8 and 13 per cent of wives earn more than their husbands; in 70–80 per cent of families it is the husband who has the larger pay-packet (Sakharova, 1973, pp. 30–1). Cherkasov also suggests that in only 15 per cent of families do women earn more than their husbands. He comments, 'the wife's earnings do not so much play the role of a supplement to the family budget as that of affording her economic independence, freedom and equality' (Cherkasov, 1975, p. 24). Finally, Kotlyar and Turchaninova put the proportion of wives who earn more than their husbands at between 5 and 30 per cent, depending upon the town and enterprise involved (Kotlyar and Turchaninova, 1975, pp. 139–40). These last authors also suggest that sex-linked earnings differences are less in small towns than in large ones. This is apparently due to the absence of high-wage jobs for men in such places rather than of greater job opportunities for women (ibid., p. 136). This result, if generally applicable, would imply that the estimates of Table 2.1 might contain an upward bias since those living in large towns are overrepresented. None of these references provides conclusive proof that Soviet women earn less than Soviet men, but the frequency with which the relationship is mentioned and the size of the difference reported makes it difficult to suggest plausible reasons for believing the contrary.

The figures given so far, if they are accepted as valid for the USSR as a whole, suggest that the disparities in earnings between men and women in the Soviet Union are about the same as, or somewhat larger than, those to be found in other socialist countries in Eastern Europe. (See Table 2.2.) Although the statistics for the different countries given in the table are not strictly comparable, taken at face value they suggest that inequality in the USSR was almost certainly greater than in Scandinavia, but possibly somewhat less than in Western Europe. On the other hand, there is little evidence of a trend towards reduced inequality such as appears to have been taking place in the United Kingdom in the past decade. (See Table 2.2 and the sources cited therein.)

Table 2.2    *Gross Earnings Differentials between Men and Women: Various Countries, 1959-76*

| Year | Country and Labour Force Group | Female Earnings as % of Male Earnings |
|---|---|---|
| 1953 | Great Britain | 54·0 |
| 1968 | Great Britain | 53·0 |
| 1975 | Great Britain | 62·0 |
| 1969 | Norway: manufacturing | 74·0 |
| 1968 | Sweden: industrial workers | 79·0 |
| 1966 | France: employees | 63·0 |
| 1964 | Switzerland: workers | 63·0 |
| 1959 | Czechoslovakia: socialist sector | 66·2 |
| 1970 | Czechoslovakia: socialist sector | 67·1 |
| 1972 | Poland: socialist sector | 66·5 |
| 1972 | Hungary: state sector | 72·5 |

*Sources:* Rows (1) to (3) Moroney, 1979, p. 605; Rows (4) to (7) Galenson, 1973, *passim*; Rows (8) to (11) Michal, 1975, p. 267.

Figures on longer-term trends within the USSR are also scarce, but those that exist perhaps suggest that differentials in the 1960s are less marked than in the 1920s or before the revolution. For instance, it is reported that in 1928 the average earnings of female textile workers in Leningrad were some 72·6 per cent of those for men; in Ivanovo oblast they were as much as 94·5 per cent (Rashin, 1930, p. 86). Before the revolution, it is reported that in St Petersburg the earnings of women textile workers were only 68 per cent of those of men; in Moscow Guberniya they were reported to be 65 per cent. Since both in 1913 and in 1928 the textile industry was not known for the low wages that it paid to *women* workers, while it was among the less well-paid sectors for men, these figures underestimate the extent of earnings inequality in each of these years (Kharchev, 1964, p. 128).

For the Stalin period proper even less information is available, but the following figures, derived from family budget studies of industrial workers in Leningrad, are suggestive (ibid., p. 247):

|  | *1940* | *1953* | *1957* | *1958* |
|---|---|---|---|---|
| Earnings of respondent | 66·9 | 62·8 | 56·9 | 57·0 |
| Earnings of other family members | 21·2 | 21·0 | 24·9 | 26·2 |
| Other receipts | 11·9 | 16·2 | 18·2 | 16·8 |
| Total money income | 100·0 | 100·0 | 100·0 | 100·0 |

On the face of it, these figures suggest that the earnings of secondary workers (primarily wives) have risen from about a third of those of the breadwinner in 1940 to approximately a half in 1958. But there are two factors that should be taken into account. Not all the families included in the sample will have had two earners. (For the USSR as a whole, there were 1·76 earners per family in 1959.) And some of the families will have been headed by a woman. (In the USSR as a whole in 1959, some 28 per cent of families were headed by a woman.)

If one assumes that all respondents were men and that all secondary workers were women and that for the sample, as for the USSR as a whole, only three families in four had second workers, one obtains an estimate of the ratio of women's to men's wages in 1958 of 60·5 per cent – clearly of the same order of magnitude as the figures in Table 2.1. If, on the other hand, one assumes that a quarter of the respondents were women and that they had the same earnings as secondary workers, one arrives at an estimate of 54 per cent for the ratio of women's and men's earnings. This may be on the low side. The 1959 Census records that in 1939 in the USSR as a whole, a fifth of families were headed by a woman (*Itogi ...*, USSR vol., 1959, p. 244). Assuming somewhat arbitrarily that there were 1·6 wage-earners per family and applying the same logic as above, one obtains the range 47–53 per cent for the ratio of female to male earnings in 1940. Slender as the evidence is, it seems to suggest some improvement in the position of women over the period 1940–60 – an improvement that, judging by Table 2.1, did not carry on into the 1960s.

Earlier in the chapter I suggested that differences in the average earnings of men and women could be ascribed to one of three factors, rate discrimination, occupational segregation, or differential participation. Since rate discrimination has been excluded, the differences reported in Table 2.1 must be ascribable to a combination of the other two factors. Now, occupational segregation itself can be subdivided into a tendency for men and women to work in different sectors and a tendency for women in any sector to be employed at the less well paying jobs. Some indication of the importance of this last factor is given by the figures in Table 2.3. These estimates, drawn from a variety of Soviet sources, refer to the differences in the earnings of men and women in individual sectors or enterprises. Unfortunately the figures

Table 2.3   *Gross Differentials in Male–Female Earnings: USSR, 1955–73*
            *(single-sector samples)*

| Date | Location and Labour Force Group Covered | Male Earnings (R per month) | Female Earnings (R per month) | Female as % of Male Earnings |
|------|------------------------------------------|-----------------------------|-------------------------------|------------------------------|
| 1956–7 | Moscow; food processing employees* | 90–93 | 52–57 | 61–64 |
| 1964 | Novosibirsk; machinebuilding: | | | |
| | new hires, workers | 97·4 | 74·1 | 76·0 |
| | quits – lathe operators | 89·4 | 73·6 | 82·0 |
| | – labourers | 94·7 | 67·8 | 72·0 |
| | – 5 occupations | 93·2 | 73·1 | 78·0 |
| 1968 | Ukraine; metallurgy employees* | 127·0 | 86·3 | 67·9 |
| 1970 | Leningrad; machinebuilding: | | | |
| | married workers | 149·1 | 108·1 | 73·0 |
| | unmarried workers | 132·6 | 98·6 | 74·0 |
| 1973 | Kiev; cotton-spinning: | | | |
| | basic process workers | n.a. | n.a. | 86·0 |
| | auxiliary workers | n.a. | n.a. | 57·0 |
| | knitwear: | | | |
| | basic process workers** | n.a. | n.a. | 86·0 |
| | auxiliary workers** | n.a. | n.a. | 67·0 |
| | confectionery: workers | n.a. | n.a. | 90·0 |

*Sources:* Row (1) Maslov and Karapetyan, 1959, pp. 69–70 and 129–30; Row (2) Kalmyk, 1969, p. 136; Rows (3) to (5) Antosenkov and Shchenko, 1969, pp. 101–3; Row (6) Kurman, 1971, p. 91; Rows (8) to (9) Yanowitch, 1977, p. 170; Rows (10) to (14) Sakharova, 1973, p. 29.

*Note:* An asterisk denotes that the estimate has been calculated; two asterisks denote that the comparison refers to wage rates rather than earnings.

are almost exclusively confined to industrial workers in urban areas in the European part of the country; they are also restricted to a limited number of occupations. But they do cover a somewhat longer timespan than the figures in Table 2.1.

On balance, the figures in Table 2.3 appear to be somewhat higher than those in Table 2.1. This implies that some part of the difference in the earnings of men and women can be ascribed to administrative segregation and to differential participation. Also, although it is hazardous to generalise on the basis of so little information, there appears to have been some reduction in single-sector differentiation in the past twenty or thirty years. Heroically, one might infer the following sequence: in the 1950s, before the wage reorganisation of 1957–65, in individual sectors, women's earnings were as little as 60 to 70 per cent of those of men. This will have been due both to the importance of bonuses in take-home pay and also to the substantial differentiation in basic rates built into the wage scales in use at that time. After 1960–2, that is, when the wage reorganisation had been completed in industry, women in any particular branch may have earned some 65–75 per cent of what men in that branch received. The relative improvement would have been due to a reduction in the weight of bonuses in earnings and to a narrowing of differentials built into wage scales. More recently, after the minimum wage hike of 1968, if not after the completion of the 1972-6 wage revision, the gap may have closed further. The earnings of women in individual sectors may be as high as 75-80 per cent of those of men in the same sectors. [5]

But this chronology is largely speculative. Differences in the estimates given in Table 2.3 may be due to differences in industrial affiliation, in geographical area, or in sample design. There is a great deal of uncertainty attached to all of these aspects. For example, neglecting differences between Novosibirsk and Leningrad (which is legitimate since, at least in principle, wage scales are nationally determined) the figures in rows (6), (9) and (10) of the table suggest that the differential in male-female earnings in machine-building increased between 1964 and 1970. This increase occurred in spite of a substantial contraction in wage differentials in the industry due to the increase in the minimum wage in 1968 which should have affected the comparison since women are to be found disproportionately in the lower-skill grades of the industry (Kotlyar and Turchaninova, 1975, p. 67). This apparent paradox is probably the result of differences in the ratios of the earnings of quits and non-quits for the two sexes; at least, a higher proportion of men advance 'dissatisfaction over pay' as the reason for leaving their jobs. (See, for example, Kurman, 1971, pp. 104-5.)

Similarly Swafford's analysis suggests that, in Erevan in the early 1960s at least, differences in the earnings of men and women were least in light industry and in plants producing consumer goods. This, together with the fact that the figures refer to individual (and possibly specially selected) enterprises, and also that in some instances comparisons are made between rates rather than earnings, may explain the generally small differentials reported by Sakharova. On balance, however, I believe it plausible to assume that intra-sectoral differentials between the sexes have declined in the past twenty years or so.

The evidence adduced so far, then, suggests that sex-linked earnings disparities in the Soviet Union are substantial, on a par with those to be found in Western Europe in the 1960s. They may have fallen in the period 1940-60 but there is little to suggest that the trend has continued since then. In part these differentials can be attributed to the fact that women are more heavily concentrated in low-paying sectors, in part they are due to the fact that, in any sector, women are to be found doing the worse-paid jobs. On the evidence available, it is not possible to say how much of the gross differential is attributable to each factor. There are some grounds for assuming that intra-sectoral differences in pay have fallen since 1960 - but this must imply that the concentration of women in low-pay sectors has increased. Up to now, no evidence has been adduced relating to the contribution of differential participation to disparities in earnings. This issue is taken up in the next section.

### Overtime and Part-Time Work in the State Sector

It was suggested above that part of the observed disparity in the earnings of men and women in the Soviet economy could be attributed to the lower participation of women. There are three ways in which the labour force attachment of the sexes might differ. First, due to their greater domestic responsibilities women may work less overtime than men; similarly they may be more likely to work on a part-time basis. Available evidence on the prevalence of part-time and overtime work in the USSR is reviewed here. Secondly, women may work for fewer weeks in any year than men. In the USSR, part-year working is largely confined to agriculture and this question is taken up in Chapter 6. Finally, women's working lives may be shorter than those of men due to interruptions for childbirth and to earlier retirement built into social security programmes. These topics are dealt with in Chapters 9 and 10.

Official statistics are silent on the question of part-time work in the USSR - at least in sectors other than agriculture. This in itself should be taken as evidence that the phenomenon is unimportant. But recently a semi-official study of the practice has been published and it is on this that the present discussion is based. The study itself was confined to the RSFSR and while its results might generalise to other parts of European USSR they are unlikely to be applicable to Central Asia or the Transcaucasus. This should be borne in mind in interpreting the various figures given.

It is reported that in 1971 some 28,000 persons were employed on a part-time basis in the RSFSR; in 1973, the figure had risen to 170,000 (Maikov and Novitskii, 1975, p. 14). How far this represents a genuine increase and how far it is a result of differences in definition is unclear. But even the higher figure amounts to less than one half of 1 per cent of the state-employed labour force.[6] The Soviet Union thus differs from most industrial market economies in which a substantial proportion of employed women work part-time.

Table 2.4　*The Structure of Part-Time Employment: RSFSR, 1971*

| Population Category | % of Part-Time Employment in | | | Part-Time Employees (thousands) |
|---|---|---|---|---|
| | Industry | Services | Total | |
| Students | 15·5 | 15·8 | 31·3 | 8·9 |
| Pensioners | 5·6 | 24·6 | 30·2 | 8·6 |
| Housewives | 4·6 | 7·3 | 11·9 | 3·4 |
| Other | 7·8 | 18·7 | 26·5 | 7·5 |
| Total | 33·4 | 66·5 | 100·0 | 28·4 |

*Source:* Maikov and Novitskii, 1975, pp. 13, 14, 92. Based on data supplied by the RSFSR State Committee on the Use of Labour Resources.

Some indication of who it is that works part-time and of the sectors in which they are employed is given in Table 2.4. This shows that little more than 10 per cent of part-time workers are housewives - although substantially more will be women. Although Maikov and Novitskii do not say so explicitly,

I would suggest that the residual category in the table consists of moonlighting state employees. Some of these will be women, but a majority are likely to be men, that is, if the figures given below are at all reliable.

Further, two-thirds of all part-time jobs are located in the services sector, and somewhat more than half of these, it is claimed, are provided by the post office. This latter body is apparently a major employer of students who work for some two or three hours a day delivering the mail. Trade and catering, local services and local industry are also large employers of part-time labour. But, given the magnitude of the figures cited so far, part-time work cannot account for more than a minute proportion of the difference in men's and women's earnings in the USSR; there is little point in elaborating further.

Officially, the Soviet authorities frown on the use of overtime in industry and other sectors. In consequence there are elaborate regulations governing its use and no regularly published official statistics relating to its incidence. None the less, given the importance attached to the timely fulfilment of plans and the frequency with which such practices as *shturmovshchina* are referred to, it seems plausible to assume that it is widespread. And there is some evidence in the literature that confirms this conjecture.

It is reported that in 1971 workers in Soviet industry worked an average of 12·6 days overtime in the year and that in 1972 the figure was 15·2 days (Rogovskii, 1973, p. 23). On the assumption that one day is equal to 7 hours, this implies a total of 88·2 and 106·4 hours for the two years (1·8 and 2·1 hours per week respectively.) This is substantially more than the 15 hours per year reportedly worked in 1966 in Novosibirsk (Cherkasov, 1970, p. 147). But it is also claimed that there is extensive unauthorised or hidden overtime in industry; indeed, it is suggested that the 15–21 hours per year officially reported (for the engineering industry in Novosibirsk) and derived from official reports, should be compared with 72 hours per year calculated from a sample survey of some 2,294 workers in the same town and industry (Cherkasov, 1970, p. 148).

Comparing the numbers given above, we can either conclude that there has been a substantial increase in overtime working since the mid-1960s (from 2·1 days in 1966 to 15·2 days in 1973) or that the official statistics now record overtime more accurately – in which case, the increase is less marked (from 72 hours per year in 1966 to 106 hours in 1973). Alternatively, one might assume that Novosibirsk is not typical of the USSR as a whole.

The figures given above provide estimates of the average number of hours of overtime worked per worker in industry. But not all workers work overtime. For the 1966 sample from Novosibirsk, for instance, it is reported that those actually working overtime put in an average of 210 hours during the year, that is, about 4 hours per week (Cherkasov, 1970, p. 148). This implies that about 34 per cent of the sample was actually involved. Some additional information about the scale and incidence of overtime working in the USSR can be extracted from a survey of recent Jewish emigrants undertaken by Ofer and Vinokur. These data should be treated with extreme caution, however, as the sample is far from representative of the Soviet urban population. With this in mind, the Ofer-Vinokur figures indicate that on average 1·3 hours overtime per week were worked – 1·7 hours for men and 0·9 hours for

women. (The sample data relate to the year 1972-3.) These figures correspond
roughly with those given by Rogovskii, but this similarity may be misleading.
First, Rogovskii's figures refer to 'official' overtime and are presumably
under-recorded, while the Ofer-Vinokur data come from a sample of workers
and therefore do not suffer from that source of bias. However, the Ofer-
Vinokur sample is biased against industry (and, indeed, against material
production where one would expect overtime to be most prevalent). When
one restricts attention to the hours worked by those actually reporting
overtime, the figure rises to 12·6 hours per week (12·8 hours for men and
12·2 hours for women). These are substantially higher than the figures for
Novosibirsk given above. At the same time, the proportion of the sample
doing overtime is smaller - 10·6 per cent.

In part, these inconsistencies might be accounted for by an increase in the
scale of overtime since the mid-1960s (due, perhaps, to growing labour
shortages in particular areas). And differences in the share of the sample
reporting an involvement in the practice might be due to sample bias.
Cherkasov also claims that the amount of overtime worked increases with
income (*sic*; but he may mean earnings) and with improvements in housing
conditions, and so on. Since the Ofer-Vinokur sample is more highly educated
and more highly skilled than the urban population of the USSR as a whole,
this effect may also contribute to the higher amounts of overtime recorded.
At all events, two conclusions can be drawn. First, that for those workers
actually involved, overtime constitutes a substantial addition to the working
week - perhaps as much as 1-2 hours a day; this would imply a commensurate
increase in take-home pay. Secondly, men are more likely to be involved than
women. The Ofer-Vinokur figures indicate that those women who work overtime put in almost as many hours as the men - but women are half as likely
to be involved. In this sense, then, it is plausible to assume that differential
participation will account for some of the difference in reported earnings.

But differential participation includes more than just overtime. It was
suggested above that all forms of moonlighting would be less prevalent among
women than men. That this is the case is indicated by the figures in Table 2.5,
also taken from the Ofer-Vinokur study. This shows that while for those
women actually involved, overtime, second jobs in the public sector and, to
a lesser extent, work in the private sector take up as much time as for men,
women are only half as likely to work overtime or in the private sector - and
only a quarter as likely to have a second public job. Since these figures
include voluntary and political work, this entry perhaps goes some way
towards explaining the relatively poor representation of Soviet women in
political office.

A long conclusion to this chapter would be out of place. I hope that the
figures speak for themselves. But it may be useful to summarise the main
points of the argument. In the first section I attempted to show that the goal
of sexual equality has been subordinated to the wider objectives of Soviet
wages policy. These in turn have emphasised the desirability of differentials,
of material incentives, of a relatively narrow concentration on the interrelation-
ship between wages and output. Attempts to secure sexual equality have been
restricted, for the most part, to the prohibition of rate discrimination. That

Table 2.5   *The Incidence of Overtime and Supplementary Work: USSR, 1972-3*

| | | The number of hours worked in | | | | |
| | | Main Job | | | Additional Jobs | |
| | *Total* | *Total* | *Regular* | *Overtime* | *Public* | *Private* |
| | | Those involved in each specific category | | | | |
| Males | 44·1 | 41·6 | 39·9 | 12·8 | 12·0 | 10·4 |
| Females | 39·7 | 38·8 | 38·0 | 12·2 | 12·0 | 9·0 |
| Ratio % | 90·0 | 93·3 | 95·2 | 95·3 | 100·0 | 86·5 |
| | | The sample as a whole | | | | |
| Males | 44·1 | 41·6 | 39·9 | 1·7 | 1·5 | 1·0 |
| Females | 39·7 | 38·7 | 37·8 | 0·9 | 0·4 | 0·5 |
| Ratio % | 90·0 | 93·3 | 94·7 | 52·9 | 26·7 | 50·0 |
| Female/Male Wage Ratio % | 65·7 | 67·0 | 66·4 | 70·5 | 71·4 | 64·0 |

*Source:* Ofer and Vinokur, 1979, Tables 5 and 15.

this is inadequate has been brought out by the evidence given later in the chapter. Disparities in earnings have been shown to be substantial, on a par with those in Western Europe; and there is little to suggest that recent reductions in intra-sectoral differentials have resulted in reductions in gross sex-linked earnings disparities. For the most part, these can be attributed to occupational segregation of one form or another, rather than to differences in hours worked. And this raises two further questions. Are the differences in the occupations commonly chosen by men and women attributable to prior differences in wage rates or are the differences in wage rates and earnings attributable to differential patterns of recruitment? And secondly, whatever the cause of occupational segregation, how far can it be termed rational - or is it a reflection of sex discrimination in a wider sense? These questions are taken up in later chapters. But first I consider changes in the level and structure of female employment.

## Notes: Chapter 2

1  Kapustin, 1974, p. 259. This statement was originally made by Lenin in 1921, but it has been cited more than once to add authority to this point of view. See, for example, Sukharevskii, 1974; see also Kulikov, 1972, p. 50, for a different quotation from Lenin.

2  Until 1976 this body (the Soviet analogue to a ministry of labour) was known as the State Committee on Labour and Wages. Since 1956 it has been responsible for the determination of wage and salary scales in the Soviet Union and, more generally, for

overseeing Soviet labour policy. Its role is discussed at greater length in McAuley, 1979, ch. 8.

3 In an attempt to increase the number of women working as tractor drivers, etc., the Soviet authorities reduced output-norms for women in these occupations by 10 per cent in 1970–1 (Fedorova, 1975, p. 63). As far as I am aware, this was the first breach of the principle of equal treatment for the sexes with respect to employment tasks. For further discussion of the reasons for this move and its consequences, see below, Chapter 6.

4 Since the position of women in agriculture raises problems that differ from those related to female employment in non-agriculture sectors, at least in Soviet conditions, estimates of earnings differences in this sector are deferred until Chapter 6 when these problems are discussed at length.

5 The three phases of Soviet wages policy mentioned in this paragraph are discussed at greater length in McAuley, 1979, chs 8–9.

6 Actually, it is probably a good deal less than that. Maikov and Novitskii refer to bodies, making no adjustment for the number of hours per week that they work. A proper comparison should surely adjust for this.

*Chapter 3*

# Female Employment and Participation, 1939-75

In Chapter 1 it was suggested that the Soviet strategy for achieving equality between the sexes involved the greatest possible expansion in female employment and the provision of equality of opportunity in the choice of occupations. The next four chapters are devoted to an analysis of the extent to which these goals have been achieved. In this chapter I deal with the question of female participation, Chapters 4 and 5 take up the question of employment opportunities and occupational segregation while Chapter 6 deals with the place of women in Soviet agriculture.

There are four aspects of female employment that are relevant to the assessment of the success of Soviet policy in this field. First, there is the question of the numbers of women in gainful employment. The measurement of the occupied female labour force in the USSR is complicated by the administrative distinction that Soviet statisticians make between state and collective-farm employment in agriculture. It is also affected by the difference between the census definition of employment (having a job on enumeration day) and the concept of annual average employment used in the current labour statistics. This latter concept makes some allowance for part-time and part-year working. These matters introduce a certain spread in estimates of the female labour force; they do not give rise to conceptual problems.

Secondly, one is interested in female participation rates, in the proportion of the female population that is in gainful employment. Since some women in the USSR continue to work after reaching the legal retirement age, the calculation of participation rates also raises the problem of the appropriate base population. But again this does not pose conceptual problems. However, since Soviet policy is designed to secure the maximal participation of women, assessment of that policy involves a determination of the allowances that should be made for differences in the functions of the sexes in the production and rearing of children. And this question does raise issues of principle. Some of these are discussed below, other are deferred until Chapter 9.

The remaining two aspects of female employment, the share of women in total employment and the broad sectoral affiliation of the female labour force, are straightforward. Let us now examine each of these aspects in greater detail.

**The Growth of Female Employment, 1939–75**

The growth of female employment in the USSR since 1940 is set out in Figure 3.1. The figure contains information on the three different indices of

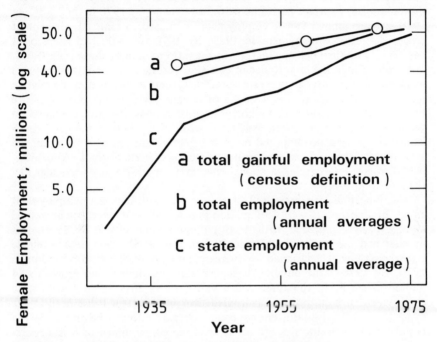

Figure 3.1    *The Growth of Female Employment, 1928–75.*

*Sources:* Female employment (census definition) from *Itogi* . . . , 1959, Table 48, and *Itogi* . . . , 1970, Vol. VI, Table 18; state employment (annual averages) *NK SSSR za 60 let*, p. 469; total employment (annual averages) ibid., *Zhenshchiny* . . . , 1975, p. 39.

female employment that can be derived from published Soviet statistics. First, using the population census definition of employment, it shows that the number of women with jobs increased from 34·1 million in 1939 to 47·6 million in 1959; the number of employed women increased by another 9·8 million in the next inter-censal period. These figures imply that the gainfully occupied female population increased at an average rate of 1·6 per cent per annum between 1939 and 1959 at the slightly faster rate of 2·1 per cent per annum in the next decade.

But the census figures given in the last paragraph make no allowance for part-time and part-year working. The second index given in the chart attempts to adjust for these influences. It provides estimates of annual average female employment in the state – and collective-farm sectors for a number of years since 1940. In this index employment is measured in woman-years so that, for example, a woman who works only three months in a given year is counted as a quarter of a woman; similarly, a woman working three days per week throughout the year would be counted as half a woman. According to this indicator, female employment grew from 27·8 million in 1940 to 40·5 million in 1960; it grew by another 14·1 million in the following decade. By 1974, the last year for which complete data are available, female employment had increased by a further 4·9 million to a total of 59 million. This index shows how unimportant part-time work had become by 1970 in the USSR. In 1940, average annual female employment amounted to some 81 per cent of census definition employment in 1939. By 1970 the ratio had risen to 94 per cent. More than half the increase in the ratio took place during the 1960s. This reduction in the importance of part-time (or, more accurately, part-year) work can be attributed to two processes. First, there is a decline in the relative importance of agriculture as a sphere of female employment; secondly, since the late 1950s a number of kolkhozy have been converted to state farms. In general, conversion has been associated with an increase in the earnings of labour but it has also imposed more stringent conditions of work upon the agricultural labour force. Agricultural workers, particularly sovkhoznitsy, have less freedom of choice about whether to work on any particular day than do kolkhoznitsy.

The final indicator presented in Figure 3.1 relates to state employment alone. In 1940, there were 13·2 million female state employees, on an annual average basis (compared with 14·6 million kolkhoznitsy); by 1960, this number had more than doubled to 29·2 million. In the next decade female state employment continued to increase rapidly, reaching 45·8 million in 1970. By 1976–7 the number of female state employees had grown to 54 million. That is, in the three and a half decades after 1940, female state employment has more than quadrupled. Part of this growth has been at the expense of collective-farm employment and part reflects the growth in the population of working age, but as we shall see below, much of it is a consequence of recruiting an increasing proportion of available women into paid employment.

Readily available Soviet data allow one to push the state employment index back to 1928, the beginning of the period of central planning and rapid industrialisation in the USSR. As Figure 3.1 shows, the rate of growth of female state employment in this decade was even more rapid than in the following thirty to forty years. Between 1928 and 1940 the number of female state employees more than quadrupled from 2·8 million to 13·2 million. It is not possible to determine how much of this growth was at the expense of agricultural employment since the collectivisation of agriculture was not substantially completed until the mid-1930s and the definition of female participation in a peasant economy raises a number of difficulties. Equally, problems over the publication of earlier population censuses make it difficult to ascertain how much of the growth in female state employment merely reflects growth in the population of working age. Certainly, the use of this index would overstate increases in gainful employment and participation. None the less, it is clear that the decade of the 1930s (and not the years 1941–5) witnessed the major breakthrough in female employment.

**Female Participation Rates, 1939-75**

Figure 3.1 recorded the sustained growth in female employment that has occurred in the USSR since the end of the 1930s. But the volume of gainful employment provides only part of the information necessary for the assessment of the success of the Soviet authorities in encouraging the incorporation of women into the social economy. For this, one needs to know not only how many women were employed, but also what proportion of women of working age were gainfully occupied; that is, one needs to calculate participation rates.

The Soviet statistical authorities do not publish annual estimates of the female labour force or population of working age. But the decennial censuses do contain such a figure. Thus, using census data, there are estimates of the crude female participation rate for only three years. (In fact, since I have been unable to find statistics on the age-composition of the Soviet population broken down by sex for 1939, only two reliable estimates are available.) However, working with published census data, Western demographers have produced age- and sex-specific projections of the Soviet population for non-census years. These can be combined with estimates of annual average employment to generate estimates of female participation for periods when census figures are not available. Although this series is not consistent with that derived from the census, there is no reason to suppose that it is internally inconsistent. It therefore allows us to trace the course of female participation, for example, for the years since 1970.

In addition to the crude participation rates discussed so far, the detailed breakdown of the population by age, sex and employment status permits the calculation of age-specific participation rates. Unfortunately, because the published returns for the 1970 census did not contain data on the age distribution of the employed population broken down by sex, one must rely upon Soviet estimates of age-specific participation rates. These have been published only for the USSR as a whole. Most of the other participation indicators can be calculated on a regional or republican basis. Age-specific participation rates cast light on the way in which women reconcile their conflicting roles of worker and mother. It would be of interest to trace the impact of regional variations in birth rates upon the employment of women of different ages; but available statistics do not permit that degree of detail.

Using census definitions of employment and population of working age (from 16 to 54 years inclusive), 73·5 per cent of working-age women in the USSR were employed in 1959. In 1970, the analogous figure was 86·3 per cent. If one assumes that the ratio of women of working age to the total female population was the same in 1939 as it was in 1959 (which is dubious) then the crude female participation rate in the earlier year was 60·9 per cent. By international standards, even the figure for 1939 is very high; the figures for 1959 and, even more, for 1970, are unapproached in industrial market economies. They suggest that the Soviet authorities have gone a considerable way towards realising their goal of incorporating women into the social economy.

The figures in Table 3.1 cast further light on these high levels of female participation in the USSR. Note first that to allow for the fact that many women above the age of retirement continue in gainful employment, participation rates are defined with reference to the population aged 15–70 years and not the population of working age given in the census. This accounts for the differences between the crude rates given in the previous paragraph and those given in the table. But even using this wider definition, a participation rate of 60–65 per cent is extremely high by international standards.

Table 3.1    *Age- and Sex-Specific Participation Rates: USSR, 1959, 1970*

| Age-Group | 1959 | | | 1970 | | |
|---|---|---|---|---|---|---|
| | Males | Females | Total | Males | Females | Total |
| 15–19 | 85·8 | 60·2 | 59·5* | 41·8 | 37·4 | 39·6 |
| 20–29 | 91·0 | 75·1 | 83·0 | 89·5 | 85·1 | 87·3 |
| 30–39 | 94·9 | 71·6 | 81·6 | 97·6 | 91·2 | 94·3 |
| 40–49 | 92·6 | 65·8 | 76·1 | 95·9 | 88·6 | 91·8 |
| 50–54 | 87·0 | 52·9 | 66·0 | 89·4 | 74·2 | 79·9 |
| 55–59 | 80·5 | 30·0 | 46·8 | 79·5 | 23·5 | 43·4 |
| 60–69 | 68·0 | 18·2 | 35·6 | 29·3 | 7·8 | 15·1 |
| Total | 85·8 | 60·2 | 71·2 | 79·9 | 65·0 | 71·8 |

*Note:* *As given in the source.
*Source:* Quoted in Newth, 1975.

At first glance, the fact that there are still substantial differences between male and female participation rates might be thought to suggest that there is scope for substantial further expansion in female employment. But the crude rates are misleading. Even in 1959, the difference was to a substantial extent attributable to difference in effective retirement age; in the prime working (and childbearing) ages differences are much less marked. And this is more true of 1970 than of the earlier year.

Differences in effective retirement age are influenced by the legal retirement age as laid down in the social security legislation. In 1970, the legal age of retirement was 60 for men and 55 for women. The figures in Table 3.1 show that between three-quarters and four-fifths of the occupied population remains at work until it attains this age. Between a quarter and a third continue to work after becoming eligible for a pension. In both cases, men are more likely to remain in employment than women (a reflection, perhaps, of the Soviet practice of leaving children to be looked after by their grandmother) but differences are not great when due allowance is made for the age of official retirement. The rather higher participation rates in the upper age-groups in 1959 can be attributed to the fact that at this date kolkhozniki were not entitled to retirement pensions.

A striking feature of the age-specific female participation rates recorded in Table 3.1 is that they do not indicate a participation trough for the peak childbearing ages. In many Western industrial economies the typical employment profile for women is one characterised by relatively high participation among the young followed by a decline that accompanies marriage and the birth of children; this, in turn, is followed by a rise as women return to work after completing their families. Although the presence of such a trough in the Soviet case might be partially masked by the fact that only ten-year-age groups are given, in fact, the actual statistics give no hint of such a pattern. Labour force separation in order to raise a family does not appear to be a Soviet phenomenon.

Finally, the changed participation pattern among the youngest age-group should be noticed. Participation here is most affected by continuing education. The figures in Table 3.1 reveal a substantial increase in the incidence of education beyond the age of 15 for both boys and girls. They also suggest that by 1970 the experience of both sexes was similar. This topic is discussed further in Chapter 8.

So far, the discussion has focused on participation rates for the USSR as a whole; but the Soviet Union is a large country characterised by considerable ethnic, cultural and economic diversity. And this affects the position of women both in the labour market and in society at large. Some idea of the scale of regional disparities in female participation rates is given by the figures in Table 3.2. The table also casts some light on changes in participation since

Table 3.2    *Trends in Female Participation: USSR and Subdivisions, 1960-75*

| | Base: Female Population Aged 16-54 years | | | | Base: Female Population Aged 15-70 years | | | |
| --- | --- | --- | --- | --- | --- | --- | --- | --- |
| | *1960* | *1965* | *1970* | *1975* | *1960* | *1965* | *1970* | *1975* |
| USSR | 62·7 | 72·7 | 81·6 | 83·1 | 50·3 | 56·8 | 61·5 | 64·3 |
| RSFSR | 66·7 | 76·0 | 85·1 | 86·9 | 53·7 | 59·2 | 63·7 | 66·7 |
| Ukraine | 60·0 | 70·3 | 81·1 | 84·1 | 47·7 | 54·3 | 59·9 | 63·6 |
| Byelorussia | 66·8 | 76·8 | 87·6 | 88·1 | 52·9 | 59·3 | 66·1 | 68·8 |
| Moldavia | 60·0 | 70·9 | 81·3 | 82·0 | 49·8 | 58·2 | 64·4 | 66·0 |
| Kazakhstan | 49·6 | 63·0 | 71·8 | 72·5 | 40·7 | 51·1 | 56·9 | 58·9 |
| Baltic | 65·0 | 78·2 | 88·4 | 90·7 | 50·0 | 59·0 | 66·1 | 69·8 |
| Caucasus | 53·0 | 58·2 | 63·4 | 64·2 | 43·3 | 46·7 | 49·8 | 52·0 |
| Central Asia | 60·1 | 67·4 | 66·5 | 65·4 | 47·2 | 52·9 | 52·2 | 53·2 |

*Notes and Sources:* Each entry is computed as ratio of annual average female employment in state and collective-farm sectors to the appropriate base population. Female collective-farm employment was derived by multiplying annual average employment by the proportion that was female according to the 1970 Census (Vol. V, Table 11); employment from *NK SSSR*, various years; population from Baldwin, 1975, and back-projection.

the 1970 Census. (Note that in Table 3.2 participation rates are calculated as the ratio of annual average female employment in the state and co-operative sectors to the female population of working age on various definitions. This explains the inconsistencies between All-Union rates given in Tables 3.1 and 3.2.)

First, at the All-Union level, Table 3.2 shows that female participation has continued to increase since 1970 – albeit slowly. Secondly, the difference between the figures for 1970 given in the two tables (61·5 per cent and 65·0 per cent using the broader definition of working age population) is a measure of the scale of part-time and part-year working among Soviet women. It can thus be seen to be of minor importance. Finally, the figures in the first panel of the table confirm what was said above: by 1970 and even more by 1975, there was little further scope for expanding female employment.

Turning now to regional variations in female participation: Table 3.2 shows that these were present in 1960 and that they have grown more marked in the last twenty years. There has also been some change in the ranking of various regions. In 1960, the regions of lowest female participation were Kazakhstan and the Transcaucasus; the Ukraine, Moldavia and Central Asia occupied an intermediate position while the RSFSR, Byelorussia and the Baltic states were areas of high participation. Over the next ten to fifteen years female participation increased in all regions – but at differing rates. The RSFSR, Byelorussia and the Baltic are still areas of high female employment and these have now been joined by Moldavia. The Ukraine and possibly Kazakhstan now occupy the intermediate positions while the Transcaucasus and Central Asia are now the regions of low female employment. According to the second panel of Table 3.2, participation in Central Asia has barely changed since 1965 (according to the first panel, it even fell slightly between 1965 and 1975).

These changes in female participation rates are a consequence of differing paths of demographic development in the different regions and an apparent change in the determinants of female employment. In 1959 (and also in 1939, for all the limitations of the data relating to that year) there was a weak positive correlation between the crude female participation rate and the proportion of women employed in the manual agricultural job categories. In 1970 the correlation, although still weak, was negative.[1] As might be expected, in 1970 at least there was a much stronger negative correlation between female participation and the birth rate ($r^2 = 0.5363$). These relationships would seem to suggest that in 1959 (and also in 1939, although the data are not good enough to establish it conclusively) regional disparities in female participation were determined by the greater propensity of women in agricultural communities to take part in productive activity. By 1970, the declining role of agriculture in the Soviet economy meant that this factor was no longer strong enough to outweigh the socially determined role conflict between woman-as-mother and woman-as-worker. The weak negative correlation mentioned above is to be explained by the fact that the regions in which the birth rate was highest in 1970 were also the least developed. This suggests a positive correlation between the birth rate and the importance of agriculture in the republican economy.

The discussion of the last few pages has shown that in the past thirty or forty years the Soviet authorities have been successful in their attempts to expand female employment. Participation rates for women in the USSR are now extremely high by international standards. I have suggested that there is now very little scope for the further recruitment of women into the gainfully occupied labour force. That is, the USSR is approaching maximal female participation; in some republics, this may have been exceeded. This issue is explored at greater length in the next section.

**Is Female Participation Excessive?**

As I argued in Chapter 1, the Soviet strategy for achieving sexual equality is predicated upon the incorporation of women into the social economy. Participation in work outside the home serves two functions: it is a means of overcoming the dependent status of women within the family and it contributes to women's psychological and social development. By giving women their own source of income, employment renders them at least partially independent of their husbands. It thus allows the family to evolve into a union of equal partners.

But, the social roles of men and women cannot be restricted to participation in collective work. If society is to continue, children must be born and reared. Individuals must reconcile their employment and parental roles. How far the rearing of the next generation will conflict with active participation in the labour force is partly a matter of biology and partly determined by social attitudes and the availability of alternative child care facilities. As a matter of biological fact, the bearing of children impinges primarily upon a woman's capacity for work outside the home. It is also the case that Soviet social conventions regard the subsequent nurture of children as primarily the woman's responsibility. And this too will tend to reduce female participation rates below those for males.

How great a difference in sex-specific participation rates there will be under such social arrangements depends upon a number of factors. It depends upon the amount of time that one or other parent must devote exclusively to their offspring and upon the number and spacing of offspring produced, that is, upon the birth rate. It may also depend upon the existence of other factors leading to sex-specific differences in participation. All these issues are complex and the relationship between employment and women's domestic responsibilities will be discussed at length in Chapters 9 and 10. Here I report on some calculations that cast light upon the strain that maternity imposes upon women in Soviet conditions.

According to Soviet social security regulations, employed women are entitled to 112 days paid maternity leave per child. They are also entitled to take further unpaid leave until their child's first birthday without loss of their job or seniority. These legal norms provide two estimates of the time that the Soviet authorities believe should be devoted to the exclusive care of a child. In the 1970s there has been some discussion among Soviet specialists of the problems associated with the communal care of very young children and some authors have advocated that the emphasis of government policy should change towards the universal provision of pre-school child care facilities for those aged 3 to 7 together with only restricted provision of facilities for the under-3s. The implications of these debates for female employment are discussed at greater length below; here I note them only to derive a third (more liberal) estimate of the time that should be devoted to the exclusive care of children in Soviet conditions.

If one assumes that it will be the mother who looks after the children, then by multiplying the figures derived in the previous paragraph by the number of live births, one will obtain three estimates of the number of woman-years that should be devoted to the exclusive care of the next generation. If one further assumes that there are no other reasons why male and female participation rates should differ, then dividing these figures by the female population of working age, one obtains three estimates of the hypothetical difference in male and female participation rates that can be attributed to the rearing of children. If the actual difference corresponds to one of these estimates, one can infer that, given the birth rate, and the arrangements for child care, female participation is maximal. If the difference between actual sex-specific participation rates is less than the estimate, one may infer that, given the birth rate, female participation is excessive.

In interpreting the results of such comparisons, there are three reservations to be borne in mind. It seems fairly safe to claim that the lowest estimate of 112 days per child relates to the length of time that a woman would find it physically difficult to combine pregnancy and child care with paid employment. Indeed, it may be an underestimate. There is some doubt however, about whether women would find it *physically* necessary to devote themselves exclusively to child care for as long as a year. It is presumably possible for fathers to assume responsibility for their offspring – at least after they have been weaned. Thus the middle estimate contains an element of social convention. This is even more true of the upper estimate. The three-year separation period is an overestimate for another reason; where families have more than one child, there is no reason to assume that the interval between them will be as great as this. Finally, it should be pointed out that all three estimates are derived from Soviet official actions or attitudes. It is at least possible that the opinions of Soviet families (and of Soviet women in particular) will differ. They may regard what appears on these considerations to be maximal female participation (and hence a success of Soviet employment policy) as excessively burdensome.

Alternatively, one might assume that women's detachment from the labour force may be restricted to late pregnancy and a few weeks following the birth of a child. Certainly, by the time that the child is weaned, the duties of child care can be shared equally by both parents. For the purposes of calculation, one may take either the official Soviet paid maternity leave period or the ante-natal leave period plus five months (the date on which the social security grant designed to defray part of the cost of weaning is payable) as the length of time for which the care of children is exclusively the mother's responsibility. Thus, if later child care duties are shared equally, one might expect a labour force detachment of 0·306–0·57 woman-years per child in addition to whatever reduction in participation there was on the part of both women and men to look after their families. Given data on male and female participation rates, the birth rate and the population of working age, one can calculate the implied separation time per child. If this falls short of the figure given above, I suggest that, even assuming an equal distribution of the burden of child care duties (which is certainly not the case in the USSR), female employment is excessive.

The results of carrying out the calculations described here are given in Table 3.3. The first column gives the difference in sex-specific participation rates on census definitions for each of the fifteen Soviet republics in 1970;

Table 3.3  *Participation Differentials and the Birth Rate: USSR and Republics, 1970*

|  | Differences in Sex-Specific Participation Rates | Differences Ascribable to Child Care Assuming Separation is: | | | Implied Separation Time per Child (years) |
|---|---|---|---|---|---|
|  |  | 0·306 years | 1 year | 3 years |  |
| RSFSR | 2·05 | 1·57 | 5·12 | 15·35 | 0·40 |
| Ukraine | 3·30 | 1·62 | 5·29 | 15·87 | 0·83 |
| Byelorussia | 2·35 | 1·81 | 5·92 | 17·77 | 0·40 |
| Uzbekistan | 8·46 | 4·83 | 15·78 | 47·35 | 0·54 |
| Kazakhstan | 10·58 | 2·86 | 9·34 | 28·03 | 1·13 |
| Georgia | 10·33 | 2·18 | 7·13 | 21·40 | 1·45 |
| Azerbaijan | 18·07 | 4·07 | 13·29 | 39·88 | 1·36 |
| Lithuania | 9·10 | 1·96 | 6·42 | 19·27 | 1·42 |
| Moldavia | 3·55 | 2·13 | 6·96 | 20·88 | 0·51 |
| Latvia | 0·97 | 1·56 | 5·11 | 15·33 | 0·19 |
| Kirgizia | 8·18 | 4·20 | 13·73 | 41·20 | 0·60 |
| Tadjikistan | 16·41 | 5·03 | 16·44 | 49·32 | 1·00 |
| Armenia | 12·92 | 2·79 | 9·12 | 27·37 | 1·42 |
| Turkmenistan | 11·50 | 5·02 | 16·39 | 49·18 | 0·70 |
| Estonia | −0·37 | 1·72 | 5·64 | 16·91 |  |
| USSR (1939) | 22·63 | 3·25 | 10·62 | 31·87 | 2·13 |
| USSR (1959) | 20·03 | 2·46 | 8·03 | 24·09 | 2·49 |
| USSR (1970) | 4·05 | 1·94 | 6·33 | 18·98 | 0·64 |

*Notes:* Entries in Column (2) give the difference (in percentage points) between male and female participation rates on census definition in 1970. Entries in Columns (3) to (5) give the difference in sex-specific participation rates that would occur if only women looked after children, if child care was the sole reason for differences and if exclusive child care lasted for the time stated. Entries in Column (6) give the period of time for which exclusive child care lasts if male and female participation rates are otherwise assumed to be equal.

analogous figures are given for the USSR in 1970, 1959 and (with some degree of error) for 1939. Thus, in 1970, the male participation rate for the USSR as a whole was 90·35 per cent, the female one was 86·30 per cent and the difference, recorded in the table, was 4·05 percentage points. The next three columns give the percentage point difference to be expected, given the birth rate in 1970, if the care of children was the exclusive responsibility of women, if child care was the sole source of disparities in participation and if exclusive child care involved respectively 0·306 years (i.e. 112 days), one year and three years. Thus, given the number of live births in Byelorussia in 1970 and given the size of the female population of working age, if each birth resulted in a woman leaving gainful employment for one year, one would expect the female participation rate to be 5·92 percentage points lower than the male one.

In all but two republics the actual difference in participation rates exceeds what would have been observed if women had restricted themselves to the legal minimum maternity leave.[2] However, for the USSR as a whole and for almost all of the more developed (and hence better-off) republics, actual differences fall short of those that would have been observed if all women had availed themselves of the legal opportunity to take a full year off after giving birth to a child. And nowhere does the gap approach that implied by a three-year separation period. In this, the situation is very different from 1959 (for the USSR as a whole).

The figures in the last column of the table report the implied separation time per child (in woman-years) on the assumption that childbirth and child care are the only reasons for the differences in participation rates reported in Column (2). In the RSFSR, Byelorussia and the Baltic states these fall short of the 0·57 years per child suggested as indicative of equality in the burden of child care. Separation times of the order of 0·5–0·6 years per child are recorded for Uzbekistan, Moldavia and Kirgizia. For all of these areas (and for the USSR as a whole in 1970) these figures suggest that female employment is excessive given the birth rate, what is known about men's attitudes to looking after children and the availability of social care facilities.

It is my belief that in Soviet conditions (given the character and extent of the services sector, the availability of pre-school child care facilities, and so on) it is reasonable to expect the birth of a child to result in the mother's separation from the labour force for a year. Therefore I would suggest that female participation is excessive in all those republics in which the entry in the last column of Table 3.3 is less than unity. In the more industrialised non-Muslim republics there has been a marked fall in the birth rate in the past two decades. If this is to be seen as one aspect of Soviet women's reaction to the conflict imposed by the attempt to reconcile motherhood with paid employment (and I think that it can be), then the figures in Table 3.3 suggest that this decline is likely to continue. Similarly, in Central Asia one may expect a fall, and perhaps a dramatic fall, in birth rates or participation as urbanisation continues. That is, if large families are culturally determined it is female employment that will give way as the agricultural imperative diminishes in strength. More plausibly, it will be population growth that will feel the effects. This is likely to exacerbate an already difficult labour supply problem that the planners in the USSR face. And, notice that any attempt to increase the supply of labour in the short term by the greater employment of women will only make the long-term problem more acute. The solution to this problem lies in the expansion of those aspects of the services sector that would make it easier for the average Soviet woman to combine the roles of mother and worker (or the acceptance of permanently lower female participation rates – that is, the abandonment of one of the objectives of Soviet employment policy!).

Low and declining birth rates are only one consequence of excessive female participation, however. Another plausible response of women to the excessive demands of job and family is the non-acquisition of skills. Thus, these factors will influence the quality of the female labour force and the character of the jobs that they do. This issue will be discussed in Chapters 4–6. But first I turn to the remaining aspects of female employment in the USSR that are of interest.

**Sex Ratios in Employment, 1939-75**

Figure 3.2 provides information on the share of women in total employment since the beginning of the period of central planning. As in Figure 3.1, three

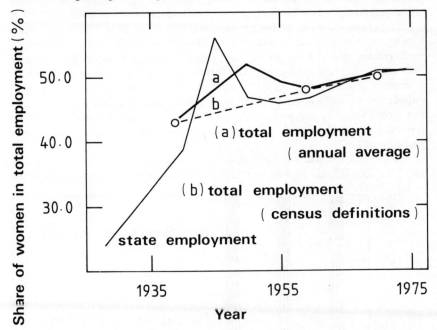

Figure 3.2 *The Share of Women in Total Employment, 1928-74.*

*Sources:* Female employment – see sources listed for Figure 3.1; total employment (census definitions) *Itogi* . . . , 1959, Table 47, *Itogi* . . . , 1970, Vol. VI, Table 2; state employment (annual averages) *NK SSSR 1975*, p. 531; total employment (annual averages) ibid., p. 440, *NK SSSR 1970*, p. 404, *Zhenshchiny* . . . , 1975, p. 39.

different definitions of employment are given. Although, due to the absence of data on female employment in the co-operative sector in 1945 and the absence of a census in 1949, the first impression created by the chart is misleading, on closer examination three things become clear.

In 1939 agriculture in the USSR was overwhelmingly organised on a collective-farm basis. The fact that at that date the share of women in total employment was greater than their share in state employment indicates that women were disproportionately employed in agriculture. This is a reflection of the recruitment patterns of the period according to which it was the men who left the villages first, going to work in state enterprises, while their wives and daughters stayed behind to provide a labour force for Stalin's farms. The disparity in sex ratios is even more marked in 1950 after conscription had created an added channel of male migration. By 1959, however, and even more by 1970, both shrinkage in the relative importance of the collective-farm sector and female rural-urban migration had restored sex ratios in the kolkhoz sector to those in the economy as a whole.

The rapid growth in the share of women in state employment during the 1930s parallels the growth of female employment recorded in Figure 3.1; it reflects the incorporation of urban housewives into the gainfully occupied population during the period of falling real wages and family incomes that accompanied the early five-year plans. The impact of the Second World War on the sex-composition of the civilian labour force in the USSR is also clear. Finally, in the postwar years, the conflicting effects of increasing female participation and the return to demographic normalcy (after the excess of male deaths occasioned by war, revolution and political repression) are clear.

Similar charts can be drawn to show the share of women in the employed population of different republics. Predictably, they indicate that this share has grown virtually everywhere since the 1930s and that it is highest in those republics where the female participation rate is greatest. Such charts are not reproduced here.

So far this chapter has been concerned with the scale of female employment in the USSR. Figures 3.3 and 3.4 illustrate a different aspect – the

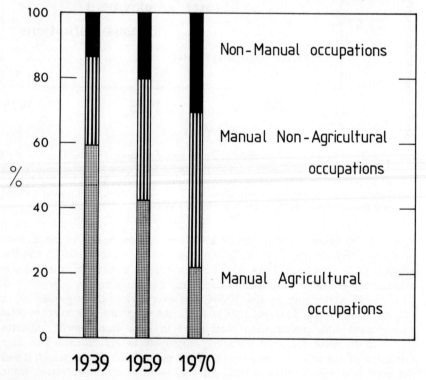

Figure 3.3    *The Sectoral Structure of Female Employment: USSR, 1939–70.*

broad sector in which women work. In Figure 3.3 the structure of female employment for the USSR as a whole in the last three census years is displayed. Figure 3.4 gives similar information for each of the union republics in 1970.

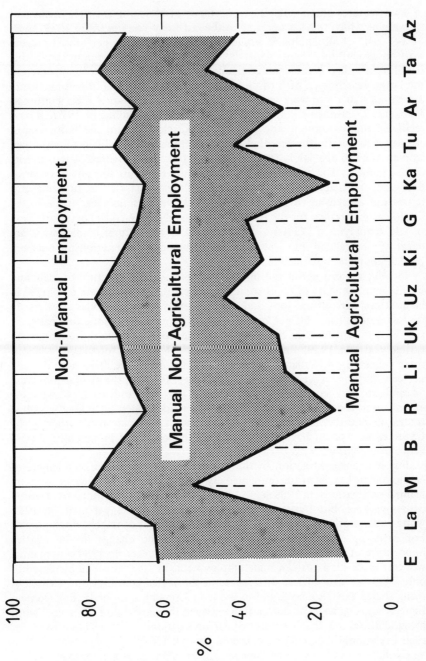

Figure 3.4   *The Sectoral Structure of Female Employment: by Republic, 1970.*

*Note:* The republics are arrayed from left to right in order of decreasing female participation rates.

Two features stand out: the importance of agricultural employment and the rate at which this has declined in the last forty years or so. In 1939, some 60 per cent of all employed women in the Soviet Union performed manual work in agriculture; twenty years later, this had declined to about two-fifths. It fell by another 20 percentage points between 1959 and 1970, but even in the latter year fully a fifth of employed women worked on the farm. Figure 3.4 shows that there were wide variations in the importance of agriculture as a sphere for women's employment between the republics in 1970. It was relatively unimportant in the RSFSR, in Kazakhstan and the Baltic states; elsewhere it was still the case that between a third and two-fifths of employed women worked the land. There is another feature of Figure 3.4 that merits brief comment. The republics are arrayed in it from left to right in order of decreasing participation rates. With one or two reversals this ordering also represents decreasing living standards. Yet there is no clear evidence of declining importance for the role of non-manual (white-collar) occupations in female employment. Clearly, white-collar and agricultural employment are negatively correlated, but there appears to be no strong relationship between participation and non-manual employment.

Finally, a word about the differences between the structure of male and female employment: in 1970 some 46 per cent of women were employed in manual non-agricultural jobs and 32 per cent were white-collar workers. In the same year, some 60 per cent of employed men were in the first category and 22 per cent were in the second. Differences were even more marked in earlier years; in 1939, for example, almost 50 per cent of the male labour force was engaged in manual non-agricultural work while little more than 27 per cent of women were in the same category. In 1959, the proportions were 54 and 36 per cent respectively. Thus in the past and, to a considerable extent, even today non-agricultural manual work (which includes the skilled trades in industry, construction and transport) has been men's work in the USSR while women have continued to be concentrated in agricultural (and hence unskilled) work.

For women, contraction in the importance of agriculture as a sphere of employment has been accompanied by growth in the significance of non-manual occupations. In 1939 some 14 per cent of employed women were white-collar workers, but by 1970 this had increased to 32 per cent. In 1959 white-collar workers accounted for about 22 per cent of female employment. For men, in contrast, there has been almost no change in the relative importance of white-collar work in the last forty years. In 1939 non-manual workers made up a fifth of male employment; in 1970 this had increased to only 22·3 per cent. These differences in the sexual composition of employment shares can also be found in individual republics in 1970. For women, there is a strong negative correlation between the importance of manual work in agriculture and that of non-manual occupations ($r^2 = 0·8311$); for men, such a relation, though negative, is weak ($r^2 = 0·1807$).

Explanations of this phenomenon will be taken up at greater length in the next chapter. But, since non-manual work consists of both management functions and the provision of various services, and since there is no reason to suppose that there are diminishing returns to scale in the exercise of higher management, it is at least consistent with the suggestion that men have retained control of executive decision-making in the Soviet Union although women have made up an increasing proportion of the labour force of a growing services sector.

The analysis of this chapter has shown how successful the Soviet authorities have been in securing high levels of female employment and participation. Women now account for about half of the gainfully employed population in the Soviet Union and between two-thirds and four-fifths of all women (depending upon the definition of working age population that one adopts) were employed in 1970. Since then, participation rates have increased further. But this success has been achieved at a price. In many parts of the country, female participation rates would seem to be excessive; and this may have had (and may still be exerting) an adverse effect on the birth rate. It also appears that women have been disproportionately recruited into low-skilled sectors. But the measurement and even the meaning of occupational segregation raises a number of problems. These will be the subject of the next two chapters.

### Notes: Chapter 3

1  Using census definition employment and the female population aged 16–55 to calculate participation rates, the correlation coefficient for the fifteen Union republics in 1959 was 0·2535; for the thirteen republics that were part of the USSR in 1939 it was 0·1719. In 1970 the correlation coefficient was —0·3654. On a standard test none of these coefficients differed significantly from zero at the 5 per cent level; but the changed slope of the regression line is suggestive.

2  The very low figure for Latvia and the negative one for Estonia are a consequence of the fact that the table makes use of census definition participation rates. For these, the female population aged 16–54 years is used as a denominator while actual employment is used in the numerator. If a higher proportion of women aged 55+ than men aged 60+ remain in employment, the gap in participation rates will be artificially narrowed.

*Chapter 4*

# Horizontal Segregation in the Labour Market, 1939-70

The popular image of the employed woman in the Soviet Union is made up of two possibly inconsistent components. On the one hand, there is the belief that women have successfully penetrated all the male occupational preserves, that sex is no barrier to the able and ambitious girl wishing to pursue any career not positively harmful to her health. This is the world of smiling female tractor drivers, of women enterprise managers or control engineers; it is the world of Valentina Tereshkova, the first woman in space. This belief is fostered by many official Soviet publications and by such books as *Soviet Women* (Mandel, 1975). On the other hand, there is the belief that Soviet women are still largely excluded from positions of power and influence in their society, that they are confined to menial or physically exacting jobs demanding little skill or training. This is the world of women street-cleaners, construction workers, agricultural labourers, the world of waitresses, cooks and shop-girls. This belief is fostered by the accounts of many Western journalists, the writings of Western academics and, increasingly, by the works of Soviet sociologists concerned with the position of women in the USSR. If one is to assess how far the goal of sexual equality set out in the 1936 Constitution has been achieved in the USSR it is important to determine which of these components contains the greater element of truth. This is the purpose of the next two chapters.

The second strand of Soviet policy designed to achieve equality between the sexes, as set out in Chapter 1, involved the guarantee of equal employment opportunities for men and women. In attempting to ascertain how far this has been achieved, one runs into a conceptual problem: what does one mean by employment opportunities? Are they best defined in terms of the jobs that most women do? Or should one rather concentrate on the jobs most commonly done by women? Perhaps I can best explain the distinction by means of a slightly far-fetched example. The occupation of ballerina is open only to women - and hence it is an example of an employment opportunity in the second sense given above. But only a small minority of Soviet women are ballerinas. Agricultural labour, on the other hand, or local government manual work are job categories that contain large numbers of Soviet women - indeed, they are two of the most common job categories in the census returns. They are therefore employment opportunities in the first sense mentioned. But both job categories also contain large numbers of men. They are certainly not exclusively female employment opportunities.

If the focus of one's interest is on the real employment possibilities open to the average Soviet woman, it seems plausible to argue that preference should be given to the first definition. Surely, the jobs that women actually do provide the best indication of the opportunities open to them. On the other hand, where one is concerned with role-models and the formation of aspirations, the second definition might be more relevant. It is surely of importance to note that a high proportion of Soviet physicians are women, even though a very small minority of Soviet women are doctors. In any case, the primary emphasis in this book will be on employment opportunities in the first sense; but some attention will be paid to the character of overwhelmingly and exclusively female occupations.

Given that one has decided to measure employment opportunities in terms of the jobs that most women do, there are three further issues that are relevant to the assessment of equality of opportunity. First, there is the extent to which the jobs done by women differ from those done by men. I shall call this *horizontal segregation*. Secondly, there is the extent to which the jobs done by women call for less skill or involve less responsibility than those done by men. I shall call this *vertical segregation*. Finally, there is the extent to which women's jobs are concentrated in different economic sectors than those of men. This will be called *administrative segregation*. Together, these three elements make up what is frequently called occupational segregation.

In the broadest sense of the term, equality of employment opportunity requires the absence of all three aspects of occupational segregation. But the presence of either horizontal or administrative segregation need not necessarily be a cause for social concern. The jobs done by women may differ from those done by men, but in a certain sense both sets of occupations may involve similar levels of skill; both may yield similar levels of job satisfaction.

Equally, men and women may perform similar operations, they may do the same jobs in a certain sense, but because these are located in plants classified into different industries, their jobs may be called by different names. In Soviet conditions, administrative segregation may give rise to earnings differences (and this, surely, would be a cause for concern) but other aspects of job satisfaction may not differ too greatly.

On the other hand, it seems more plausible to assume that differences in job description reflect differences in job content and that the presence of substantial horizontal or administrative segregation should be taken as *prima facie* evidence of inequality in employment opportunities. Further, if there is a positive relationship between the wage or salary that a job pays and the level of satisfaction that it affords (and this seems a reasonable general hypothesis to maintain in spite of the exceptions for dirty or degrading work that one can think of) the earnings disparities between men and women reported in Chapter 2 are symptomatic of a wider inequality in the Soviet labour market.

The material presented in Chapters 2 and 3, then, suggests that the Soviet authorities have been unable to guarantee equality of opportunity to women in the labour market. In the rest of this chapter I attempt to chart the changes in horizontal segregation that have taken place in the last thirty or forty years and also to explore how it varied between the different Soviet republics in 1970. Changes in the scale of vertical and administrative segregation are taken up in Chapter 5. Taken together, these two chapters provide a clearer picture of the sources of sexual inequality in the Soviet labour market, of the problems that remain to be explained.

### The Measurement of Horizontal Segregation

The measurement of horizontal segregation in the USSR (or, for that matter, in any other economy) poses both conceptual and empirical problems. First, it calls for detailed information about the occupations of employed men and women and this is not always available. But it also requires a method for reducing this detailed information to a single statistic – or at most a few parameters. It is only in this way that one can readily ascertain whether segregation has increased or decreased, whether it is higher in one area or another; it is only in this way that one can relate changes (or differences) in segregation to changes (or differences) other economic and social variables. That is, only in this way can one search for explanations of horizontal segregation – and thus cast light on the policies likely to reduce it.

The most detailed published information on the occupations of men and women in the USSR is to be found in the population censuses. This is probably true of many other countries as well, in the past if not at the present time. Since census data suffer from certain shortcomings as a source of information on the extent of horizontal segregation, it is as well to spell these out if this discussion is to have any general relevance.

Population censuses are relatively infrequent; they permit, then, only infrequent estimates of the scale of horizontal segregation. As mentioned in the last chapter, information is available on only three or four Soviet censuses. Censuses were held in 1939, 1959 and 1970 and although the 1939 Census was not published, data on the occupational structure of the employed population are given in the census for 1959. (A census was also held in 1926, but structural change in the Soviet economy between that year and 1939 makes comparisons for this period of less interest than for later years.)

The census classification of the employed population is in terms of what may be called job categories. In some areas of employment the classification refers to occupations – that is, descriptions of what people do. For example, the Soviet tables contain information about the numbers of cooks, waitresses, shop assistants or weavers. Elsewhere, the classification refers only to the sector of employment. For example, in the Soviet case again, the tables refer to the number of manual workers in the food-processing industry, to printing trade operatives or to manual workers in rail transport. In those employment fields (presumably those of most interest to the compilers) where job categories are specified in some detail, one has some confidence that they refer to homogeneous occupations and, therefore, that reported sex ratios correspond to those found 'on the ground' as it were. In other areas, much less detail is given and disparate occupations are combined into miscellaneous job categories. This can lead to bias in reported sex ratios. (Consider the consequences of a common agglomeration – beauticians, barbers and hairdressers.)

These inconsistencies in the classification principle employed also result in the reporting of job categories of widely different sizes. Soviet censuses may be particularly remiss in this respect but inconsistencies can be found in those of other countries too. This is not a particularly satisfactory state of affairs, but census data still constitute the most comprehensive source of information on the jobs that people do.

Also, in most countries, there have been changes in both the number and descriptive titles of the job categories listed. In part, these are a reflection of economic growth, of structural change; new occupations arise and traditional ones diminish in importance or disappear. These changes ought to find a reflection in the classification system. But one suspects that other factors are at work. On the one hand, changes in the focus of interest of policy-makers or those responsible for taking the census may lead to the adoption of finer or coarser classification schemes. And improvements in enumeration technology, the use of punch-card systems or, most recently, electronic computers, should permit a much more detailed breakdown of occupations to be provided.

Finally, a specifically Soviet weakness: rather than printing a single table in which the number of men and women in each job category is given (or using a common schema to report the occupational structure for each of the sexes), Soviet censuses include two separate tables, one referring to the employed population without regard to sex and the other reporting on employed women alone. This second table is markedly shorter than the first, in part as a result of the omission of job categories, in part due to their amalgamation. A breakdown of the employed population by job category by sex is available only because the table relating to female occupations also gives the proportion of each category that are women. Thus, we have less information about the sexual composition of Soviet occupations than about the occupational structure as a whole. The fact that fewer job-categories are explicitly included in tables referring to employed women than employed men in itself constitutes indirect evidence for the existence of horizontal segregation in the Soviet Union.

Thus, in order to measure the extent of segregation in the Soviet labour force, one has available information on the numbers of men and women to be found in some 100–120 job categories. This is substantially less than would be available for most industrialised countries (British censuses list some 200–225) and, of course, grossly oversimplifies the variety of occupations actually to be found in the economy; but it is much more detailed than the information available from any other published source. (Note that since the Soviet censuses provide information about the structure of employment in each of the Union republics, one is able to analyse regional variations in horizontal segregation.)

In view of the fact that the classification schemas used in Soviet (and other) censuses are based on inconsistent principles of disaggregation and, especially, since job categories contain substantially different numbers of workers, it does not seem appropriate to use the job category as the unit of measurement in determining the extent of horizontal segregation. That is, it is not very illuminating to be told that, for example, in Britain in 1901 thirty-four job categories contained no women workers (Hakim, 1978, p. 1265). Rather, in the spirit of the definition of employment opportunities suggested at the beginning of this chapter, it seems preferable to ask what proportion of men or women were registered in job categories with specified characteristics. That is, it is of more interest to be told that in Britain in 1901 11 per cent of employed women were listed as working in exclusively female occupations (Hakim, 1978, p. 1265).

Accepting this principle, it is possible to specify a number of measures of horizontal segregation. Perhaps the simplest and most direct are the proportions of men (women) in exclusively, overwhelmingly or predominantly male (female) job categories. Clearly there is an element of choice in specifying what one means by an overwhelmingly (predominantly) male or female occupation and one's definition should take into account the degree of disaggregation, and hence likelihood of bias, in the job categorisation with which one is working. Bearing this in mind, one might suggest, for Soviet data, that overwhelmingly female (male) occupations are those containing at least 90 per cent women (men). In the same spirit, predominantly female (male) job categories are those that are at least 75 per cent female (male). Exclusivity would mean that the job category is 100 per cent male or female. Alternatively, some authors have defined predominantly female job categories to be those in which the share of women is greater than their share in the labour force as a whole. I shall not adopt this usage here. A formal specification of the various measures of segregation used in the remainder of this chapter is given in an appendix.

**Horizontal Segregation in the USSR, 1939-70**

In the last section a number of measures of horizontal segregation were introduced. In this section I present estimates of their value for the years 1939, 1959 and 1970. Since these estimates are based on published census returns and since there are two alternative occupational classifications for 1959 (one from the census of that year and one from the 1970 Census) two values are given for that year. Further, the Soviet census returns distinguish between 'those primarily engaged in physical labour' and 'those primarily engaged in mental labour' (approximately blue-collar and white-collar occupations) and that distinction has been retained here. In addition, in every case, those reported as engaged in manual agricultural occupations have been excluded from the first category. There are two reasons for this. First, as was shown in the previous chapter, large numbers of men and women were employed in agriculture, particularly in the early years; yet, the census classification provides little detailed information about their occupations (almost nine-tenths of the total being recorded in the job category 'agricultural occupations not elsewhere specified'). Thus the approach to horizontal segregation adopted here tends to break down in this case. Secondly, I believe that agriculture is a special case, that both climate and administrative structure raise special problems; these are taken up in Chapter 6.

Some idea of the way in which the relative sizes of different segregation classes have changed in the USSR since 1939 can be gained from Figure 4.1.

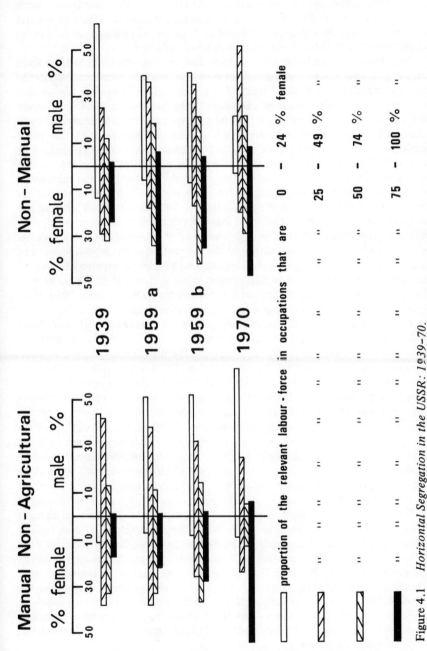

Figure 4.1    *Horizontal Segregation in the USSR: 1939–70.*

*Note:* The distribution labelled 1959a is derived from the occupational classification given in the 1959 Census, that labelled 1959b is derived from the classification used in the 1970 Census.

In effect it contains sixteen histograms, eight relating to the male labour force and eight to the female. Four of the histograms for each sex relate to manual non-agricultural job categories, the other four to non-manual ones. Let us consider, first, the manual non-agricultural part of the figure.

Two features stand out. The lowest bar on the left-hand side in each histogram corresponds to $\beta(0.75)$, that is, the proportion of women registered in job categories that were at least 75 per cent female. The chart shows that this increased in magnitude in each intercensal period. In 1970 more than half of all women engaged in manual non-agricultural labour were in job categories in which women made up at least 75 per cent of the total. Analogously, the highest bar in each of the histograms on the right-hand side corresponds to $\gamma(0.25)$, that is, the proportion of men in job categories that were less than 25 per cent female. The figure shows that this was substantial in 1939 and has increased in each intercensal period. In 1970 more than 60 per cent of male manual non-agricultural workers in the USSR were in job categories in which men made up at least 75 per cent of the total. As is to be expected, the growth in relative importance of these extremal categories has been accompanied by a contraction of the proportion of the labour force to be found in others. In 1970, between a quarter and a fifth of both men and women worked in job categories in which women made up from 25 to 50 per cent of the total. This is not negligible, but is substantially different from 1939 when 38 per cent of women and 42 per cent of men were in this category.

The situation with non-manual occupations is somewhat different. Once again, the value of $\beta(0.75)$ increased in each intercensal period. More generally, it can be seen that the centre of gravity of the distribution shifted towards the more segregated end of the scale. But in 1970 it was still true that less than half of all women 'white-collar' workers in the Soviet Union were in job categories in which the labour force was more than 75 per cent female. Developments among male white-collar workers reveal a pattern that differs strikingly from that of male manual workers. In 1939 more than three-fifths of all male non-manual workers were in job categories in which men made up at least 75 per cent of the labour force; by 1970 this proportion had fallen to a fifth. In the latter year approximately half of all male white-collar workers were registered in job categories in which women made up from 25 to 50 per cent of the labour force.

This intuitive impression is confirmed by a more formal statistical analysis whose results are reported in Table 4.1. Here the values of the various measures of horizontal segregation defined in the appendix are given for each of the census years. For manual non-agricultural job categories all but one of the measures listed indicate that horizontal segregation increased in each intercensal period. (The table suggests that relative excess segregation fell between 1939 and 1959.) Although one might hesitate to rely too much on inferences based on a single indicator (especially one whose sampling properties were poorly understood), such uniformity suggests that we can accept the conclusion with some confidence.

As might have been expected from an examination of Figure 4.1, the position with regard to non-manual job-categories is less clear. The proportion of women in job categories that were at least 75 per cent female and those that were at least 90 per cent female increased in each intercensal period. The average degree of segregation $(\overline{\theta}_i)$ is also shown to have increased. But these are the measures that are least sensitive to the changes that were taking place among men at this time. They are also unresponsive to the substantial expansion of female non-manual employment which, as was reported in Chapter 3, took place between 1939 and 1970. As the table indicates, both

Table 4.1   *Alternative Measures of Horizontal Segregation: USSR, 1939-70*

|  | 1939 | 1959[a] | 1959[b] | 1970 |
|---|---|---|---|---|
|  | *Manual Non-Agricultural Employees* | | | |
| $\beta(0{\cdot}75)$ | 0·173 | 0·223 | 0·285 | 0·539 |
| $\beta(0{\cdot}90)$ | 0·106 | 0·169 | 0·174 | 0·291 |
| $\overline{\theta}_i$ | 0·483 | 0·555 | 0·597 | 0·673 |
| $\hat{\theta}_i$ | 0·183 | 0·185 | 0·207 | 0·253 |
| $\theta_i^*$ | 1·595 | 1·500 | 1·538 | 1·587 |
| $H$ | n.a. | n.a. | 1·798 | 1·977 |
| $S$ | n.a. | n.a. | 0·429 | 0·558 |
|  | *Non-Manual Employees* | | | |
| $\beta(0{\cdot}75)$ | 0·245 | 0·422 | 0·347 | 0·471 |
| $\beta(0{\cdot}90)$ | 0·118 | 0·188 | 0·205 | 0·244 |
| $\overline{\theta}_i$ | 0·530 | 0·691 | 0·676 | 0·706 |
| $\hat{\theta}_i$ | 0·190 | 0·151 | 0·156 | 0·116 |
| $\theta_i^*$ | 1·558 | 1·280 | 1·300 | 1·196 |
| $H$ | n.a. | n.a. | 1·495 | 1·312 |
| $S$ | n.a. | n.a. | 0·511 | 0·488 |

*Notes:* Defining $f_i$ and $m_i$ as the numbers of women and men in the $i^{th}$ job category and $F(M)$ as the number of women (men) in the labour force, we define

$$\theta_i = f_i/(f_i + m_i) \text{ and } \theta = F/(F + M)$$

Then the alternative measures are defined as follows:

$$
\begin{aligned}
\beta(0{\cdot}75) &= F^{-1} \Sigma f_i & (i \text{ such that } \theta_i \geqslant 0{\cdot}75) \\
\beta(0{\cdot}90) &= F^{-1} \Sigma f_i & (i \text{ such that } \theta_i \geqslant 0{\cdot}9) \\
\overline{\theta}_i &= F^{-1} \Sigma f_i \theta_i \\
\hat{\theta}_i &= \overline{\theta}_i - \theta \\
\theta_i^* &= \overline{\theta}_i/\theta
\end{aligned}
$$

$$H = \theta^{-1} \Sigma f_i / \Sigma(f_i + m_i) \text{ (for } i \text{ such that } \theta_i > \theta)$$

For more detail see Hakim, 1978.

$$S = \tfrac{1}{2}(| f_i/F - m_i/M |)$$

For more detail see Fuchs, 1975, pp. 105-11.

absolute and relative excess segregation fell in each period; also, for the years in which they are given, both $H$ and $S$ show a fall.

Combining the insights from both Figure 4.1 and Table 4.1, one may draw the following conclusions. There is extensive horizontal segregation among those who work in manual non-agricultural job categories in the Soviet Union. And this has almost certainly increased since 1939. The greater employment of women, occasioned both by war and by its demographic consequences on the one hand and by conscious government policy on the other, far from resulting in the emergence of women from the female employment ghetto, has rather resulted in an expansion of the sorts of jobs that are regarded as 'women's work'.

Progress has been made, however, among white-collar workers. Certainly it is true that almost half of all female non-manual workers in 1970 were classified as belonging to predominantly female job categories whereas in 1939 slightly less than a quarter had done so. But it is also true that the proportion of male non-manual workers in predominantly male job categories has fallen; whereas in 1939 over three-fifths of men were in this class, by 1970 the proportion had fallen to about a fifth. As a result, at least on some measures, horizontal segregation among white-collar workers has fallen.

As pointed out above, the census materials on which the measurement of horizontal segregation are based permit the derivation of estimates not only for the USSR as a whole but also for each of the Union republics. The results

Table 4.2    *Alternative Measures of Occupational Segregation: USSR and Republics, 1970*

| | Manual Non-Agricultural | | | | Non-Manual | | | |
|---|---|---|---|---|---|---|---|---|
| | $\bar{\theta}_i$ | $\theta^*$ | $\beta(0.75)$ | $\beta(0.90)$ | $\bar{\theta}_i$ | $\theta^*$ | $\beta(0.75)$ | $\beta(0.90)$ |
| USSR | 0.673 | 1.587 | 0.539 | 0.291 | 0.706 | 1.196 | 0.471 | 0.244 |
| RSFSR | 0.69 | 1.57 | 0.562 | 0.287 | 0.717 | 1.175 | 0.611 | 0.235 |
| Ukraine | 0.65 | 1.55 | 0.527 | 0.297 | 0.705 | 1.236 | 0.493 | 0.255 |
| Byelorussia | 0.68 | 1.58 | 0.557 | 0.310 | 0.709 | 1.244 | 0.505 | 0.241 |
| Uzbekistan | 0.61 | 1.60 | 0.206 | 0.144 | 0.595 | 1.240 | 0.300 | 0.178 |
| Kazakhstan | 0.70 | 1.71 | 0.591 | 0.295 | 0.703 | 1.213 | 0.463 | 0.275 |
| Georgia | 0.61 | 1.65 | 0.260 | 0.107 | 0.690 | 1.301 | 0.476 | 0.252 |
| Azerbaijan | 0.58 | 1.81 | 0.218 | 0.107 | 0.604 | 1.314 | 0.330 | 0.184 |
| Lithuania | 0.66 | 1.65 | 0.546 | 0.315 | 0.690 | 1.190 | 0.596 | 0.250 |
| Moldavia | 0.65 | 1.67 | 0.397 | 0.287 | 0.682 | 1.196 | 0.470 | 0.232 |
| Latvia | 0.70 | 1.63 | 0.613 | 0.354 | 0.743 | 1.216 | 0.660 | 0.358 |
| Kirgizia | 0.68 | 1.70 | 0.380 | 0.232 | 0.670 | 1.219 | 0.343 | 0.238 |
| Tadjikistan | 0.58 | 1.70 | 0.279 | 0.196 | 0.580 | 1.336 | 0.297 | 0.169 |
| Armenia | 0.57 | 1.50 | 0.259 | 0.103 | 0.656 | 1.276 | 0.332 | 0.250 |
| Turkmenistan | 0.65 | 1.86 | 0.350 | 0.226 | 0.603 | 1.273 | 0.315 | 0.226 |
| Estonia | 0.70 | 1.59 | 0.631 | 0.333 | 0.745 | 1.227 | 0.653 | 0.404 |

of such an exercise (based on the 1970 Census) are given in Figure 4.2 and Table 4.2. What do they indicate about regional variations in the scale of segregation?

In Figure 4.2 the republics are arrayed in diminishing order of the share of

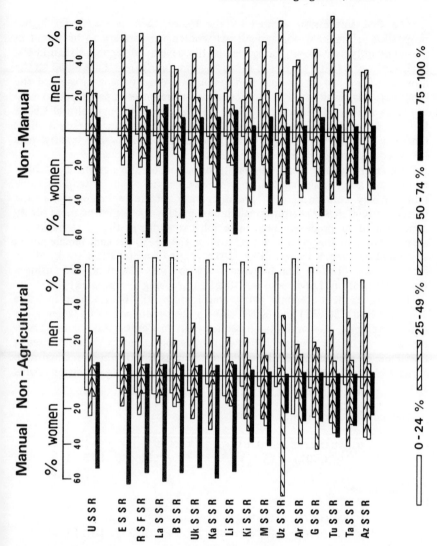

Figure 4.2    *Distribution of the Male and Female Labour Force by Degree of Feminisation: Soviet Republics, 1970.*

women in manual non-agricultural employment. That is, women made up the largest proportion of the manual non-agricultural labour-force in Estonia and the smallest proportion in Azerbaijan. In general terms at least, this order also corresponds to levels of industrialisation and per capita incomes (although in this respect Kirgizia is placed too high and both Latvia and Lithuania are placed too low). Again, in general terms, the first seven republics (from Estonia to Lithuania) may be classed as developed and relatively well-off while the remaining eight are backward and relatively poor.

The first impression created by the figure, then, is that a far higher proportion of manual non-agricultural women workers are to be found in predominantly female job categories in the developed republics than in the backward ones. (Note that since the histograms in Figure 4.2 are based on the number of women in manual non-agricultural employment in each of the republics, this result is not a consequence of differences in participation rates nor does it depend, directly at least, on the size of the agricultural labour force.) Although the results are less clear, the figure also suggests a slight tendency for men to be more heavily concentrated in predominantly male job-categories in the more developed republics.

The figure also presents similar information on the non-manual labour force. One notes a similar tendency for women non-manual workers to be more heavily concentrated in predominantly female job categories in the better-off republics. *Per contra* male non-manual workers may be more highly concentrated in predominantly male job categories in the more backward areas – although this class is not as large as the 25–50 per cent female one in any republic except Latvia. (This is the result of a statistical freak, of the fact that the dividing line between categories was placed at 0·25; using a finer classification, Latvia does not stand out as being exceptional.)

These inferences are only partly confirmed by the figures given in Table 4.2. First, both $\beta(0·75)$ and $\beta(0·9)$ show a clear tendency to be larger in the more developed Slav or Baltic republics than in Central Asia or the Trans-caucasus. Also, the average degree of segregation increases with increases in the share of women in the labour force. This is true for both manual non-agricultural and non-manual job categories, as the following regression results show:

Manual Non-Agricultural

$$\overline{\theta}_{ij} = 0·2398 + 1·0361\ \theta_j$$
$$\quad\quad (3·01)\quad\ (5·13) \quad\quad\quad\quad\quad r^2 : 0·6650 \quad DF: 13$$

Non-Manual

$$\overline{\theta}_{ij} = 0·1762 + 0·9144\ \theta_j$$
$$\quad\quad (4·81)\quad\ (13·62) \quad\quad\quad\quad\quad r^2 : 0·9357 \quad DF: 13$$

where $\overline{\theta}_{ij}$ refers to the index of segregation as defined above for the $j$th republic and $\theta_j$ refers to the share of women in total employment in the $j$th republic (in either manual non-agricultural or non-manual job categories). The values of the $t$-statistics show that both coefficients in each equation are well-determined and the correlation coefficient is really quite high for a cross-section regression; the equation for non-manual job categories is particularly well determined. Neither of the coefficients on $\theta_j$ differs from unity at the 5 per cent level; equally, there is no significant difference between the constants in the two equations. This implies that (at least as far as the regression equation allows one to carry out hypothesis-testing) there was no difference in absolute excess segregation between the republics for either manual non-agricultural or non-manual job categories. It also implies that absolute excess segregation was the same for both sections of the labour force.

Thus, once again the conclusions are mixed. There certainly appears to be horizontal segregation in all republics and in both sections of the labour force. Horizontal segregation is probably more pronounced in the more developed republics than it is in the poorer areas of Central Asia and the Transcaucasus. This suggests that the increase in segregation among manual non-agricultural employees in the USSR as a whole in the past forty years may be associated with Soviet-style economic development. On the other hand, the cross-sectional analysis does not support the conclusion that horizontal segregation was more pronounced among manual non-agricultural workers than among non-manual employees. All the same, on the basis of the All-Union figures and other material reported below, I believe that this is the most plausible inference to draw.

There is another way in which one might approach the question of horizontal segregation and the way that this has changed through time. As reported in Chapter 3, between 1939 and 1970 there was a substantial increase in both the number of women employed in the USSR and also in female participation rates. From successive censuses, it is possible to identify the job categories that recorded the largest increases in female employment and thus determine something of the character of the expansion in women's work in the Soviet Union. This is taken up in the next section.

## Employment Growth and Segregation, 1939-70

It is commonly believed that as a result of sex-role specialisation and, possibly, sex discrimination women are largely confined to domestic activities in pre-industrial societies. Industrialisation leads to their emergence from the home but, at least initially, their employment is largely confined to occupations analogous to their traditional domestic concerns. In consequence, it is argued, a majority of employed women will be found in occupations in which women make up a large or even overwhelming proportion of the labour force. The fuller integration of women into the labour force or the successful pursuit of policies that expand the range of occupational choice open to them will lead to an increasing proportion of women entering occupations in which a majority of the workforce is male. It should result in a decline in occupational segregation.

But there is a possibility that this will not occur. Those who believe that sex discrimination in the labour market is primarily a result of the aversion that men feel for working with (and particularly under) women suggest that if the share of women in any given occupation reaches some critical level, it is likely to become completely feminised. Men will no longer seek to join that occupational group and existing male members may transfer to other work. It is true that even if this occurs, the range of occupational choice open to women has expanded; but horizontal segregation has not diminished and the possibility of earnings differentiation remains.

In an attempt to ascertain how far either or both of these processes have been true of the growth of female employment in the USSR in the past forty years or so, all job categories were classified into five groups. A detailed statement of the criteria used to assign job categories to groups is given as an annexe to Table 4.3 but in general terms they were distinguished as follows.

Table 4.3    *Analysis of the Growth in Female Non-Agricultural Employment: USSR, 1939–70*

| % of the growth in female employment occurring in: | Manual Non-Agricultural | | Non-Manual | |
|---|---|---|---|---|
| | *1939–59* | *1959–70* | *1939–59* | *1959–70* |
| 1  Job categories that were predominantly male | 9·73 | 12·71 | 5·79 | 2·15 |
| 2  Job categories showing penetration by women | 34·53 | – | 20·12 | 23·38 |
| 3  Job categories that were mixed | 7·92 | 24·65 | 4·33 | 29·39 |
| 4  Job categories undergoing a process of feminisation | 34·50 | 23·68 | 49·85 | 15·02 |
| 5  Job categories that were predominantly female | 13·32 | 39·34 | 19·91 | 30·49 |
| Total | 100·00 | 100·00 | 100·00 | 100·00 |

The categories are defined according to the following scheme, writing $\theta_{it-1}$ for $\theta_i$ at the beginning of an intercensal period, etc.:

| | $\theta_{it} < 0.25$ | $0.25 \leqslant \theta_{it} < \theta_t$ | $\theta_t \leqslant \theta_{it} < 0.75$ | $0.75 \leqslant \theta_{it}$ |
|---|---|---|---|---|
| $\theta_{it-1} < 0.25$ | (1) | (2) | (4) | ✕ |
| $0.25 \leqslant \theta_{it-1} < \theta_{t-1}$ | *(1) | (3) $\Delta\theta > 0.15$ / (2) $\Delta\theta < 0.15$ | (2) | ✕ |
| $\theta_{t-1} \leqslant \theta_{it-1} < 0.75$ | ✕ | (3) | (3) $\Delta\theta > 0.15$ / (4) $\Delta\theta < 0.15$ | (4) |
| $0.75 \leqslant \theta_{it-1}$ | ✕ | ✕ | *(5) | (5) |

*Note:* The cells marked with an asterisk contained only three job categories; those marked with a cross contained none – in either intercensal period.

The first and last groups are the predominantly male and female job categories of the preceding section. The fourth group (consisting of job categories undergoing a process of feminisation) includes those that become predominantly female during an intercensal period or in which growth in the share of women is particularly rapid. The second group (consisting of job categories in which women are penetrating previously male occupational preserves) includes those in which the share of women was less than for the labour force as a whole but in which that share grew at a faster-than-average rate. The final group consists of those job categories in which the share of women was about the same as that for the labour force as a whole and showed little tendency to change over the intercensal period. Having established these categories, the intercensal growth in female employment was allocated between them. This analysis was carried out separately for manual non-agricultural and non-manual job categories for each of the two intercensal periods. The results are given in Table 4.3.

If it is the case that increased female participation is associated with an expansion in employment opportunities, one would expect to observe that a high proportion of the increase in female employment takes place in the first two groups. On the other hand, if female employment growth is occasioned by a growth in demand for those skills that already characterise 'women's work' or if it is accompanied by an expansion of what I have called the female employment ghetto, it will be concentrated in the last two groups. Finally, growth in the third group can be regarded as neutral.

If we look now at the figures in Table 4.3, it appears that for manual non-agricultural workers in the period 1939-59 female employment growth was divided more or less equally between the first two and the last two groups and that very little of the growth can be attributed to so-called mixed job categories. The picture is very different in 1959-70. In the latter period, almost two-thirds of the growth in female employment took place in the last two groups, a further quarter occurred in mixed occupations and little more than an eighth could be associated with the expansion in employment opportunities. Notice also that almost a quarter of the expansion in female employment in this period was associated with the process of feminisation referred to above.

In some ways, the experience among non-manual job categories reveals a reverse pattern. In 1939-59 almost 70 per cent of the expansion in female employment occurred in the final two categories and only a quarter can be associated with assumption by women of largely male roles. Note that virtually half of the expansion in this period was associated with the process of feminisation. In 1959-70, on the other hand, the expansion in female employment was somewhat more balanced. Again, a quarter of growth could be associated with expanding opportunities and somewhat less than half fell into the final two categories. Notice, finally, that as with manual non-agricultural job categories, much more of the growth in 1959-70 occurred in the mixed group than was true of 1939-59.

This analysis reveals a sharp cleavage between the experience of those women employed on manual (non-agricultural) work and those in white-collar jobs. For the former there appears to have been some expansion in employment opportunities in 1939-59, but since then the growth in jobs has been largely confined to the female ghetto. This is consistent with the maintenance if not an increase in the degree of horizontal segregation. For the latter, expansion in job opportunities appears to have been greater in the more recent intercensal period.

There is one further way in which the analysis of employment growth can cast light on the process of feminisation and the expansion in female employment. According to the argument developed at the beginning of this section, if the process of feminisation is a consequence of the aversion that men are reported to feel about working with women, an increase in female employment should be accompanied by a reduction in male employment in the same occupational groups. Alternatively, it might be argued that the rapid expansion in female employment in the USSR reflects the scarcity of male labour. As a result of population losses due to revolution, political oppression and war, men have been in short supply in the USSR; the authorities have been forced to recruit substantial numbers of women in order to attain their ambitious industrialisation goals.

If the latter is a more correct explanation of the underlying factors at work in the Soviet labour market over the past thirty or forty years, one might expect to observe that the bulk of the expansion in female employment took place in those job categories that grew most rapidly in absolute size (that is, where male and female employment, taken together, grew most rapidly). On the other hand, if 'aversion' and discrimination are involved, female employment growth will be more heavily concentrated in those job categories that grow more slowly. Women will replace rather than supplement men.

Which of these explanations is more consistent with Soviet experience can be tested as follows. All the job categories listed in the population censuses were classified into four groups: those in which employment growth had been sluggish, those where it had been approximately the same as for the labour force as a whole, those in which it had been substantially more rapid and those in which it had been very fast indeed. The actual boundaries chosen for these groups are to a large extent arbitrary, but they should suffice for a preliminary analysis. Thus, if labour scarcity dominates we would expect to see female employment growth concentrated in the second two groups, whereas if discrimination is important the first two will be large. Once again the analysis is carried out for manual non-agricultural and non-manual job categories separately and the results are given in Table 4.4.

Table 4.4    *Employment Growth and the Growth of Female Employment: USSR, 1939–70*

| | Manual Non-Agricultural | | Non-Manual | |
|---|---|---|---|---|
| *% of the growth in female employment occurring in:* | *1939–59* | *1959–70* | *1939–59* | *1959–70* |
| 1  Job categories whose overall growth was less than 25% | 38·90 | 32·45 | 21·30 | 5·61 |
| 2  Job categories whose overall growth was between 25% and 75% | 20·20 | 27·46 | 35·06 | 47·14 |
| 3  Job categories whose overall growth was between 75% and 150% | 26·67 | 36·68 | 11·53 | 24·54 |
| 4  Job categories whose overall growth was greater than 150% | 14·25 | 3·41 | 32·16 | 22·71 |
| Total | 100·00 | 100·00 | 100·00 | 100·00 |

It should be noted at the outset that the discriminatory power of this test is not great. Quite apart from the problem of specifying an appropriate statistical test of significant differences in the shares of employment growth occurring in the different groups, a ready explanation can be advanced for any finding of the apparent importance of discrimination. It could be argued that the traditional industrial or white-collar occupations (that is, those in which employment growth was slowest) were somehow less dangerous or demanding than the newer ones. Thus, in periods of labour market tightness, men were transferred to the newer jobs while women took their places in the old ones. (This avoids the accusation of discrimination on the part of the labour force at the expense of discrimination on the part of employers – in the Soviet case, of course, the state.)

As can be seen from Table 4.4, among manual non-agricultural occupations, between a third and two-fifths of the expansion in female employment took place in sectors where the overall growth in the intercensal period was less than 25 per cent. A further fifth to a quarter of the growth in female employment occurred in job categories that grew at approximately the same rate as the labour force as a whole. Only two-fifths of the expansion in female employment took place in the most rapidly growing sectors. At this broad level of analysis there seems little difference between 1939–59 and 1959–70.

Contrasts are less marked for non-manual job categories, but it is still the case that in both intercensal periods a higher proportion of the expansion in female employment occurred in the lower growth categories than in the others. The difference was slightly more marked in 1939–59 than in the later period and, further, as many as a fifth of the new jobs for women at this time were to be found in categories that grew only slowly. In 1959–70 only 5 per cent of the growth was of this type. Once again there are differences between manual non-agricultural and non-manual job categories. Once again it appears that the evidence of discrimination against women is stronger for the former than for the latter group.

This chapter has explored various aspects of horizontal segregation among the non-agricultural labour force in the USSR. Among manual job categories it appears to have increased unambiguously. It may also be associated with sex discrimination on the part of male workers. Among non-manual job categories, the evidence is less clear. On the one hand, the proportion of women working in predominantly or overwhelmingly female occupations has increased. There has been a substantial feminisation of white-collar work in the USSR. But a more sophisticated approach suggests that this might be due in large part to increases in female participation. Also, the evidence in favour of discriminatory attitudes on the part of male co-workers is less strong.

The analysis offered here has demonstrated, however, that there is no necessary connection between increases in female participation rates and decreases in horizontal segregation. The increased employment of women does not necessarily lead to an expansion in job opportunities for women. The Soviet policy of incorporating women into the social economy needs to be accompanied by measures designed to secure access to more and different jobs if it is to lead to a reduction in sexual inequality.

Further, both the extent and persistence of horizontal segregation in the

USSR are consistent with the disparities in earnings reported in Chapter 2.

Finally, however, it should be pointed out that all that has been done in this chapter is to establish that the jobs done by women in the USSR differ from those done by men. Nothing has been said about the quality of those jobs, about whether women's work demands more or less skill than men's work, involves more or less responsibility, confers more or less job satisfaction. All these are aspects of what I have called vertical segregation (and, to a lesser extent, administrative segregation). And that is the subject of the next chapter.

### Appendix: The measurement of horizontal segregation

It will be helpful to set out the argument of section 4.2 in formal terms. To that end, let $f_i$ and $m_i$ be the number of women and men in the $i$th job category and let $F$ and $M$ be the number of women and men in the employed labour force as a whole. Then, for each job category, one can define a female share index

$$\theta_i = f_i/(F_i + m_i) \tag{1}$$

One can now define $\beta(k)$ as the proportion of women in the $k$ segregation class

$$\beta(k) = F^{-1} \Sigma_i f_i \text{ (for } i \text{ such that } \theta_i \geq k) \tag{2}$$

For example, for $k = 0.75$, $\beta(k)$ is the proportion of women in predominantly female occupations. (One can define $\gamma(h)$ analogously as the proportion of men in the $h$ segregation class; i.e. $\gamma(h) = M^{-1} \Sigma m_i$, for $i$ such that $\theta_i \leq h$.)[1]

Now $\beta(k)$ and $\gamma(h)$ are certainly statistics that measure the extent of horizontal segregation in the labour force and have been used for such a purpose by several authors. But they suffer from certain drawbacks. First, the specification of the boundary (i.e. the selection of $k$ or $h$ is to some extent arbitrary. It is possible that the use of different values for $k$ or $h$ would lead to conflicting inferences being drawn about the extent of horizontal segregation within a given labour force. Secondly, as is also true of percentile measures, $\beta(k)$ and $\gamma(h)$ are unaffected by the shape of the distribution below $k$ (or above $h$). And, again, these may affect one's assessment of the extent of horizontal segregation or the way that it has changed over time.

One way of taking account of these objections is to proceed as follows. Each individual man or woman in the labour force is employed in a job category characterised by a certain value of $\theta_i$. One can therefore think of a distribution of the labour force with respect to $\theta_i$; more to the point, one can calculate the mean value of $\theta_i$ for men and women in a given labour force, regarding it as the 'average degree of horizontal segregation' characteristic of a given occupational structure. That is, proceeding formally, for women one can calculate

$$\overline{\theta}_i = F^{-1} \Sigma f_i \theta_i \tag{3}$$

This measure does not depend upon the arbitrary specification of boundaries. It is also responsive to changes in the shape of the distribution in the same way that any mean value is. It therefore meets both the objections raised above.

But $\bar{\theta}_i$ still suffers from one weakness. One can show that it is bounded from below by $\theta$, the share of women in the labour force as a whole.[2] This implies that, in certain circumstances, measured horizontal segregation may increase as female participation (and hence the share of women in total employment) increases. This is clearly an undesirable property for a measure to possess. Perhaps the simplest way to overcome this problem is to use $\theta$ to normalise one's measure of horizontal segregation. In this way I finally define two indices

$$\hat{\theta}_i = \bar{\theta}_i - \theta \qquad \text{absolute excess segregation} \qquad (4a)$$

$$\theta_i^* = \bar{\theta}_i / \theta \qquad \text{relative excess segregation} \qquad (4b)$$

Each of these statistics measures the excess of average horizontal segregation over the minimum consistent with a given degree of female participation. Although the sampling properties of these statistics (and hence inferences about the significance of changes in their value) are unknown, they do take account of the major shortcomings of the measures that have been widely used to assess the extent of segregation in labour markets by other investigators. Estimates of the value of all three indicators, as well as $\beta(0.75)$ and $\beta(0.9)$ for the USSR in the last three census years, are given above.

Mention should be made of two further measures of horizontal segregation that have been suggested recently. In a study of occupational segregation in Britain since the turn of the century, Catherine Hakim suggests that one compute the ratio of observed to expected employment in those sectors in which the share of women was greater than in the labour force as a whole (Hakim, 1978). That is, in terms of the notation used above, she suggests the use of

$$H = \frac{\Sigma f_i}{\theta^{-1} \Sigma \ (f_i + m_i)} \qquad \text{(for $i$ such that $\theta_i > \theta$)} \qquad (5a)$$

A number of authors have proposed that one use half the sum of the absolute values of the differences in percentage shares of men and women in all job categories:

$$S = \tfrac{1}{2}\Sigma \ (|f_i/F - m_i/M|) \qquad (5b)$$

(See, for example, Fuchs, 1975). The measure $S$ has a relatively straightforward interpretation: it represents the proportion of men (or women) that must change job categories if the occupational distribution of the two sexes is to be made identical. Estimates of the value of $H$ and $S$ for the USSR in 1959 and 1970 are also given above.

## Notes: Chapter 4

1   In the notation adopted here, the alternative definition of the proportion of women in predominantly female occupations, say, $\beta^*(\theta) = F^{-1}\Sigma f_i$ (for $i$ such that $\theta_i \geq \theta$) where $\theta = F/(F + M)$.

2   To see this, define the sex ratio in the $i$th job category $a_i = m_i/f_i$ and let $a = M/F$ be the sex ratio for the labour force as a whole. Then simple substitution will establish the following

$$\text{(i)} \ \bar{a}_i = F^{-1}\Sigma f_i a_i = a$$

$$\text{(ii)} \ \theta_i = (1 + a_i)^{-1}$$

$$\text{(iii)} \ \theta = (1 + a)^{-1}$$

Finally, from Jensen's inequality it follows that:

$$\bar{\theta}_i = F^{-1}\Sigma f_i(1 + a_i)^{-1} \geq (1 + a)^{-1} = \theta \text{ (with equality if and only if } \theta_i = \theta \text{ for all } i).$$

*Chapter 5*

# Vertical Segregation in the Labour Market, 1939-75

In the last chapter it was established that the jobs done by Soviet women are substantially different from those done by men. But the mere fact of difference does not, by itself, necessarily imply that women's work in the USSR is worse than men's work, is less skilled or less demanding, yields lower pay or less job satisfaction. To establish how far this is true of occupational segregation in the USSR requires a separate analysis. Such an analysis is the subject of this chapter.

Assessing the extent of vertical segregation in the Soviet Union (or any other country for that matter) is difficult for two reasons. First, there is no general agreement about those attributes that make some jobs better than others, about what it is that the analysis should concentrate on. Secondly, in view of this lack of agreement, there is no easily available body of data that can be used to determine the nature of the disparities in men's and women's work. One must be content with a more heuristic approach.

In this chapter I shall assume that the three aspects of a job that are most important in determining its quality are the wage it pays, the satisfaction it affords and the conditions in which it is carried out. The first two of these are not directly observable for the USSR and only limited information is available about the third; nevertheless, it can be argued that pay and satisfaction are positively correlated with factors such as skill and executive authority – and on these a certain amount of information is available.

It is an ultimate goal of socialism so to change both human psychology and working conditions as to make labour desirable in itself, to make it a 'prime necessity of life' as Marx put it. But Soviet social theorists and ideologists realise that such a transformation has not yet been achieved. In the USSR as elsewhere, people work in order to earn the money necessary to buy the good things in life. This is recognised in the emphasis that the authorities place upon material incentives, in their attitudes towards the distribution of income. The State Committee on Labour and Social Problems (the body responsible for determining wage and salary scales) attempts to set wages in a way that reflects skill differences. It also pays attention to differences in responsibility and to what is called the economic significance of the occupation. The first of these means that managers are paid more than those that they manage; the second means that those working in high-priority sectors earn more than those in low-priority ones. Priorities, in this case, are of course determined by the state.[1]

In the West it is commonly accepted that the exercise of a skill confers job satisfaction; indeed, *ceteris paribus* it is usually assumed that satisfaction increases with skill. Skilled craftsmen are presumed to derive greater pleasure from their work than the unskilled; and professionals or creative artists are supposed to enjoy their work more than craftsmen. Similarly, the exercise of authority over others, possession of the power to make decisions, is thought to confer satisfaction in itself, quite apart from the privileges that usually accompany such positions. Similar conclusions emerge from Soviet sociological studies of attitudes to work in the USSR. (See, for example, *Chelovek . . .*, 1967, especially chs 2–3.)

Finally, it seems reasonable to suppose that individuals would prefer to avoid jobs that involve arduous physical labour, that *ceteris paribus* they would prefer to work in clean, dry, warm surroundings. And, again, it is to be presumed that Soviet workers in this respect are like their West European or American colleagues.

Thus, from the point of view of the worker, it seems reasonable to argue that the quality of a job is determined by its pay, the satisfaction it affords and the conditions in which it is carried out. Further, although there is little direct information about how the first two of these vary between occupations in the USSR, it seems plausible to assume that skilled jobs will rank higher on both than unskilled jobs. Also, one may infer that managerial and executive jobs are ranked more highly in both respects than are most non-managerial jobs. And arduous or unpleasant working conditions detract from the quality of the job. In the rest of this chapter I shall examine a number of the jobs commonly done by men and women in the USSR to see how far they differ in these respects.

Ideally, of course, one should not consider pay, satisfaction and conditions of work in isolation from each other. Trade-offs between them are possible and it is the resultant that determines the quality of the job. That is, it is possible to compensate workers for unpleasant conditions or monotonous and repetitive work by offering them higher pay. Similarly, it is possible to trade upon people's sense of vocation, or upon their desire for a modicum of personal autonomy, and pay them less than in other circumstances they might receive. It is frequently suggested, for instance, that in Britain it is possible to pay nurses less than might be indicated by a job description of the tasks that they perform, since the young women who go into nursing possess a strong sense of vocation. (Nurses in the USSR are also relatively poorly paid.) In what follows it is seldom possible to take account of these inter-relationships. The available data do not permit it. But too much should not be made of this limitation. Although it may be theoretically correct to postulate the possibility of pecuniary compensation for unpleasant working conditions, and so forth, the fact of the matter is that in global terms the 'better' jobs everywhere offer higher pay and more satisfaction.

One would like, then, to assess the extent of vertical segregation between men and women in the Soviet Union in terms of skill, responsibility and working conditions. But there is no source that provides consistent information on all of these aspects for the employed population as a whole. This is not due to any particular shortcoming of Soviet statistics; such information is not available for other countries either. One must, therefore, be satisfied with a more impressionistic approach. One must marshal the available evidence and hope that it is sufficient to demonstrate the existence of significant differences in the skill, responsibility and conditions of the jobs most commonly done by the two sexes. Here I make use of three sorts of material. In the next section I examine a selection of the census job categories that contain the largest number of men and of women. An examination of their descriptions conveys some idea of typically male and female jobs in the USSR. Then I turn to an account of differences between the jobs done by male and female industrial workers, concentrating upon their rated skill and levels of mechanisation. This analysis relies upon recently published work by Soviet labour economists and industrial sociologists. The fourth section of the chapter takes up the question of status hierarchies among non-manual workers. This makes use of both census materials and data published in annual statistical handbooks. The final part of the chapter deals with the third dimension of occupational segregation set out above: the extent to which men and women work in different administrative sectors in the USSR.

## Men's and Women's Work, 1939–70

In Chapter 4 it was suggested that the best measure of the employment opportunities open to women in the Soviet Union was given by the jobs that most women do. In this section an attempt is made to meet that criterion by examining the five job categories in each of the last three censuses that contained the largest number of women. Information is also provided on the five categories employing the largest number of men. As in the previous chapter, agriculture is excluded and the distinction between manual and non-manual occupations is maintained. It was decided to restrict the number of categories to five in order to avoid overburdening the chapter with statistics.

Of the five most prevalent female manual non-agricultural occupations in 1939, only two were industrial and both of these were in what may be regarded as traditionally women's sectors (see Table 5.1). The skills involved in at least four out of the five job categories were analogous to those used by women in domestic activity. It is not clear what is the full range of activities included under the first category, but it is probable that the skills involved here were similar to those exercised in the home too.[2] It probably also includes all those women who keep the streets of Soviet cities clear of snow, about whom Western journalists write so frequently.

In part, the listings in Table 5.1 are a consequence of the inconsistent disaggregation discussed in the last chapter. It is because the census gives information about specific occupations in the textile industry that so few of these appear. If one restricts oneself to industry-level job categories, then both textiles and the rather more unconventional 'metallurgical and metal-working trades' take precedence over cooks and those employed in food-processing (see Table 5.1, note a).

According to the 1959 Census, cooks had been replaced by those employed on power plants and lifting machinery as the fifth most populous occupation among manual women. That is, there appears to have been some expansion

Table 5.1   *The Five Most Prevalent Female Non-Agricultural Manual Occupational Groups:ᵃ USSR, 1939, 1959, 1970 (thousands)*

|  | 1939 | 1959[b] | 1959[c] | 1970 |
|---|---|---|---|---|
| Workers in municipal and economic services | 2,280 | 3,343 | 3,661 | 4,320 |
| Cleaners, orderlies and nursemaids | 410 | 869 | 869 | 1,569 |
| Tailors and seamstresses | 344 | 756 | 1,013[d] | 1,481[d] |
| Cooks | 274 |  |  | 986 |
| Workers in food-processing | 274 | 525 |  |  |
| Those employed on power plants and on lifting-transporting machinery |  | 557 |  |  |
| Sales staff, managers of stalls, booths and buffets |  |  | 952 | 1,945 |
| Warehousemen, storemen, weighers, etc. |  |  | 532 |  |
| % of female non-agricultural manual employment accounted for | 38 | 36 | 40 | 39 |

*Notes:*   a   The table omits residual categories and also industrial groups where these are broken down by sub-occupations. If the latter are included, the following groups should be borne in mind:

|  | 1939 | 1959a | 1959b | 1970 |
|---|---|---|---|---|
| Metallurgical and metalworking trades | 522 | 1,451 | 1,304 | 2,376 |
| Textile trades | 805 | 958 | 958 | 1,003 |
| Garment workers | 555 | 1,172 | 1,172 | 1,726 |
| Construction trades |  | 905 | 905 | 1,482 |
| Catering trades (including retail sales staff in 1959b and 1970) | 474 | 704 | 1,657 | 3,269 |

b   Figures in this column are based on the 1959 Census classification.
c   Figures in this column are based on the 1970 Census classification.
d   Includes modistes and milliners.

*Sources: Itogi vsesoyuznoi perepisi naseleniya 1959 goda*, Moscow, 1962, Vol. *SSSR*, Table 48 and *Itogi vsesoyuznoi perepisi naseleniya 1970 goda*, Moscow, 1973, Vol. VI, Table 18.

of female employment into unconventional (if semi-skilled) industrial areas. But just how dependent these results are on the detailed classification used is shown by the third column of the table; here, the only industrial occupation included is to be found in the traditional area of garment manufacture. Again, the use of a less disaggregated classification results in changes: in 1959 both metalworking and construction employed more women than catering (although not trade and catering).

Finally, in 1970, there is still little evidence of the mass expansion of female employment into skilled industrial work. Rather, the resurgence of catering and retail trade suggests a reversion to more traditional patterns of female employment. However, the number of women recorded as working in

Table 5.2    *The Five Most Prevalent Male Non-Agricultural Manual Occu-*
*pational Groups:*[a] *USSR, 1939, 1959, 1970 (thousands)*

|  | *1939* | *1959*[b] | *1959*[c] | *1970* |
|---|---|---|---|---|
| Workers in municipal and economic services | 2,281 | 1,647 | 1,803 | 1,148 |
| Rail transport employees (manual) | 745 | 1,155 | 1,155 | 921 |
| Drivers (road transport) | 655 | 3,152 | | |
| Electricians, network supervisors | 468 | 1,308 | | |
| Those employed on power installations and lifting-transporting machinery | 450 | 1,184 | | |
| Fitters, assembly-workers, installers | | | 2,955 | 5,087 |
| Turners | | | 774 | 1,233 |
| Tool-setters, adjusters, tuners of equipment and machinery (workers) | | | 519 | 1,034 |
| % of the male non-agricultural manual labour force accounted for: | 21 | 30 | 26 | 26 |

*Notes:*  a   The table excludes residual and generic categories; since the groups are derived from the female employment table this leads to some distortion. The main omitted groups are:

|  | *1939* | *1959*[a] | *1959*[b] | *1970* |
|---|---|---|---|---|
| Metal trades | 3,828 | 7,613 | 7,389 | 12,476 |
| Woodworking trades | 821 | 1,125 | 1,125 | 1,105 |
| Construction trades | 2,285 | 4,124 | 4,124 | 4,005 |
| Road transport | 698 | 3,395 | 2,965 | 6,272 |
| Other manual occupations | 7,973 | 6,714 | 7,288 | 7,659 |

b    Figures in this column are based on the 1959 Census classification.
c    Figures in this column are based on the 1970 Census classification.
*Sources:* As for Table 5.1.

both construction and metalworking should be noted. Expansion in this latter job category is almost certainly due to the recruitment of large numbers of semi-skilled female assembly-workers.

It is the differences between the occupations listed in Tables 5.1 and 5.2 that are more striking than the similarities. In 1939 four out of the five most populous categories for men were to be found in industry and transport. And the same pattern has persisted throughout the period covered by the table. The impression given is that the most prevalent male manual non-agricultural occupations in the USSR involve substantially more industrial training and higher levels of skill than do their female counterparts. Also, the size of the residual 'other manual occupations' should be noted. Since Table 5.2 was derived from lists of job categories done by women, this presumably represents jobs in which female participation was so small that the Soviet compilers did not think it worth listing them separately. This in itself suggests the presence of horizontal if not vertical segregation.

These tables suggest that women manual workers in the USSR are less skilled than their male counterparts. They also provide little evidence to support the contention that there has been a large-scale process of skill acquisition among women over the past thirty to forty years – at least in areas of non-traditional female employment. They thus imply that the horizontal segregation among manual non-agricultural workers, established in Chapter 4, is associated with considerable vertical segregation.

Table 5.3    *The Five Most Prevalent Female Non-Manual Occupational Groups:[a] USSR, 1939, 1959, 1970 (thousands)*

|  | 1939 | 1959[b] | 1959[c] | 1970 |
|---|---|---|---|---|
| Accountants, accounts clerks | 662 | 1,300 | 1,300 | 2,021 |
| Teachers in primary, 7-year and all secondary educational establishments (including directors of primary schools) | 658 | 1,467 | 1,467 | 2,176 |
| Sales personnel, managers of stalls, booths, buffets and departments | 408 | 995 |  |  |
| Clerks, secretaries | 378 | 497 |  |  |
| Cashiers | 182 |  | 364 |  |
| Nurses (qualified) |  | 689 | 689 | 1,275 |
| Laboratory staff |  |  | 377 |  |
| Engineers (including chief engineers/special) |  |  |  | 1,121 |
| Directors and staff of children's homes and kindergartens; staff of boarding schools |  |  |  | 825 |
| % of female non-manual employment accounted for | 49 | 45 | 42 | 40 |

*Notes:*  a   Residual and generic categories (like ITR, for example) have not been included.
b   Figures in this column refer to the 1959 Census classification.
c   Figures in this column refer to the 1970 Census classification.
*Sources:* As for Table 5.1.

Table 5.3 brings out the dominance of just two job categories, book-keeping and teaching, among women engaged in non-manual work. In 1939 more than 1·3 million women (between a quarter and a third of all female white-collar workers at the time) were to be found in these occupations. In 1970 the number of women so employed had increased to 4·1 million (but their share had declined to a fifth). More generally, the figures in Table 5.3 suggest that between 1939 and 1959 there was substantial growth in the number of women with some special training (what the Russians refer to as secondary specialist education); indeed, this trend continues through to 1970. Two further features stand out: the relatively small number of women employed as (or at least classified as) secretaries and typists. Such a job category was not listed in the 1959 Census and even in 1970 there were barely a quarter of a million of them. This is in marked contrast to most market economies. In part, this represents a real difference, in part it is a consequence of the classification schemas used. (Since the centrally determined salary for secretarial staff in the USSR is low, it is reported that enterprises and organisations have difficulty in recruiting sufficient women for such jobs. To get round this difficulty it is claimed that some managers reclassify the job as that of technician or assistant. If this is widespread, typists and secretaries will be listed under other job categories in the census returns.) Secondly, the emergence of the female engineer is striking. (The disappearance of the retail trade occupations between columns 2 and 3 of the table is a result of their having been classified as manual in the 1970 Census.)

There are differences between the most prevalent male and female non-manual occupations in the USSR, but perhaps the most striking feature of Table 5.4 is the degree of overlap between the sexes. Until 1959 book-keeping and teaching were the most popular professions for men as well as for women and in 1939 the distributive trades were also important. But Table 5.4 also reveals the importance of managerial and technical occupations among male white-collar workers. These were unimportant for women before 1970. Finally, note the difference between the sexes in respect of 'nurturing' or 'caring' roles. Both nursing and pre-school child care figure in Table 5.3; they have no equivalent in Table 5.4.

Table 5.4    *The Five Most Prevalent Male Non-Manual Occupational Groups:*[a]
*USSR, 1939, 1959, 1970 (thousands)*

|  | 1939 | 1959[b] | 1959[c] | 1970 |
|---|---|---|---|---|
| Accountants, accounts clerks | 1,127 | 506 | 506 | |
| Teachers in primary, 7-year and all secondary educational establishments (including directors of primary schools) | 538 | 542 | 542 | 846 |
| Sales personnel, managers of stalls, booths, buffets and departments | 308 | | | |
| Foremen (technical personnel) | 252 | 577 | 577 | 1,155 |
| Engineers (including chemical engineers/specialists) | 220 | 570 | 570 | 1,682 |
| Heads of shops, sections, workshops and departments | | 307 | 307 | 556 |
| Technicians (excluding agricultural, zoological and veterinary technicians) | | | | 407 |
| % of male non-manual employment accounted for | 27 | 27 | 27 | 36 |

*Notes:* a   Residual and generic categories (like ITR, for example) have not been included.
b   Figures in this column refer to the 1959 Census classification.
c   Figures in this column refer to the 1970 Census classification.
*Sources:* As for Table 5.1.

At this very crude level of analysis, certain conclusions emerge. Distinctions between the most prevalent white-collar jobs for men and women in the Soviet Union are less marked than among manual non-agricultural job categories. This is consistent with the findings of the last chapter. The levels of education or training required (or rather, attained) appear to have risen over the years; this applies to women's jobs as much as to men's. But similar levels of education conceal substantial differences in job content. Women are more involved in the care of the sick and the young and in clerical work. Men are more concerned with the exercise of managerial and technical functions. Finally, the last rows of Tables 5.3 and 5.4 hint at the possibility that there exists a greater diversity of white-collar job opportunities for men than for women. If this is so, however, disparities between the sexes appear to have diminished over the past thirty or forty years.

It is possible that the apparent increase in the variety of white-collar jobs open to women is a result of the policies pursued by the Soviet government, the detailed provisions of which are to be found in the Labour Code. Alternatively, it might be a consequence of industrialisation and development. In this case, it would still be attributable to government policy – but not to specifically labour-market policies. Also, one might expect to observe similar patterns in other social systems. That is, with the process of industrialisation and development, one might expect to observe women venturing beyond the confines of occupations that call for the exercise of 'domestic' skills and penetrating previously male occupational preserves. With only three observations, it is not possible to carry out any formal statistical test of this hypothesis at the level of the USSR as a whole. But the Soviet Union is a federal state made up of fifteen Union republics at different levels of development and the population censuses provide breakdowns of the occupational structure by sex for each of them. These provide a basis for the more formal tests referred to above.

Since, with minor modifications, the same code of labour law operates in all fifteen republics and since the law has been the main vehicle through which the authorities in the USSR have sought to influence and control industrial relations, if expanding employment opportunities for women are attributable primarily to the operation of labour policy one would expect to observe little difference between the republics in this respect. If, on the other hand, the growth in job opportunities is attributable to the more general process of industrialisation and development, one would expect to observe a wider variety of employments for women in the more developed republics. The Soviet republics differ in more than the level of development; they differ in language and culture and these may affect the way in which the legal system is operated. Considerations such as these undermine the clarity of the test proposed above and should be borne in mind in interpreting its results.

An examination of the five job categories employing the largest number of women manual workers in each of the republics in 1970 reveals a considerable degree of uniformity. In all but Armenia the following four are included: local government manual work, tailoring, retail sales staff and cleaners. Six of them also yield cooks as the fifth category. In the RSFSR and Estonia there were somewhat more women recorded as 'storemen, weighers and distributors' than cooks and in both Lithuania and Latvia 'workers in food-processing' was the larger category, but for the rest it was the less developed republics that showed the greater deviations. In Uzbekistan it was 'painters and plasterers' that constituted the fifth category, in Tadjikistan it was 'weavers', in Turkmenistan 'rug-makers'; in Armenia both 'other metalworking trades' and 'workers in food-processing' contained more women than 'cooks' and 'cleaners'. Georgia displayed a pattern similar to that of Latvia and Lithuania. Looked at in general terms, these results suggest that there is considerable uniformity of employment structure in all the republics but that industrial occupations are somewhat more important in the *less* developed regions.

The five largest job categories for women in non-manual occupations in each of the Soviet republics in 1970 were considerably more uniform in character than for manual non-agricultural workers. They coincided with those for the USSR as a whole in all but four of them. (See Table 5.3 for the list.) In Georgia, however, *laboranty* (possibly laboratory assistants) were more numerous than pre-school child care staff; in Moldavia *laboranty* outnumbered engineers and in both Latvia and Byelorussia there were more cashiers than there were personnel in pre-school child care institutions.

These results suggest that in spite of considerable differences in levels of development, in culture and language, membership of the Soviet Union imposes a substantial degree of similarity upon the economic structure of the various republics. They would seem to imply that the industrialisation hypothesis advanced above is incorrect. But this conclusion is misleading. So far, we have considered only which five occupational groups contain the largest number of women; we have not considered how many women they contain (or what proportion of the female labour force is recorded as belonging to these populous professions). Yet if industrialisation and development are to result in an expansion of the job opportunities open to women, we would surely expect the proportion of women found in traditional semi-skilled or unskilled employments to fall. And that, in general terms, is what we find in the USSR.

In Table 5.5 I report the results of regressing the proportion of women in the five largest job categories on per capita monthly income in 1970. For the regression the same five job categories were used for each of the republics and they were the ones that contained the largest number of women for the USSR as a whole. (They are listed in Tables 5.1 and 5.3.) As independent variables, two alternative definitions of income were used. (The table only reports the results of the one that gave the better fit for each labour force group.) For manual non-agricultural categories, this was personal per capita income. This is defined as the value of resources, in cash and kind, that pass through the household's budget; it thus excludes state expenditures on education and welfare. But income here is used as a measure of development and it is possible to argue that a large and profitable private agricultural sector is not indicative of a high level of development. Personal income, then, will overstate the level of development in those republics in which households depend heavily upon the private plot. As an alternative measure of development, therefore, a new income variable was defined: personal income

Table 5.5    *Relationship between Female Employment in Selected Job Categories and Republican Per Capita Incomes: 1970*

| Dependent Variable | Constant | Per Capita Income (1) | Per Capita Income (2) | $R^2$ |
|---|---|---|---|---|
| Manual Non-Agricultural | | | | |
| Full Regression | 53·7943 | −0·1961 | | |
| | (10·77) | (2·38) | | 0·3182 |
| | | | | (DF 13) |
| Limited Regression | 70·8190 | −0·4754 | | |
| | (12·62) | (5·11) | | 0·7436 |
| | | | | (DF  9) |
| Non-Manual | | | | |
| Full Regression | 56·5086 | | −0·2464 | |
| | (20·27) | | (4·87) | 0·6467 |
| | | | | (DF 13) |
| Limited Regression | 58·6061 | | −0·3008 | |
| | (29·97) | | (8·18) | 0·8781 |
| | | | | (DF 9) |

*Notes:* The dependent variable in each case was the proportion of all women in the relevant labour force group recorded as being employed in the five job categories that contained the largest number of female employees in the USSR as a whole.

Per capita income (1) was personal income as defined in McAuley, 1979; per capita income (2) was personal income less the value of output in private subsidiary economic activity.

For manual non-agricultural job categories the limited regression excludes observations on Uz. SSR, La. SSR, Ta SSR and E SSR; for non-manual, G.SSR, Ar.SSR, Ta SSR and E.SSR. See text for a discussion of the reasons for their exclusion.

net of receipts from private subsidiary economic activity. An extended discussion of the methods used to construct these estimates and values of the indices used can be found in McAuley, 1979, chapters 5 and 6.

When the regressions described in the previous paragraph were carried out, it was found that personal income resulted in a better fit in the case of manual non-agricultural job categories while personal income net of private receipts performed better for non-manual occupations. Also, while for both sections of the labour force the coefficient on the index of development had the predicted sign and, according to the *t*-statistics, all coefficients were well determined, the proportion of the variance explained was low. This was particularly true of non-agricultural manual categories where the $R^2$ was only 0·3182. An examination of the scattergram underlying the regression revealed the existence of a negative relationship between the two variables for most republics but also suggested that the experience in some of them differed. In particular, it appears that the proportion of women in these five occupations in Estonia and Latvia (the two richest republics) is substantially higher than would be expected on the basis of their per capita incomes. Similarly, the proportion of women in these occupations in Tadjikistan and Uzbekistan (two of the poorer republics) is lower than would be predicted from their level of development. I have no idea why these republics should be 'different', but if they are excluded from the regression the fit improves considerably.

The fit of the regression relating the five most populous non-manual job categories to the level of development is substantially better than that for manual non-agricultural occupations; but here, again, the scattergram revealed the presence of outliers. In this case it was Georgia, Armenia and Estonia that recorded a substantially higher proportion of women in the five most populous professions than one would have expected on the basis of their per capita income, while Tadjikistan (and, possibly Azerbaijan) recorded proportions that were too low. In the case of Georgia it is possible that part of the explanation lies in the fact that the census returns do not report separately the number of women registered as nurses and those registered as *feldshers* and midwives. But, since Armenia also appears to be a 'rogue' this may not be the only factor at work. In any case, exclusion of the two Transcaucasian republics, Tadjikistan and Estonia, leads to a substantial improvement in fit.

These regression results can be taken to imply that, in Soviet conditions, the process of development does lead to a widening of employment opportunities for women. It is still the case that even in the more advanced areas some 35–45 per cent of women are to be found in semi-skilled non-industrial occupations (or in routine jobs concerned with the care of the sick and the young and in clerical work) but other opportunities are apparently opened up. It remains to be seen whether these offer substantially higher rewards and satisfaction, whether they demand the acquisition of new skills and more exacting professional competence. And, of course, expanded opportunities in the sense used here do not conflict with the persistence of or increase in horizontal segregation established in the last chapter.

The analysis of this section has suggested that there is still considerable vertical segregation in the Soviet Union. Women are still more heavily concentrated in low-skilled non-industrial manual work than men. And the occupations that are traditionally regarded as women's work in market economies are overwhelmingly female in the USSR as well. There is a greater prevalence among men of occupations that require industrial training and the acquisition of skills. In the white-collar professions, too, jobs that are regarded as women's work elsewhere are done by women in the Soviet Union. A high proportion of women are also engaged on routine clerical work. For men, on the other hand, management functions are important.

But the situation is not wholly bleak. Further analysis suggests that the process of development, if not the labour policies of the Soviet government, has led to an expansion of job opportunities for women. Among manual workers the proportion engaged in low- and semi-skilled non-industrial work appears to be lower in the better-off republics and it is possible to hypothesise that this cross-section result would also apply to a time-series analysis. For non-manual workers, expansion in job opportunities seems to have involved predominantly the acquisition of greater professional expertise. There is less evidence of an expansion of female employment in managerial or supervisory roles. But this analysis is largely heuristic. It has concentrated upon developments in a few selected job categories and it has relied upon a subjective assessment of their attributes. By making use of the results of recent research by Soviet labour economists and industrial sociologists it is possible to provide a more objective (but less sanguine) assessment of the extent of vertical segregation in industry. This topic is taken up in the next section.

### Vertical Segregation among Industrial Workers

The analysis of vertical segregation given in the previous section was impressionistic; it relied heavily upon subjective interpretation for determining the quality of the jobs done by men and women. This was an almost inevitable consequence of the data upon which it was based. There are no published statistical sources that provide information about job quality defined in a consistent way in all sectors of the Soviet economy. And I doubt whether any such sources exist in an unpublished form. But consistent information of this type does exist for one sector, industry, and some of it has been published in monographs and academic journals.

As a by-product of the Soviet wage determination process almost all manual occupations in Soviet industry are assigned a skill grade. These are certainly consistent within industrial branches and some attempt has been made within the past twenty years or so to ensure that jobs of comparable skill in different branches are assigned to the same skill category. By extension, the skill grades assigned to jobs are transferred to the workers who perform them. Thus, skill-grading provides one way in which the quality of the jobs done by male and female workers in the USSR can be compared.

Secondly, it is the practice of Soviet statisticians to classify industrial jobs into one of five categories, depending upon the degree of mechanisation of the operations that they entail. Some labour force censuses have included tables which present a distribution of men and women workers by the degree of mechanisation of the jobs they hold. This also provides an objective measure of differences in job quality.

Finally, Soviet statisticians also distinguish between basic production workers and auxiliary personnel. The latter category is often broken down into finer occupational groups. Although the assessment of quality in this case is more subjective, this categorisation may also be used to explore the extent of sex-linked disparities in skill and satisfaction. Information on all three aspects of job differentiation is given below.

Although similar classifications exist for workers in construction, state agriculture and some branches of transport, much less has been published about these sectors (and what is available is in a much less systematic form) so that only passing reference can be made to conditions in these sectors here. But industry, on the Soviet statistical definition, is somewhat broader than manufacturing, the term used by Western statisticians. In approximate terms, industry, *promyshlennost*, consists of manufacturing, mining and quarrying and part of public utilities. (The production and distribution of electricity is classified as industry in the USSR, for example.) Therefore, the discussion here covers more of the economy than would be true in Western Europe or North America.

The first of the indicators mentioned above that can cast light on disparities in job quality was skill-grading. Here, I outline the function that skill grades play in the Soviet wage system and then consider the available evidence about differences in the skill grades of men and women workers in Soviet industry.

Wage rates in the USSR are centrally determined. This means that the same structure is applied in virtually all branches. For our purposes two elements are relevant, the *stavka* and the *tarifnaya setka*. The first of these is the basic rate (in robles and kopeks) paid for the least skilled work in any individual branch. *Stavki* are differentiated by industry, with generally higher rates being paid in mining and quarrying, metallurgy and other branches of heavy industry, and lower ones assigned to light industry and food-processing.

The *tarifnaya setka* consists of a set of coefficients, typically six, indicating by how much the rate for any particular job exceeds the basic *stavka*. For the branches employing most workers, these coefficients range from 1·0 to 1·8 or 2·0; that is, the top wage in any sector is from 80 to 100 per cent above the lowest one. Individual jobs are assigned to a particular point on this scale on the basis of a job evaluation procedure. That is, if a particular job in the food-processing industry is deemed to be of Grade III standard, those doing that job will receive a wage that is 1·2 times the basic *stavka*. A worker doing a job of Grade III standard in some other sector, say, metalworking, will also receive a wage that is 1·2 times the basic *stavka*. But the two workers will only receive the same basic wage if the *stavki* for the two sectors are identical.

Jobs are assigned to grades on the basis of a job evaluation procedure that is supposed to use common criteria to evaluate occupations in all branches. Thus, Grade III work should involve the same intrinsic levels of skill (and possibly the same training time), irrespective of the branch in which it is performed. Further, the grades are supposed to reflect increases in skill; the first step or two, it is claimed, involve little more than the acquisition of experience and good working habits while at the top increases involve the learning of substantially new skills (Rabkina and Rimashevskaya, 1972, p. 83). As a result, all recent Soviet scales have displayed both increasing relative and absolute differentials. (The step sizes get larger.)

In so far as this skill-grading has been carried out on a uniform basis, the discussion here indicates that the *razryad*, skill grade, should act as an admirable proxy for the skill involved in a particular occupation. It should also serve as an indicator of the monetary benefit that occupation offers. If, as argued at the beginning of the chapter, job-satisfaction is positively correlated with skill, the *razryad* should serve as a measure of job quality. There is one drawback to this interpretation, however. The Soviet wage system also includes premia for work performed in arduous or unpleasant conditions but it is frequently alleged that these premia are insufficient to attract the necessary labour. In consequence, enterprise managers sometimes overgrade particular occupations, thus permitting the enterprise to pay those who undertake them higher wages. Since, due to protective legislation, a majority of the workers in this category are likely to be men, estimates of vertical segregation based on *razryady* are likely to be biased. How significant this source of bias is likely to be is unclear.[3]

Table 5.6    *Distribution of Male and Female Industrial Workers by Skill Grade: Various Sectors, RSFSR, 1970-2 (%)*

|  | I-II | III | IV | V-VI |
|---|---|---|---|---|
| Engineering |  |  |  |  |
| Men | 23·0 | 24·6 | 26·6 | 25·8 |
| Women | 67·7 | 26·8 | 4·4 | 1·1 |
| Textiles |  |  |  |  |
| Men | 25·9 | 12·0 | 17·6 | 44·5 |
| Women | 8·3 | 50·0 | 36·7 | 5·0 |
| Baking |  |  |  |  |
| Men | 2·4 | 7·5 | 37·1 | 53·0 |
| Women | 13·6 | 21·1 | 27·8 | 37·5 |
| Meat-Processing |  |  |  |  |
| Men | 4·2 | 27·1 | 31·2 | 37·5 |
| Women | 9·4 | 63·5 | 23·4 | 3·7 |

*Source:* Kotlyar and Turchaninova, 1975, pp. 68–71.

Some recent figures on differences in the skill grades of jobs done by men and women in Soviet industry are given in Table 5.6. Ideally, one would like to have figures relating to industry as a whole for the USSR as a whole, but these proved impossible to locate. And one can have some confidence that the figures in the table do not understate the quality of women's jobs too much. First, the RSFSR is the largest single Soviet republic, containing about half the population of the USSR and perhaps three-fifths of its industrial capacity. It is also one of the more developed republics. Secondly, it is reported that in 1972 some 69 per cent of all women manual workers in industry were to be found in the three branches machinebuilding and metalworking, light industry and food-processing (Kotlyar and Turchaninova, 1975, p. 37). These are the branches referred to in the table. Nor does the RSFSR differ from the rest of the Soviet Union in this respect. In 1969 the Soviet Central Statistical Administration reported that 68·6 per cent of all female industrial workers were in these same three branches (Kotlyar *et al.*, 1973, p. 382).

The figures in Table 5.6 show that there are substantial differences in the skill grades of men and women workers. In engineering, for instance, more than two-thirds of all female employees were in the lowest two classes. Moreover, although this is not shown by the table, women made up between 80 and 90 per cent of all workers in these categories (Kotlyar and Turchaninova, 1975, p. 68). More than half of all male engineering workers, in contrast, were in the top three categories, and more than a quarter were rated Grade V-VI. Men accounted for between 80 and 95 per cent of all workers in the top three *razryady*.

The position in the other sectors listed in Table 5.6 is not perhaps as extreme as in engineering, but in no sector is there as high a proportion of skilled women as skilled men and only in baking are more than half the female workers to be found in Grades IV–VI. (This is true of men in all the listed sectors.) A similar state of affairs has been reported by a number of other Soviet economists and sociologists. (See, for example, Danilova, 1968, p. 23; Frolov *et al.*, 1975, p. 41; Kasimovskii, 1975, p. 134; Shishkan, 1976, p. 137.) And in construction, too, women are disproportionately concentrated in the lower-skilled jobs – at least on one major construction site in Siberia. It is reported that the modal skill grade for men involved in the construction of the Krasnoyarsk Hydroelectric Station was Grade IV with approximately equal numbers in Grades III and V–VI. Sixty per cent of women, on the other hand, were in Grades I–II and a further quarter were classified as Grade III (Zayonchkovskaya, 1970, p. 249). One eminent Soviet sociologist has gone so far as to suggest the following skill structure as typical of industrial towns in the USSR (Sonin, 1973, p. 362):

|  | Men (%) | Women (%) |
|---|---|---|
| Highly skilled (Grades V–VI) | 31 | 4 |
| Semi-skilled (Grades III–IV) | 50 | 30 |
| Unskilled (Grades I–II) | 19 | 66 |

(The author only provided the verbal descriptions of the skill categories; it is I who have assigned the grade designations.) These distributions suggest that the average skill grade of male workers is 3·7 as opposed to 2·3 for female workers.

As mentioned earlier in this chapter, Soviet statisticians have long been preoccupied by the degree of mechanisation in Soviet industry. To study this

Table 5.7  *Relationship between Female Employment and the Character of Industrial Employment*

|  |  | *% of Women in* | | |
|---|---|---|---|---|
|  | *% of labour force in 1972* | *Paper industry, no date* | *Karaganda oblast, 1969* | *Ki SSR, 1972* |
| Working on automatic machines |  | 1·1 | 3·0 | 1·8 |
| Working on non-automated machines | 44·3 | 42·6 | 43·4 | 45·5 |
| Working by hand, assisted by machine | 7·1 | 29·0 | 10·0 | 8·4 |
| Working by hand, not assisted by machine | 36·0 | 24·3 | 40·6 | 41·9 |
| Working on maintenance and repair | 12·6 | 3·0 | 3·0 | 2·4 |

*Sources:* Col. (1) Shishkan, 1976, p. 127; Col. (2) Uchastkina, 1975, p. 33; Cols (3) and (4) Mailibaeva, 1975, pp. 35, 46.

they have introduced a set of five categories designed to distinguish the more mechanised (and hence more productive, more desirable) jobs from less mechanised jobs and those involving primarily physical labour. The actual categories used are set out in Table 5.7. It should be noted that the last category, although it involves mainly manual (non-mechanised) labour, is none the less highly regarded since in order to be able to maintain and repair machines a worker must understand something about how they function.

This classification system gives some idea of official attitudes towards the quality of various industrial jobs and, to the extent that Soviet workers share these official values, it presumably corresponds to their personal assessments. Information on the proportion of men and women in jobs of different categories will therefore cast some light on vertical segregation. Unfortunately, complete classifications of the labour force in different sectors or regions by degree of mechanisation by sex are not easy to find. Three partial distributions of women workers are given in Table 5.7 together with data on the Soviet labour force as a whole which is included for purposes of comparison. These show that while the proportion of men and women working on automated and non-automated machines is about the same, women are substantially more likely than men to be engaged in manual work (whether or not assisted by machine). They also show that men are much more likely than women to be engaged in the skilled activities of maintaining and repairing machines.

The female distributions given in Table 5.7 refer to rather special subpopulations of industrial workers, but there is nothing to suggest that they are atypical. It is reported, for instance, that in 1969 21·3 per cent of male industrial workers (in the RSFSR) were engaged on maintenance and repair work while only 1·3 per cent of women were (Kotlyar and Turchaninova, 1975, p. 43). Even in those sectors in which women account for a large proportion of the labour force, few of them are employed as tool-setters (*naladchiki*) or on maintenance work (Mikhailyuk, 1970, p. 68):

|                 | % of women in labour force | % of female tool-setters |
|-----------------|:--------------------------:|:------------------------:|
| Chemicals       | 47·5                       | 6·8                      |
| China-pottery   | 60·5                       | —                        |
| Light           | 80·5                       | 7·0                      |
| Food-processing | 51·5                       | 2·3                      |
| Printing        | 68·5                       | 2·9                      |

Mikhailyuk also asserts that both in industry as a whole and in a range of individual branches manual labour, *ruchnoi trud*, that is, work without the assistance of machines, is more prevalent among women than men. She gives the following figures (although she does not say to which year or region they refer) (1970, p. 66):

Those engaged in *ruchnoi trud* out of every 100 workers of given sex

|                        | men | women |
|------------------------|-----|-------|
| Logging (*lesnaya*)    | 37  | 69    |
| Building materials     | 25  | 37    |
| Peat-digging           | 10  | 56    |
| Non-ferrous metallurgy | 13  | 23    |
| Ferrous metallurgy     | 19  | 23    |
| Chemicals              | 12  | 15    |

It has also been claimed by Sukhachev (1975, p. 72) that

> According to the occupational census, held by the CSA, among women engaged on construction work or subsidiary production, 80 per cent were working in occupations that involve physical or exacting physical work and only 6 per cent were shown to have the occupations of driver, machine-operator or their assistant.

Unfortunately, Sukhachev does not indicate what proportion of men are recorded as being in these two categories. If Zayonchkovskaya's work about the Krasnoyarskii GES is typical, one suspects that it will be lower.

The evidence produced in the last few pages has been neither as coherent nor as comprehensive as one would have liked; but perhaps it can compensate by variety for what it lacks in consistency. In any case, it seems to suggest that men are more likely to be engaged on skilled mechanised work or the maintenance of machines than women; and that women are more likely than men to be engaged in manual non-mechanised work. Given the structure of Soviet wages and Soviet official attitudes, men's jobs are likely to be both more highly paid and held in higher esteem. Finally, there does not seem to have been much improvement in this state of affairs in the last ten or twenty years. It is reported that 'of the total growth in the number of workers engaged on non-mechanised work between 1962 and 1969, 96 per cent were women' (Shishkan, 1976, p. 138).

In addition to classifications in terms of *razryady* and the degree of mechanisation, Soviet statisticians also divide manual jobs in industry into the categories of basic production work and auxiliary work. (Analogous distinctions may be made in other countries too.) The former refers to jobs in which the worker contributes directly to the output of his enterprise; for example, in the textile industry spinners and weavers would be classed as basic production workers. Auxiliary work on the other hand comprises all those jobs that are essential if the factory is to operate smoothly and efficiently but which do not contribute directly to its output. In the textile industry again, maintenance and repair work would be ascribed auxiliary status – as would the manufacture of spare parts necessary to keep the looms running. If the same spare parts were manufactured in a textile machinery plant, however, the work would be classified as basic.

This brief discussion indicates that the basic/auxiliary division does not coincide with the Marxist theoretical distinction between productive and unproductive labour – however much the labels used might point in that direction. Nor does it correspond to distinctions in skill: some auxiliary workers are a good deal more skilled than the basic production workers whose machines they service. Further, it is not clear what inferences can or should be drawn from information about differences in the prevalence of auxiliary status among men and women. It has been claimed, for instance, that these status differences affect 'wage levels, the length of holidays and many other factors that directly or indirectly determine the stability of the industrial labour force, *stepen zakreplenia kadrov na proizvodstve*' (Kurman, 1971, p. 74). The implication here is that basic production workers enjoy higher esteem and greater privileges than auxiliary personnel. But this is hard to believe. Both categories contain workers with widely differing levels of skill and most other evidence suggests that privileges like holidays depend more on skill than on production status.

Nevertheless, Soviet economists and sociologists have produced information about differences in production status between male and female workers and, what is more interesting, have provided some insights into sex differentiation within these general categories. The material produced below indicates that women are likely to be engaged on low-skill work, whether basic or auxiliary, while men in both categories are likely to be more highly skilled.

Table 5.8    *Distribution of Industrial Workers by Sex and Production Status: RSFSR, 1969 (%)*

|  | Men | | Women | |
|---|---|---|---|---|
|  | *Basic* | *Auxiliary* | *Basic* | *Auxiliary* |
| Light (excluding textiles) | 35·7 | 64·3 | 88·0 | 12·0 |
| Textiles | 7·6 | 92·4 | 73·2 | 26·8 |
| Food-processing | 28·3 | 71·7 | 63·0 | 37·0 |
| Coal-mining | n.a. | n.a. | 36·2 | 63·8 |
| Ore-mining | n.a. | n.a. | 26·3 | 73·7 |
| All-industry | 43·8 | 56·2 | 60·4 | 39·6 |

*Source:* Kotlyar *et al.*, 1973, p. 390.

Information about the sex composition of the two status-groups in industry as a whole and in selected branches is given in Table 5.8. The Soviet source from which these figures were taken does not say so explicitly, but it is likely that they refer only to the RSFSR. I do not suppose, however, that the position for the USSR as a whole would be markedly different. It is also unlikely that there have been substantial changes in the distribution since 1969.

In two of the three branches that employ the bulk of women industrial workers (light industry and food-processing) women are concentrated in basic production jobs while men occupy the auxiliary positions. It is highly probable (in view of the all-industry figures) that the same situation pertains for women in engineering – although a larger proportion of the men in this branch will be classified as basic production workers. In heavy industry, on the other hand, the table shows that women are concentrated in auxiliary operations.

Some people might be surprised by the figures for industry as a whole, with a majority of males being classified as auxiliary while three-fifths of females are basic workers. This reflects, I think, the degree of mechanisation of the sector - and the inefficiency of maintenance and repair work in the USSR. Due to poor-quality workmanship and chronic shortages of spare parts, armies of men (and a significant proportion of the machine-tool stock of the country) are busy in every factory in the land keeping the machines going by make-do-and-mend methods and the literal manufacture of components.

This is brought out by a consideration of the occupations of those classed as auxiliary workers. A number of Soviet authors have commented on the clear sexual differentiation (and, I would say, vertical segregation) in this sphere:

A high proportion of female auxiliary workers is employed on loading/ unloading work, sorting and packing, control operations and warehouse management, *obsluzhivaet skladskoe khozyaistvo*. A majority of the occupations in this form of auxiliary work are of a semi- or unskilled nature and, in addition, the share of women in them is as high as 75-90 per cent . . .

Male auxiliary workers are different (repairmen, workers in energy-power and instrumentation); they work in occupations a majority of which call for special training and high skill. (Kotlyar and Turchaninova, 1975, p. 47)

The point is also made that the position in other branches of material production and the services sector is essentially similar (Litvyakov, 1969, p. 133). And Mikhailyuk has stressed how unpleasant most of these jobs are (1970, p. 67):

Women make up a majority of those workers doing subsidiary and auxiliary work that does not demand much knowledge but is connected with the expenditure of considerable physical effort . . .

Indeed, it has been alleged that both the spirit and the letter of the law are being broken here (although the protection offered to women in the USSR in this area has not been very great).[4]

. . . some bosses, *khozyaistvennye rukovoditeli*, continue to consider the use of female labour on heavy work as normal; they incline towards infractions of the code limiting women's work; they permit, from time to time, infractions of the rights of mothers. (Lysakova, 1967, p. 96)

The material presented in this discussion of disparities in production status between men and women has been impressionistic rather than comprehensive. But the general tenor of the material has been to reinforce the evidence presented earlier. Women industrial workers are either concentrated in low-skill jobs in the traditional branches of textiles, garment-making and food-processing, or they are employed as semi-skilled assembly workers in engineering, or, finally, as auxiliary workers, as loaders, packers and sorters, elsewhere in manufacturing. Nor is the situation different in other sectors of the economy. The jobs that they do are less mechanised than those of men, make little call on specific skills (as opposed, perhaps, to manual dexterity), are monotonous, repetitive and may call for considerable physical effort. It seems fair to conclude that women's work in Soviet industry is characterised by low social esteem, low pay and inferior working conditions. While I would not wish to suggest that the position of male industrial workers in the USSR is wholly satisfactory, their status and prospects do seem to be better than those of women. I believe that there is convincing evidence of vertical segregation among manual workers.

## Status Hierarchies among Non-Manual Workers

The analysis of the last section was concerned primarily with vertical segregation in industry; it was confined wholly to manual (non-agricultural) workers. This is the section of the labour force for which the clearest evidence of horizontal segregation was adduced in the last chapter. Perhaps the picture is less bleak among white-collar workers?

There exists no body of data that permits one to identify unambiguously the quality of different white-collar jobs. Soviet managerial and professional occupations are not assigned skill categories in the way that industrial jobs are. It makes little sense to talk of comparative levels of mechanisation; and, of course, there is no question of hard physical labour. But the general framework laid down at the beginning of this chapter is still relevant. It still makes sense to associate differences in the quality of jobs with differences in the pay they offer, the satisfaction they provide and the conditions in which they must be done. Only for white-collar work, the correlates of these attributes are somewhat different.

A consideration of published Soviet salary scales (and they are available only for enterprise-level management personnel and for certain groups of professionals) shows that salaries are positively correlated with the degree of authority or responsibility of the position and with the professional-technical qualifications it requires. They also increase with age or experience. Thus, the salaries of enterprise directors are higher than those of their subordinates; the salaries of directors of large enterprises are higher than those of small ones. The same is true of administrative-executive personnel in institutions like hospitals or universities. Similarly, the salaries of those with university-level qualifications exceed those of persons with only secondary-specialist training; the salaries of those with higher degrees are greater than those of persons with only a first degree; and so on. This implies that managerial-executive status can act as a proxy for salary – and thus yield information about one aspect of job quality. Information on educational attainment will also yield insight into this question.

As far as personal satisfaction is concerned, I would like to suggest that it depends on two factors. First, as a general rule I would argue that occupations requiring university-level preparation enjoy higher social esteem than those requiring only secondary training. They will also yield greater job satisfaction. Secondly, positions that confer decision-making authority, that entail a measure of managerial or executive power, also enjoy social esteem; and the greater the power the greater the esteem. I take it as axiomatic that job satisfaction and esteem are positively correlated. Thus the criteria by which I propose that white-collar occupations should be assessed are the level of qualifications required and the degree of managerial authority conferred. These will cast light on both pay and job satisfaction. I can think of no convenient way of measuring working conditions – but do not consider this dimension to be important in the case of white-collar workers.

Although Soviet data sources do not provide consistent and comprehensive information about the qualifications and authority of non-manual occupations taken as a whole, it is possible to construct a limited number of status hierarchies that relate to particular employment areas. It is also possible to determine the sex-composition of those occupying various rungs in these hierarchies. This information casts light on the extent of vertical segregation among non-manual workers.

In this section I consider status hierarchies in three fields: management, education and medicine. It is also possible to construct them in a fourth: politics. This has been excluded since the book is primarily about women's work and it is not clear how far political participation and promotion are determined by economic factors (but see Lapidus, 1975b, pp. 90–118).

Table 5.9 presents status hierarchies for the three fields mentioned above

Table 5.9  *The Share of Women in Selected Managerial and Professional Occupations (Census Definitions): 1939–70 (%)*

|  | 1939 | 1959[a] | 1959[b] | 1970 |
|---|---|---|---|---|
| Management |  |  |  |  |
| Enterprise directors | 7 | 12 | 12 | 13 |
| Shop and section heads | 9 | 15 | 16 | 18 |
| Foremen | 9 | 24 | 24 | 27 |
| ITR | 22 | 39 | 40 | 44 |
| Manual non-agricultural labour force | 30 | 37 | 39 | 42 |
| Medicine |  |  |  |  |
| Chief physicians, etc. | 39 | 52 | 54 | 53 |
| Physicians | 61 | 79 | 79 | 74 |
| Midwives and *feldshers* | 72 | 84 | 84 | 83 |
| Nurses and pharmacists | 98 | 100 | 99 | 99 |
| Education and Science |  |  |  |  |
| Heads of scientific establishments | 31 | 38 | 38 | 43 |
| University teachers, etc. |  |  | 38 | 40 |
| School principals, etc. | n.a. | n.a. | 23 | 32 |
| Primary and secondary school teachers | 55 | 73 | 73 | 72 |

*Notes:*  a Col. (2) refers to the classification given in the 1959 Census.
b Col. (3) refers to the classification given in the 1970 Census.
*Sources: Itogi* . . . , 1959, Table 48, and *Itogi* . . . , 1970. Vol. VI, Table 18.

and also shows the share of women at different levels according to the last three population censuses. Considering first that for management: the category ITR, *inzhenirno-tekhnicheskie rabotniki*, includes the three executive levels listed above it. It also includes those who perform other management functions (norm-setters, senior accountants, engineers, etc.) but who possess less authority over people. The data refer to the economy as a whole and not just to industry. The hierarchy displays two prominent features: the more senior the position, the smaller the share of women, and the more recent the year, the larger the share of women. Thus, in 1939, although women accounted for 30 per cent of manual non-agricultural workers and more than a fifth of ITR, only one in ten section heads was a woman and only one in fourteen directors. By 1970, however, the share of women among ITR exceeded their share in the non-agricultural (manual) labour force; one foreman in four was a woman, one section head in five and one director in eight. The same general pattern is true of the other hierarchies listed in the table.

Tables 5.10 to 5.12 provide rather more detailed information about status hierarchies in industry and agriculture for a more recent period. They are

Table 5.10    *The Share of Women in Industrial Management: 1963–73 (%)*

| Position | 1 December 1963 | 15 November 1973 |
|---|---|---|
| Enterprise directors | 6 | 9 |
| Chief engineers and other specialists | 16 | 10 |
| Shop and shift heads and their deputies | 12–22 | 16 |
| Departmental heads and their deputies | 20 | 26 |
| Engineers (excluding chief engineers) | 38 | 49 |
| Technicians (excluding norm-setters) | 65 | 78 |
| Foremen | 20 | 24 |
| Engineers – norm-setters, technicians – norm-setters | 62 | 75 |
| Chief and senior accountants | 36 | 53 |
| Engineer-economists, economists, statisticians, planning personnel | 79 | 86 |
| Industrial employees | 45 | 49 |

*Sources:* Col. (2) Zhenshchiny, 1969, p. 102; Col. (3) Zhenshchiny, 1975, p. 80.

derived, indirectly, from occupational censuses and regular labour force accounting. It is for this reason, as well as because they refer to a more restricted population, that the figures they give differ from those in Table 5.9.

Table 5.10, for example, shows that in 1973 only one industrial enterprise director in ten was a woman; that women were more prominent in subordinate positions; that women were more likely to be employed as 'specialists' than in a supervisory role (consider the relationship between engineers – 49 per cent

Table 5.11    *The Share of Women in Management: State Agriculture,*
              *1975-6 (%)*

|  | 1975 | 1976 |
|---|---|---|
| Sovkhoz directors | 1·5 | 1·6 |
| Section heads | 5·0 | 5·1 |
| Chief specialists | 11·6 | 11·7 |
| Agronomists | 27·8 | 28·6 |
| Zootechnicians | 44·0 | 45·6 |
| Veterinarians, etc. | 36·2 | 37·6 |
| Engineers, technicians | 6·5 | 7·4 |
| Brigade-leaders: crop-work | 17·1 | 17·8 |
| animal husbandry | 38·3 | 40·5 |
| Agricultural employees (annual average) | 45·0 | n.a. |

*Sources:* Col. (2) *NK SSSR*, 1974, p. 453; Col. (3) *NK SSR*, 1975, p. 446.

female - and foremen - 24 per cent female.) It also shows how large a
proportion of subordinate management staff in industry is in fact female - 53
per cent of senior accountants, 75 per cent of norm-setters, 78 per cent of
technicians and 86 per cent of clerical-planning personnel. Finally, note that
as with the period 1939-70 women made gains in virtually all sectors between
1963 and 1973.

A similar picture emerges from Tables 5.11 and 5.12. Although almost half
the manual labour force is female, very few of the highest managerial positions
in agriculture are occupied by women. In 1975-6 only one sovkhoz director
in sixty-five was a woman and only one kolkhoz chairman in fifty. Even at
the brigade level, men are much more prevalent than women in supervisory
roles.

This is particularly striking in animal husbandry. The vast majority of

Table 5.12    *The Share of Women in Management: Collective Farms,*
              *1975-6 (%)*

|  | 1975 | 1976 |
|---|---|---|
| Chairman | 1·8 | 1·9 |
| Deputy chairman (osvobozhdennye) | 5·8 | 6·5 |
| Chief specialists | 14·6 | 14·2 |
| Agronomists | 28·9 | 28·6 |
| Zootechnicians | 57·2 | 58·9 |
| Veterinarians, etc. | 29·0 | 30·7 |
| Engineers, technicians | 1·6 | 2·0 |
| Brigade-leaders: crop-work | 9·4 | 9·9 |
| animal husbandry | 26·7 | 28·5 |
| Labour force (annual average) | 48 | n.a. |

*Sources:* Col. (2) *NK SSSR*, 1974, p. 451; Col. (3) *NK SSSR*, 1975, p. 446.

workers in this sector are female (they make up over 90 per cent of milkmaids and poultry-workers, for example, the two categories separately identified in the census tables). Yet between 60 and 75 per cent of the supervisors are men! More generally, the tables bring out clearly the difference between specialist expertise and the management or supervision of people. Women are reasonably well represented in the former category but poorly represented in the latter.

Finally, perhaps a comment should be made about the striking difference between the proportion of industrial engineers who are women and the proportion of female engineers in agriculture. In the former sector in 1973, virtually half of all engineers were women. In 1975-6, however, only 2·7 per cent of engineers in agriculture were female. No explanation of this difference springs readily to mind.

The medical status hierarchy given in Table 5.9 calls for little comment. The information it contains is, by now, familiar. It reveals the dominance of women in the sector in the USSR. Although the share of women among physicians declined between 1959 and 1970, the decline was certainly not substantial. In the latter year, three-quarters of all Soviet doctors were still women. I suspect that the greater prominence of men among senior medical personnel is also familiar and should be seen, at least in part, as yet another example of the Soviet preference for men in the area of management.

The educational data in Table 5.9 suggest the existence of two status hierarchies, one in primary and secondary education and one in tertiary education. An attempt is made to separate these (for the postwar period) in Tables 5.13 and 5.14. Once again, one observes the same phenomenon:

Table 5.13    *The Share of Women in Selected Educational Posts: 1963/4–1975/6 (%)*

|  | 1963/4 | 1970/1 | 1975/6 |
|---|---|---|---|
| Principals — Secondary Schools | 20 | 25 | 29 |
| — 8 Year Schools | 24 | 28 | 33 |
| — Primary Schools | 72 | 56 (?) | 83 |
| Deputy Principals — Secondary Schools | 44 | 61 | 65 |
| — 8 Year Schools | 56 | 60 | 61 |
| Teachers: Classes 1–10 | n.a. | 80 | 79 |
| of which   Classes 8–11 | 67 | | |
| Classes 5– 8 | 75 | | |
| Classes 1– 4 | 67 | | |
| Music, PE, etc. | 28 | 31 | 34 |

*Sources:* Col. (2) *NK SSSR*, 1963, p.561; Col. (3) *NK SSSR*, 1970, p. 632; Col. (4) *NK SSSR*, 1975, p. 672.

within any year, the more senior the position, the more it involves the management or administration of adults (rather than the care of children), the fewer the women employed in it. But over time women have made gains in all but one category: perhaps surprisingly, there are now (1975) a lower proportion of women among senior scientific fellows than in 1950. And the share of women in this grade appears to have fallen steadily throughout the

Table 5.14    *The proportion of Women in Selected Academic Positions:*
*USSR, 1950-75 (%)*

|  | 1950 | 1960 | 1970 | 1975 |
|---|---|---|---|---|
| Academician, corresponding member, professor | 5·6 | 7·1 | 9·9 | 10·5 |
| Dotsent | 14·7 | 17·1 | 21·0 | 22·3 |
| Senior scientific fellow | 30·7 | 28·6 | 25·1 | 23·4 |
| Junior fellow, assistant | 48·0 | 50·9 | 49·8 | 49·6 |
| All scientific personnel | 36·3 | 36·3 | 38·8 | 39·9 |

*Note:* According to Russian usage 'science' includes the humanities and social studies.
The above figures include personnel in both universities and research institutes.
*Sources: NK SSSR*, 1970, pp. 656-7; *NK SSSR*, 1975, p. 165.

postwar period. I have no explanation for this trend.

The material presented in this section permits one to draw three conclusions. The reduction in horizontal segregation among white-collar workers
that was tentatively suggested in Chapter 4 has been accompanied by a
reduction in vertical segregation. This has been the result of two trends. First,
as a result of greater education, women have come to occupy an increasing
proportion of professional and specialist positions in the USSR. Secondly,
women have made more limited gains in occupations that permit the exercise
of managerial authority, broadly defined. But it is still the case that women
are under-represented in jobs that demand technical training or confer
executive power, given the scale of their participation in the labour force.
Sector by sector, then, it seems fair to conclude that women's jobs are inferior
in quality to those done by men. There is still vertical segregation among
white-collar occupations.

Finally, it should be pointed out that our analysis does not permit one to
draw conclusions about the relative merits of occupations in different status
hierarchies. Nothing that has been said so far allows one to infer that industrial
management enjoys a higher social esteem, say, than medicine or scientific
research. Thus, the fact that women have made relatively greater gains in these
last two might constitute an additional reason for arguing that there has been
a reduction in vertical segregation. On the other hand, it might be the case that
greater gains have been made in areas of lower social esteem. Although
concepts and data are not strictly comparable, this issue is discussed in the
next section which takes up the question of administrative segregation in the
USSR.

## Administrative Segregation, 1940–75

So far the focus of attention has been the job categories to which male and
female employees in the USSR are assigned. Job categories have been used as
the best available approximation to occupations. But, as the discussion of the
Soviet wage system at the beginning of this chapter noted, occupational
differentiation is not the only source of disparities in earnings in the USSR.

Differences in *stavki*, the rates paid for the least skilled work in any branch, affect levels of earnings in industry. And, although wage and salary systems elsewhere in the economy are not set out with quite such bureaucratic precision, they are similar in character. Thus it is possible that work of a similar character (entailing the same skill in terms of its *tarifnyi razryad*) will be remunerated differently when it is performed in different sectors of the economy.

Soviet labour economists justify this differentiation of *stavki* by an appeal to their interpretation of the labour theory of value. They assert that the economic significance of the sector in which a person works affects the quality and quantity of labour that he or she supplies – and hence its value. Thus one may infer that differences in *stavki* set for different branches of material production, or their analogues in the case of white-collar workers, reflect differences in the importance attached to the sector on the part of the planning authorities.

It can be argued, I think, that differences in *stavki* will correspond more or less to differences in social esteem or prestige assigned to work in different parts of the economy. As argued above, Soviet workers will work in order to make a living and a job that pays well will be regarded, *ceteris paribus*, as a good job. Nor should one assume that ordinary men and women in the Soviet Union are indifferent to the values of their government. If the whole tenor of public discussion emphasises certain attitudes, it is logical to assume that these will have been absorbed, to some extent at least, during the process of socialisation. This suggests that, in so far as personal job satisfaction is affected by sectoral affiliation, it will be positively correlated with pecuniary remuneration. Thus it is plausible to assume that there is a sectoral dimension to the assessment of job quality. If it is the case that women in the USSR are disproportionately concentrated in low-paying sectors, this should be taken to imply that there is some tendency to impute low social esteem to women's work.

The form in which Soviet statisticians record data on current employment permits some assessment of the nature and extent of administrative segregation in the USSR. For every year since 1960 (and for some earlier years) data are available on the shares of men and women in employment in twelve to sixteen standardised economic sectors. These range from branches like industry, agriculture (state employment only) and construction to education, health and government service. The number of sectors separately identified has increased slightly over the years and this may have entailed changes in sectoral definition as well as reductions in the scope of the unidentified residual. Similar data are available for most of the union republics (at least for some years.) This data is certainly not as detailed as one would like – in all years, for instance, industry is recorded as employing between a quarter and two-fifths of the labour force and it would be helpful if one could disaggregate this sector into its component branches. But the frequency with which the data are collected (and published) allows one to trace the course of segregation through time.

Given the character of the employment data available, there are two ways in which one can measure the extent of administrative segregation and the way that it has changed through time. First one can calculate the $S$ index defined in the last chapter. (This shows the proportion of the male or female labour force that will have to change sectors if the sectoral distributions of men and women are to be made identical.) An increase in the value of $S_t$ would imply an increase in administrative segregation, and so on. But $S_t$ does not indicate how far women are to be found disproportionately in 'worse' sectors than men. This is what the second indicator proposed here, $R_t$, attempts to do.

In addition to the employment data described above, the annual statistical handbooks (at both All-Union and republican level) give information on average earnings in most of the sectors for which labour force figures are given. If one takes these to represent an index of job quality, then the ratio of average notional earnings for each of the sexes[5] will indicate the extent to which women are concentrated in low-pay (and hence low-prestige) sectors.

Estimates of both $S_t$ and $R_t$ for the USSR as a whole for the period 1940–75 are given in Table 5.15. Not too much significance should be attached

Table 5.15    *Administrative Segregation in the USSR: 1940–75*

| | S-index | Standardised earnings ratio | Coefficient of variation of sectoral earnings (%) |
|---|---|---|---|
| 1940 | 0·173 | 97·2 | 33·24 |
| 1950 | 0·204 | 94·2 | 21·99 |
| 1955 | 0·231 | 96·7 | 25·31 |
| 1960 | 0·236 | 92·8 | 22·05 |
| 1965 | 0·256 | 94·1 | 15·50 |
| 1970 | 0·262 | 92·3 | 16·03 |
| 1975 | 0·267 | 90·4 | 17·22 |

*Notes:* Both indices are based on the shares of male and female employment in the twelve to sixteen economic sectors used in current labour statistics – e.g. industry, agriculture, construction, etc. As defined in Chapter 4,

$$S_t = \tfrac{1}{2} \Sigma ( |f_{it}/F - m_{it}/M| )$$

where $f_{it}$ is the number of women in the $i$th sector in year $t$, etc. The standardised earnings ratio, $R_t$, is calculated as:

$$R_t = \frac{M}{F} \cdot \frac{\Sigma_i f_{it} w_{it}}{\Sigma_i m_{it} w_{it}}$$

where $w_{it}$ is the average monthly earnings in the $i$th sector in year $t$ (and the other symbols have the significance assigned in Chapter 4).

to the figures for 1940 (or, possibly, 1950) since the data on which they are based are less ample than those for other years. Nor can much meaning be attached to the absolute value of either index in any year. Both are sensitive to the number of sectors separately identified and Soviet sources are niggardly in this respect. But the direction of change revealed by both $S_t$ and $R_t$ is striking. Both suggest that the concentration of women in particular (low-paying) sectors has increased over the last thirty to thirty-five years, that what I have called administrative segregation has increased since 1940. The evidence from the $R_t$ series is, perhaps, more ambiguous than that from $S_t$, since $R_t$ increased between 1950 and 1955 and between 1960 and 1065, but the general trend is negative and the index in 1975 was lower than in any previous year. Finally, changes in $R_t$ seem to bear little relationship to changes in the dispersion of sectoral earnings - at least as measured by the coefficient of variation. That is, there appears to be no direct relationship between inter-sectoral differentials and the extent of administrative segregation.

It is possible to calculate values for $R_k$ ($k = 1 \ldots 13$) for all but two of the republics in 1970. (I have been unable to locate wage data for Kazakhstan or Turkmenistan in that year.) These tend to show that administrative segregation is greater in the richer (more developed) regions. In fact, the relationship is somewhat more complex - as Figure 5.1 indicates. This reproduces the scattergram of $R_k$ on per capita personal income (excluding private receipts) in each republic. The scattergram reveals a clear tendency for $R_k$ to decline with income (which serves as a proxy for the level of development). But it also shows that some other factor is at work. For any given level of income, administrative segregation is greater in Central Asia and the Transcaucasus than it is in the Baltic states or Slav areas. Presumably this is a reflection of differing cultural traditions, different attitudes towards women and women's work in Muslim and non-Muslim areas. (Neither Georgia nor Armenia can be called Muslim, but their geographical location may well have resulted in the absorption of predominantly Muslim cultural attitudes in certain areas of social life.) Figure 5.1 also identifies Kirgizia and the Ukraine as 'rogues'. Perhaps a third factor is at work in these two republics; or possibly their deviance is a reflection of errors in the estimation of personal income.

The regression equations fitted to the scattergrams of Figure 5.1 are

*Slav-Baltic Area*

$$R_k = 99 \cdot 9397 - 0 \cdot 1227 y_k$$
$$(77 \cdot 72) \qquad (5 \cdot 98) \qquad \qquad r^2 : 0 \cdot 8739 \quad DF: 5$$

*Central Asia–Transcaucasus*

$$R_k = 99 \cdot 6613 - 0 \cdot 1709 y_k$$
$$(56 \cdot 17) \qquad (4 \cdot 09) \qquad \qquad r^2 : 0 \cdot 8149 \quad DF: 4$$

While the degrees of freedom are ludicrously small, both the proportion of the variance explained and the determination of individual coefficients are high. I suggest that this implies (at least in Soviet conditions) that administrative segregation is affected if not determined by the level of development, or factors associated with that concept.

This is not the place to explore in depth what those factors might be, but

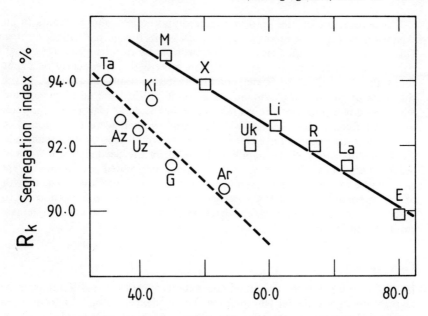

Figure 5.1   *Relationship between $R_k$ and Per Capita Personal Income (Excluding Private Receipts): Union Republics, 1970.*

*Note: Regression Equation*

$$R_k = 99{\cdot}8682 - (0{\cdot}1216 + 0{\cdot}0541 d_j) y_k \quad R^2 : 0{\cdot}8619$$
$$(104{\cdot}2) \quad\quad (7{\cdot}9) \quad\quad (5{\cdot}6) \quad\quad\quad DF : 10$$

where $d_j = 1$ for $j$ equal to 'underdeveloped'
$\quad\quad = 0$ for $j$ equal to 'developed'

in the post-Stalin period it has been observed that increases in female employment have been concentrated in the services sector (Sonin, 1973, p. 357). One might hypothesise, then, that rising real incomes in the USSR (in time or space) are associated with an expansion in demand for services. Although this increase in demand does not result in increases in prices or other market phenomena, it does lead to planners' response; that is, it results in an increase in the supply of services. Since labour productivity tends to be low in these sectors (and since there is little scope for rapid growth in productivity), this increase in supply entails an increase in the demand for labour, an increase in the number of jobs created. Because labour productivity in these sectors is low, the relative wage paid is also low; in addition, the character of the jobs offered, the fact that they frequently involve activities similar to those performed in the home, results in their being identified as 'women's work'. (The phenomenon described here is not peculiar to the USSR; *mutatis mutandis*, it is supposed to have occurred in the USA and elsewhere in the developed world. See, for example, Ginsberg, 1977.)

The expansion of the services sector, hypothesised above, results in an expansion of female employment, an increase in female participation rates. This is facilitated by the demographic transition, by the change to a low birth rate–low death rate regime of population growth that frequently occurs at about the same time. In Soviet conditions it also results in a change in the character of female employment. As a result of distorted development and relentless downward pressure on real wages in the early plan period (say, up to 1939) female participation was high and women were to be found in unconventional occupations. This tendency was reinforced by disturbances in the sex-composition of the population caused by the Second World War and other phenomena. But many of the jobs performed by women were characterised by unpleasant, even unsuitable, working conditions. The growth of job opportunities in the services sector has resulted in women choosing to move out of manufacturing and back to more traditional areas of female employment.

## Conclusion

In this chapter I have examined the extent of vertical and administrative segregation in the Soviet labour force. The evidence, though far from ideal, has tended to confirm the existence of both. Among female manual workers, there has been little change in the character of mass occupations in the past thirty or forty years; they are still heavily concentrated in semi- or unskilled non-industrial or traditional occupations. This suggests that women possess less industrial training than men. Further, for those women in industry (and, by implication, in other branches of material production) conditions of work are often unpleasant: work is monotonous and frequently involves considerable physical effort.

Among white-collar workers there has been more change. Again, women are to be found in large numbers in routine clerical occupations and in traditional 'caring' roles. But, in increasing numbers, they have moved into specialist and professional positions demanding considerable prior training. And, if they are still seriously under-represented in areas which call for or permit the exercise of managerial discretion, which confer authority over others, they have made some inroads into these positions too. (This is true up to the level of enterprise director. It is still the case that at the highest political levels in the USSR, among oblast party secretaries, ministers and the Politburo, women are almost entirely lacking.)

Both the character of the occupations that women now do in the Soviet Union and the changes that have occurred in the past thirty to forty years imply the existence of extensive occupational segregation between the sexes. And this in turn is consistent with substantial earnings disparities. The existence of these latter, established in Chapter 2, raises the question of the direction of causation. Is it the case that women are heavily concentrated in particular sectors and jobs because they are low-paying? Or are certain sectors low-paying because women predominate in them? Available data do not permit one to resolve this issue; in any case it is a chicken-and-egg question. Still, I think some arguments can be advanced in favour of primacy for the second formulation: it is the existence of an available supply of female labour that results in certain jobs either coming to be or continuing to be low-paid. But discussion of this issue will be deferred until the position of women in Soviet agriculture has been analysed. This topic is taken up in the next chapter.

## Notes: Chapter 5

1 Wage and salary determination in the Soviet Union is a good deal more complicated than is perhaps implied by the description given here. It is discussed at length in McAuley, 1979, chs 8-10. Soviet attitudes towards distribution and redistribution are analysed in McAuley, 1980.
2 In the census table relating to the occupational structure not broken down by sex this job category is disaggregated into: water and sewerage workers, hairdressers, photographers, cloakroom attendants, porters and janitors, watchmen, cleaners, stokers and furnacemen, messengers, bath-house attendants, laundry-workers and firemen. It is an open question in how many of these sub-categories the share of women was large.
3 Wage determination in the Soviet Union is rather more complicated than is suggested by the discussion in these few paragraphs. It is treated at greater length in McAuley, 1979, chs 8-10. See also Kirsch, 1972. Both sources also give details of earnings and wage relativities in various industrial branches in the USSR.
4 One should distinguish between the protection afforded women as women and as mothers. This is dealt with at greater length in Chapter 9.
5 In no sense can these 'earnings' figures be taken as estimates of male or female earnings. They are calculated by using the *same* earnings data for both sexes.

*Chapter 6*

# Women's Involvement in Agriculture, 1960-75

In previous chapters the position of women in Soviet agriculture has been largely ignored. There have been two reasons for this: first, the available Soviet information on women's earnings and, even more, the structure of female employment in agriculture is different in character and less abundant than that on the position of women in non-agricultural sectors. Although more than two-fifths of all employed women worked in agriculture in 1959, the census of that year contains very little information about the sort of jobs they did; equally, the 1970 Census is unilluminating about the specific occupations of the 20 per cent or so of women working in agriculture in the latter year. Consequently one must rely on a variety of local studies, undertaken by Soviet economists and sociologists, into conditions in particular areas, and make use of census materials to provide control totals where applicable. It is difficult to integrate this type of analysis into the approach used in Chapters 4 and 5; for that reason it was decided to deal with agriculture in a separate chapter.

But there are more fundamental grounds for arguing that agricultural employment is different from employment in other sectors, for men as well as for women, and therefore that it should be dealt with separately. As Peter Wiles has recently pointed out, for most of the world, agriculture is the *industrie mère* from which all non-agricultural occupations have separated off in the course of relatively recent history. This means that, in most countries, agricultural work and agricultural organisation are much more intimately involved with culture than is true of metal-fabricating, say, or motor-car assembly (Wiles, 1977, pp. 99ff.). As a consequence, there may well exist clearly defined cultural conventions about which occupations are 'women's work' and which are not. Such attitudes will affect one's interpretation of information about occupational segregation.[1] The fact that the USSR's ethnic minorities are largely located in rural areas, and also disproportionately engaged in agriculture, is a source of added confusion in this respect. Conflicting cultural attitudes can lead to divergent patterns of sexual specialisation.

Secondly, agriculture in virtually all countries is subject to seasonal variations in its demand for labour. In Soviet climatic conditions these variations are likely to be particularly acute; although, here, the size of the USSR and the range of climatic zones in which it is situated will introduce considerable regional differences. Since some activities are more dependent upon the weather than others, sexual specialisation may well result in differences in the month-by-month employment profiles of men and women. It may also contribute to the lower involvement of women in paid employment.

The tripartite organisation of agriculture in the USSR, with kolkhozy, state farms (sovkhozy) and private plots, means that differences in the amount of work done by men and women in the course of the year will be reflected in their earnings in a particularly complicated way. Work on private plots does not generate earnings in the sense of wages and salaries, although it contributes to both personal and money income. Members of kolkhozy are only paid for the days that they actually work and although a prescribed minimum quota exists, it is not always rigorously enforced. The position in sovkhozy is obscure but their labour forces are covered by the state's minimum wage laws and it is to be presumed that anti-absenteeism regulations are enforced. In so far as men and women are differentially represented in these three subsectors, their gross earnings will be affected.

Finally, the division between work and home is less clear-cut in agriculture than in most other areas of employment. It is sometimes possible for women (or, for that matter, men) to perform agricultural and domestic functions simultaneously. As a result, analysis of time-budget materials for the light that they cast on women's double burden and the contribution that it makes to occupational segregation should properly be undertaken separately for the agricultural and non-agricultural labour forces.

This chapter, then, attempts an assessment of the position of women in Soviet agriculture, of their earnings, of the amount of work they do, of the sorts of occupations in which they are to be found, bearing all these points in mind. In the next section I present what limited information I have been able to find on female earnings and on the gross male–female differential. Subsequent sections deal with the level of female participation and sexual differences in participation rates, the character of occupational segregation and the influence of such factors as education on women's work and wages in the sector. The evidence, taken as a whole, suggests the following conclusions. There is extensive occupational segregation in Soviet agriculture; women are still confined to manual work in the fields that demands considerable physical strength and promises little financial reward. This pattern cannot be wholly (or, possibly, even largely) explained by educational differences. Women also experience greater seasonal fluctuations in their employment than do men. As a result, differences in gross earnings are, if anything, larger than in other sectors, although when due allowance is made for differences in participation there seems little to choose between them. As was shown in Chapter 5, although women have come to play an increasingly important role as technical specialists (as agronomists, for example, or zootechnicians), they are still largely excluded from positions of managerial authority where they might exercise control over men. In the light of Soviet pay relativities, this also contributes to existing earnings disparities. (It also weakens the link between increases in education and increases in pay; that is, it undermines simple-minded versions of the human capital theory.) Finally, there is some limited evidence that the existing structure of women's employment is leading to labour force recruitment problems in some areas. This may result in changes over the next decade or so.

## The Earnings of Men and Women in Agriculture

Available information on differences in the earnings of men and women in agriculture is given in Table 6.1. It is inadequate in many respects, but it does provide a more explicit statement of the scale of earnings differentiation in rural areas of the USSR than has previously been available outside the Soviet Union. The major shortcomings of the data in the table are their restrictedness,

Table 6.1   *Sex Differences in Earnings: Agriculture, 1967–8*

| Labour force group | Male earnings (R per month) | Female earnings (R per month) | Female earnings as % of male earnings |
|---|---|---|---|
| Stavropolskii krai: kolkhozniki* | 95·60 | 46·90 | 56·7 |
| Tatar ASSR: | | | |
| Russians engaged in physical labour, | | | |
| under 35 | 69·00 | 47·00 | 68·1 |
| over 35 | 60·00 | 37·00 | 61·7 |
| Tatars engaged in physical labour: | | | |
| under 35 | 63·00 | 39·00 | 61·9 |
| over 35 | 57·00 | 22·00 | 38·6 |
| Russians engaged in white-collar work | | | |
| under 35 | 109·00 | 76·00 | 69·7 |
| over 35 | 104·00 | 80·00 | 76·9 |
| Tatars engaged in white-collar work | | | |
| under 35 | 97·00 | 79·00 | 81·4 |
| over 35 | 100·00 | 33·00 | 33·0 |

*Notes and Sources:* Row (1) Gorodetskii and Savchenko, 1974, p. 93; Rows (2) to (9) Arutyunyan *et al.*, 1973, p. 189.

The earnings figures in Row (1) were derived from a sample of 10,000 relatively well paid kolkhozniki in seven kolkhozy in Stavropolskii krai; those in Rows (2) to (9) on the rural component of a sample of 10,000 persons in the T.ASSR in August–September 1967. The latter sample will include persons who do not work in agriculture.

An asterisk implies that the figures given have been calculated from figures given in the source.

geographical, temporal and administrative. The statistics refer to 1967–68, they refer only to the North Caucasus and the Tatar ASSR and explicit differentials are given only for the kolkhoz sector. It is possible to make allowances for some of these problems, in a more or less heuristic way, by referring to other material, but the fact remains that it would be desirable to amass more evidence about the earnings of the two sexes in agriculture in different parts of the country to be able to establish the scale of disparities more firmly.

The figures for earnings in Stavropolskii Krai are derived from a sample of 10,000 kolkhozniki in seven large and relatively well-paid kolkhozy in that region. Although the sample may be representative of collectivised agriculture in the North Caucasus, it is certainly not typical of the USSR as a whole. This is brought out by the following figures on earnings, taken from Gorodetskii and Savchenko (1974, p. 90) and Tarasov and Romashchenko (1974, Table 8):

*(Earnings: Rubles per Month)*

|  | Stavropol sample | RSFSR kolkhozniki | sovkhozniki |
|---|---|---|---|
| 1966 | 66·67 | 52·3 | 80·1 |
| 1967 | 72·11 | | |
| 1968 | 76·50 | | |
| 1970 | | 74·6 | 100·0 |

These figures bring out three points. First, in the mid-1960s kolkhozniki in the North Caucasus were substantially better off than kolkhozniki in the RSFSR as a whole (although, on the whole, Russians were not particularly well paid when compared with kolkhozniki in other republics; for details see McAuley, 1979, ch. 7). Secondly, even in a relatively affluent area like Stavropolskii krai, the average earnings of kolkhozniki from collective work were markedly lower than those of sovkhozniki. In 1966 this was as a consequence of two factors: first, kolkhozniki on average worked fewer days for the collective farm than did sovkhozniki for the state farm; secondly, until that year, kolkhozniki received no wages for their work for the collective. Rather, they received a share of the residual income of the farm after all other financial obligations (including investment) had been met. This made the earnings of kolkhozniki particularly low in those farms that were in financial difficulties. In 1966 regulations were introduced making payments to labour a prior charge on the income of the farm. At the same time kolkhozy were recommended to pay their members at rates similar to those used in sovkhozy. This is the third point brought out by the figures given above. It provides a substantial part of the explanation of the increase in kolkhoznik earnings between 1966 and 1970. Gorodetskii and Savchenko cite the fact that the kolkhozy in their sample were already using wage scales similar to those employed in sovkhozy to account for the relatively slow rate of growth of earnings in the period 1966-8 (Gorodetskii and Savchenko, 1974, p. 90). In the longer term, however, the 1966 change in regulations has not conferred equality of earnings to those in different sectors of Soviet agriculture. Many kolkhozy have continued to use wage scales based on a minimum wage of 40·00 rubles per month while in state farms the minimum was raised to 60·00 rubles in 1968 and then to 70·00 rubles in 1972 (Kotov and Kvachev, 1976, p. 86; see also McAuley, 1979, pp. 33-4).

The analysis of the previous paragraph suggests that the level of earnings of kolkhozniki and kolkhoznitsy given in Table 6.1 is probably untypical of the USSR as a whole; but in itself it does not cast doubt upon the scale of differentiation. Here there is less evidence to guide us. One can advance the following propositions, however. If wage rates generally are low and individual earnings barely sufficient to support a family, there will be pressure (arising from traditional attitudes and social convention) to ensure that men's earnings are the more adequate. Earnings disparities in the collective sector may be more pronounced than in more affluent circumstances. This is likely to be reinforced by Soviet administrative arrangements. In such circumstances, peasant households depend very heavily for their subsistence upon output from their private plots. Entitlement to these is conditional upon adult members of the household supplying a minimum amount of labour to the kolkhoz or sovkhoz; but this regulation is more rigorously enforced against men than against women. Women, then, will concentrate disproportionately upon private sector activities. Differential participation will accentuate disparities in rates. Also, traditional attitudes towards the status of men and women in the Muslim areas may contribute to earnings differentiation in Central Asia where, on the whole, collectivised agriculture is reasonably well paid.

On the other hand, it might be argued that the major source of earnings differentiation in Soviet agriculture is the fact that mechanised work is very much better paid than manual work and those who work with machines are overwhelmingly male. In so far as the degree of mechanisation is less on poor farms, one might expect earnings differentials to be less. And there is some evidence to support this conjecture. A study of the earnings of kolkhoznitsy and their families on four kolkhozy in Moldavia in 1966 suggests a male-female differential of 66 per cent in annual earnings and 85 per cent in day rates.[2] And although a differential as large as that in Stavropol could emerge from the Tatar ASSR data, given appropriate weights for the different population groups, it is rather unlikely - particularly among the Russians.

Arutyunyan *et al.'s* study of the rural population of the Tatar ASSR provides further evidence of how well paid the North Caucasian kolkhozniki were in the mid-1960s. Their earnings were approaching those of the rural intelligentsia in other parts of the country. Also, since the entries in Rows (2) to (5) of Table 6.1 will include the earnings of sovkhozniki and those employed in non-agricultural sectors (e.g. transport and construction) as well as collective farm workers, all of whom might be expected to be better paid than the latter, regional disparities are greater than might appear at first glance.

Table 6.1 reveals that ethnic Russians, whatever their sex and labour force status, earn more than their Tatar equivalents. For the most part differences are not very great, but the Tatar ASSR is an area of old Russian settlement and there has been a good deal of integration. In 1970, for instance, about a third of Tatars living in rural areas in the T.ASSR claimed to be fluent speakers of Russian. This is significantly higher than the 7 per cent of rural Turkmens or 10 per cent of rural Tadjiks who made the same claim (*Itogi* . . . , 1970, Vol. IV, Tables 6, 25 and 28). One would expect ethnic differences in earnings to be greater in these Central Asian republics. The table also shows that Tatar men in any labour force category earn more than Russian women in the same category; that is, sex-linked differentials appear to be larger than those associated with what the Russians call nationality.

On balance, then, although the data are scarcely adequate to support such a generalisation, I suggest that it is plausible to assume that in the mid-1960s the gross earnings of women in Soviet agriculture were between 55 per cent and 70 per cent of those of men. My own preference is for the lower end of this range. Increases in the minimum wage, the conversion of kolkhozy into state farms and some contraction in intra-agricultural rate differentials may have led to some narrowing in this disparity over the past ten to fifteen years; but it is unlikely to be less than that found in non-agricultural sectors.

Unusually, Gorodetskii and Savchenko provide a distribution of men and women by annual earnings, rather than simply citing average figures for the two sexes. This allows one to make comparisons of earnings inequality within as well as between the sexes. Such comparisons are most instructive:

|  | *Men* | *Women* | *Ratio of Female to Male (%)* |
|---|---|---|---|
| Median (rubles per year) | 1,099·60 | 562·00 | 51·10 |
| 1st decile (% of median) | 46·40 | 35·90 | 39·60 |
| 9th decile (% of median) | 162·00 | 210·00 | 66·25 |
| Decile ratio | 3·49 | 5·84 | |

These figures (calculated from Gorodetskii and Savchenko, 1974, Table 11) show that the distribution of female earnings is more unequal than that of men. The average figure given in Table 6.1 is relatively high as a result of the exceptionally high earnings of a few women. Median earnings for women (that is, that figure such that a half of the women in the sample earned less) are approximately half the male figure. Indeed, 86 per cent of the women in the sample earned less than the male median. Further, disparities are greatest among those who earned least. The earnings of the bottom tenth of women were less than two-fifths of the bottom tenth of men whereas the top tenth of women received earnings that were, perhaps, two-thirds of those of the top 10 per cent of men. The substantial disparities at the bottom of the distribution are undoubtedly due in part to differential participation and the narrowing at the top is a reflection of the successful penetration by Russian women into male occupational preserves that we have already noticed among non-agricultural employees. All the same, these figures demonstrate the existence of considerable rural inequality both between men and women and between women and women.

Finally, there is a comment to be made on another feature of the figures in Table 6.1. Arutyunyan gives the figures to show that in the USSR – in contrast, he argues, to most capitalist countries – there is no tendency for earnings to increase with age. It is for this reason that the estimates are given by age-class as well as sex, nationality and labour force group. Gorodetskii and Savchenko also give a breakdown of earnings by age (unfortunately not broken down by sex and status). And this would appear to conflict with the one given in Table 6.1. For the Stavropol sample, average earnings increase with age for each age-group until 40–49 years; there is then a sharp fall for the 50 to 54-year-olds, a rise for the 55 to 59-year-olds (reflecting, one assumes, the retirement of substantial numbers of low-paid women) and another fall for those over 60 years old. Unfortunately, Gorodetskii and Savchenko do not give details of the age-composition of their sample so it is not possible to produce figures directly comparable with those of Arutyunyan *et al.*, but if one uses weights derived from manual agricultural workers for the RSFSR as a whole (calculated from Gorodetskii and Savchenko, 1974, p. 93, and *Itogi* . . . , 1970, Vol. VI, p. 452) the following picture emerges:

|  | *(Rubles per Month)* | | |
| --- | --- | --- | --- |
|  | *Stavropol* | *Tatar ASSR* | |
|  | *Sample* | *Russian men* | *Tatar Men* |
| Manual workers under 35 years | 70·5 | 69·0 | 63·0 |
| Manual workers over 35 years | 78·9 | 60·0 | 57·0 |

My own guess is that the Stavropol figures are more likely to be representative of the USSR as a whole – particularly in recent years. I suspect that the Tatar anomaly is to be explained first by the fact that non-agricultural workers in the sample are likely to have been disproportionately concentrated in the younger age-groups (and agricultural earnings tend to be less than those in other sectors). Secondly, in view of the date to which the figures relate, it is possible that kolkhozy in the T.ASSR did not use any formal wage scales to differentiate the shares of kolkhozniki in residual income, but were still using the old *trudoden* system. In any case, the formal wage scales used in the more progressive kolkhozy in the early 1960s (and presumably used more widely after 1966) embodied a substantial element of differentiation. Maximum daily rates were between 1·4 and 5·0 times the minimum paid. And evidence from many areas of the Soviet economy suggests that rated skills (and hence day rates) increase with age.

In conclusion, then, the data produced here suggest that in the 1960s there were substantial differences in the gross earnings of men and women in Soviet agriculture and there is every reason to suppose that these have persisted to the present day. How far these can be ascribed to differential participation and how far they are the result of occupational segregation will be explored in subsequent sections.

### Female Participation in Agriculture

Some idea of the importance of agriculture, past and present, as an area of female employment in the USSR was given in Figure 3.3; this is supplemented by the figures in Table 6.2. These show that in 1940 some 16 million Soviet women were employed in the sector, approximately the same number as in 1955. But the numbers so employed have fallen steadily, if not dramatically, since the end of the Second World War and in 1975 were only about two-thirds of what they had been at their peak. The absolute fall in female agricultural employment combined with rising female participation rates has resulted in a decline in the relative importance of the sector, but it is still, arguably, the most important single sphere of women's work and the conditions it offers them determine to a large extent any assessment of the nature of sexual equality and inequality of employment under socialism.

Table 6.2 also casts light on the relative importance of kolkhozy and sovkhozy in both female and male agricultural employment. Until 1955 the overwhelming bulk of the Soviet agricultural labour force was employed on collective farms, with all the social disabilities that this entailed. Since the late 1950s, however, the Soviet authorities have undertaken an extensive pro- gramme of conversions and this, together with rural-urban migration, has resulted in the fact that in 1975 between a third and two-fifths of the

Table 6.2   *Administrative Subdivisions in the Female Agricultural Labour Force: USSR, 1928-75*

| Year | Average annual no. of women (thousands) employed in: | | Share of average annual agricultural employment in sovkhozy | |
|------|----------|----------|-----------|---------|
| | Sovkhozy | Kolkhozy | Women (%) | Men (%) |
| 1928 | 157 | n.a. | — | — |
| 1940 | 593 | 14,627 | 3·90 | 7·57 |
| 1950 | 1,194 | 16,083 | 6·91 | 10·01 |
| 1955 | 1,293 | 14,723 | 8·07 | 11·60 |
| 1960 | 2,717 | 11,276 | 19·42 | 25·71 |
| 1965 | 3,639 | 9,341 | 28·04 | 33·15 |
| 1970 | 3,859 | 8,274 | 31·80 | 36·31 |
| 1975 | 4,281 | 7,392 | 36·67 | 39·52 |

*Sources: Trud v SSSR*, Moscow, 1968, p. 75; *NK SSSR*, 1975, p. 542; *Zhenshchiny v SSSR*, Moscow, 1975, p. 39; *Vestnik Statistiki*, no. 1, 1977, p. 87.

agricultural labour force was to be found on state farms. This conversion programme has certainly resulted in rising rural living standards (for details, see McAuley, 1979, ch. 2) and it may also have contributed to a reduction in the scale of differential participation between the sexes. But the fact that for much of the period in question a higher proportion of male agricultural workers than females were employed by the state has probably contributed to sexual inequality in the countryside. This follows because, as we have seen, average earnings in the state sector have persistently been higher than those in kolkhozy, even allowing for differences in the number of days worked in the year. State farm workers have also enjoyed more favourable coverage under various social security schemes. Differences in the type of farm on which the two sexes are employed have diminished since 1970, however, and will presumably disappear within the next decade or so. This will eliminate one source of earnings inequality between the sexes.

A majority of those Soviet women who work in agriculture are to be found in kolkhozy where they make up a majority of the labour force, as the figures in Table 6.3 show. At the beginning of the 1960s 56 per cent of all kolkhozniki were women. Their predominance in the agricultural labour force at this time is a consequence of the excess of male deaths in war, civil war and political oppression during the preceding forty years or so and also of sex-specific differences in rural–urban migration. An increase in the numbers of women leaving the villages and a return to demographic normalcy has meant that by the mid-1970s collective farm membership is almost equally divided between the sexes.

The figures in Table 6.3 also show that although women made up more than half the collective farm labour force throughout the period 1960–74 they contributed less than half the number of days worked. At the beginning of the period women on average worked only three-quarters of the number of days worked by the average male kolkhoznik and, while the gap has narrowed in recent years (largely as a result of an increase in female labour input),

Table 6.3    *Female Participation in Kolkhoz Agriculture: USSR, 1960–74*

|  | 1960 | 1965 | 1970 | 1974 |
|---|---|---|---|---|
| Kolkhoznitsy as proportion of total employment | 56 | 55 | 53 | 51 |
| Days worked per woman | 170 | 170 | 185 | 204 |
| Days worked per man | 232 | 222 | 233 | 244 |
| Row (2) ÷ Row (3) (%) | 74 | 77 | 80 | 84 |
| No. of able-bodied women not working a single day (as % of 1960) | 100 | 70 | 40 | 33 |

*Source:* Fedorova, 1975, p. 55.

women still work some forty days a year less than men. This differential participation clearly affects disparities in gross earnings. For example, Gorodetskii and Savchenko report that kolkhoznitsy in their sample worked an average of 197·5 days in 1967 while the men put in an average of 259·2 days in the same year (Gorodetskii and Savchenko, 1974, p. 100). Combining these figures with the ones given in Table 6.1 implies a daily wage of 4·42 rubles and 2·85 rubles for men and women respectively, or a female/male daily earnings ratio of 64·5 per cent.

As might be expected, the average figures of Table 6.3 conceal wide regional variations. Although it is still the case that women in all republics put in less days than men, those in Estonia worked almost three times as many hours as those in Tadjikistan. More generally, women in Estonia and Latvia worked almost 50 per cent more hours than the All-Union average, those in Lithuania and the three Slav republics (all areas of low birth rates) a quarter more, while in the Transcaucasus and Central Asia women supplied between two-thirds and three-quarters as many hours as the All-Union average (Churakov, 1972, p. 186; the figures relate to 1967, but the author claims that little has changed subsequently). Male labour supply follows a roughly similar pattern with above-average hours being supplied in the Baltic states and Slav areas and below-average hours in Central Asia and the Transcaucasus. But all variations are not as extreme and in both Kazakhstan and Uzbekistan men supply an above average amount of labour. These differences in annual participation can only accentuate whatever differences in earnings are generated by occupational segregation.

The final row of Table 6.3 refers to another phenomenon – the existence of certain kolkhozniki whose membership of the collective farm appears to be purely formal. More light is thrown on it by the figures in Table 6.4. These show that in the RSFSR in the mid-1960s some 2 to 3 per cent of kolkhozniki in any year did not work a single day for the collective farm. These 'delinquents' were four or five times as likely to be women as men – evidence, I believe, that the authorities enforce the participation regulations more vigorously against males. Similar figures exist for other republics; for example, it is claimed that in the early 1960s some 6 to 7 per cent of female kolkhozniki in Kirgizia failed to participate in collective work (Bekkhodzhaeva, 1965, p. 31; see also Akademii Nauk UzSSR, 1970, pp. 210–11, for an analysis of the

Table 6.4   *Non-Participation in Collective Agriculture: RSFSR, 1965–8 (thousands)*

|  | No. of able-bodied kolkhozniki not working a single day | | | |
|---|---|---|---|---|
|  | 1965 | 1966 | 1967 | 1968 |
| Men (16–60) | 31·90 | 35·40 | 28·30 | 24·60 |
| Women (16–55) | 164·90 | 155·10 | 124·80 | 104·30 |
| All | 196·80 | 190·50 | 153·10 | 128·90 |
| As % of annual average employment | 2·68 | 2·65 | 2·15 | 1·85 |

*Source:* Novozhenyuk, 1971, p. 215; *Selskoye khozyaistvo SSSR*, Moscow, 1971, p. 447.

situation in Uzbekistan). It appears, however, that the introduction of a guaranteed wage (and perhaps a more active policy of enforcement) has led to a decline in non-participation. It should be recognised, though, that the figures in Table 6.3 overstate the decline in this phenomenon since the number of kolkhozniki has also fallen since 1960.

So far in this section attention has been confined to only two of the three administrative subsectors of Soviet agriculture – state and collective farms. Although Soviet statisticians only count work in one of these subsectors as employment and, by and large, confine their attention to the two labour force groups discussed so far, there is also a thriving private sector in the USSR and a complete analysis of female participation in agriculture should include reference to it. Private plots are important as a source of agricultural commodities and they have also proved a vital source of peasant household income in the past. In 1960 they yielded as much as 52·5 per cent of the personal income of kolkhoznik households (McAuley, 1979, p. 131) in 1974, they still accounted for more than 30 per cent (McAuley, 1980a, Table A6). And there is reason to believe that the labour that produces this income is disproportionately female.

It is not only kolkhozniki that are entitled to private plots; state farm workers receive them also. In addition, in certain circumstances, they can be acquired by members of the non-agricultural labour force. A lower bound on their importance as a form of agricultural employment in the USSR in the last forty years is given by the figures in Table 6.5. It is a lower bound because it includes in the private sector only those recorded in the relevant census as depending upon private subsidiary agriculture for their 'means of subsistence'. Since kolkhozniki, sovkhozniki and even non-agricultural state employees work part-time on private plots, the labour input into this subsector is surely greater than that shown in the table.

At all events, Table 6.5 shows that in 1939 the private sector accounted for a fifth of all agricultural employment (and, perhaps surprisingly, for about a tenth of all employment in the USSR). Its relative importance has fallen since then, of course, but in 1959 it still accounted for more than 10 per cent of all agricultural work. Of more importance to the theme of this chapter, however, the figures show that throughout the period the private agricultural

Table 6.5    *Agricultural Employment\* in the USSR: 1939–70*

|  | The Share of Agriculture in Total Employment for each Labour Force Group (%) | The Share of Agricultural Employment (%) in: | |
|---|---|---|---|
|  |  | The State Co-operative Sector | The Private Sector |
| **1939** |  |  |  |
| Both sexes | 49·92 | 79·16 | 20·84 |
| Men | 34·01 | 94·12 | 5·88 |
| Women | 67·07 | 70·98 | 29·02 |
| **1959** |  |  |  |
| Both sexes | 37·38 | 87·02 | 12·93 |
| Men | 27·76 | 98·52 | 1·48 |
| Women | 46·85 | 80·37 | 19·63 |
| **1970** |  |  |  |
| Both sexes | 21·05 | 92·16 | 7·84 |
| Men | 17·79 | 97·71 | 2·29 |
| Women | 24·26 | 88·17 | 11·83 |

*Note:* Agricultural employment is defined to consist of two components – those registered in manual agricultural job categories and those whose means of subsistence are given as 'subsidiary private agriculture'. Since the latter category are not listed as employed in the USSR censuses, total employment has been adjusted to allow for this in calculating the percentages given in the table.
   *Sources:* Calculated from *Itogi* ..., 1959, USSR Vol., Tables 31, 47 and 48, and *Itogi* ..., 1970, Vol. V, Table 10, and Vol. VI, Tables 2 and 18.

labour force has been disproportionately female. In 1939 almost a third of all women in agriculture were in the private sector (and a fifth of all employed women). Even in 1970 the private sector still accounted for more than a tenth of female agricultural employment.

The figures given in the last paragraph refer to women exclusively engaged in the private sector. But, as figures given below show, both kolkhoznitsy and sovkhoznitsy devote more time to private plots that do their male colleagues. This in part accounts for their lower participation in collective work (and hence their lower average earnings). It also constitutes a significant additional burden on their time and therefore may help to explain their relatively poor performance in the acquisition of skills. On the other hand, in so far as the sale of privately produced output is more lucrative than working for the sovkhoz or kolkhoz, women's work may contribute more to the family budget than that of their husbands.

The discussion so far has concentrated on global indicators of female participation and has shown that throughout the postwar period women have worked fewer days in the state collective sector than have men. These average figures are a reflection of substantially different seasonal patterns of employment for the two sexes. The analysis of these differences is taken up in the next section.

## Seasonal Variations in Agricultural Employment

The marked seasonal variation in demand for labour experienced by a large part of Soviet agriculture is the largest single source of part-time work in the country. Since variations in the amount of time worked can be responsible for differences in gross earnings, it is desirable to determine how far the experience of the two sexes differs in this respect.

In Soviet conditions, both state and collective farms employ three devices to adjust their labour supply to current demand. First, they can vary the number of 'able-bodied' workers that they call upon to work; secondly, they can vary the number of days in the month that those called upon to work actually put in; and finally, they can recruit temporary and seasonal workers either from the retired population and schoolchildren living in rural areas (or among those who live in the countryside but work in the towns) or from among the urban population through the assistance of the political authorities. The existence of these various channels makes the analysis of available data on seasonal variations in labour utilisation more complicated.

The most complete data on seasonal variations in the use of labour on kolkhozy are to be found in a survey undertaken in 1967 and devoted to this topic. The survey covered 684,000 kolkhozniki and its findings were published in the 1971 handbook of agricultural statistics. Although the survey was undertaken nearly fifteen years ago now, its findings are thought to be valid still; at least, Soviet economists still refer to them as if they were. Table 6.6 contains figures relating to seasonal variations in labour supply that have been condensed from the ones published in 1971.

Table 6.6    *Seasonal Variations in Kolkhoz Labour Input: USSR, 1967*

|  | Quarter I | Quarter II | Quarter III | Quarter IV |
|---|---|---|---|---|
| No. of days worked in quarter (as % of Qu. III) | | | | |
| Able-bodied men | 79 | 93 | 100 | 86 |
| Able-bodied women | 55 | 90 | 100 | 77 |
| Average no. of kolkhozniki taking part in social labour as % of Qu. III) | | | | |
| Able-bodied men | 86 | 98 | 100 | 90 |
| Able-bodied women | 60 | 94 | 100 | 80 |
| Average no. of days worked by participating kolkhozniki | | | | |
| Able-bodied men | 57·4 | 59·4 | 62·8 | 59·8 |
| Able-bodied women | 51·0 | 53·7 | 55·7 | 53·9 |

*Note:* In addition to able-bodied (men aged 16–60, women aged 16–55) kolkhozniki, Soviet kolkhozy also employ the old, the young and non-members. According to the survey, the old and young made up some 16 to 22 per cent of those taking part in social labour and supplied between 11 and 18 per cent of the total number of days worked in various months. Also about half a million non-members (on an annual average basis) are recruited for work in kolkhozy and sovkhozy each year. See *Sel'skoe khozyaistvo SSSR*, Moscow, 1971, p. 446.

*Sources: Sel'skoe khozyaistvo SSSR*, Moscow, 1971, pp. 450 and 469–70; quarterly figures given here were condensed from monthly figures given in the source. Based on a sample 684,000 kolkhozniki in 1,036 kolkhozy carried out in 1967.

These figures show that while male kolkhozniki supply four-fifths as much labour in the first quarter (January–March) as they do in the third quarter (July–September), kolkhoznitsy supply little more than half as much. The major mechanism through which labour supply adjustments are achieved is variations in the number of kolkhozniki who take part in collective work. This is true for both sexes. And again, there are wider variations among women than among men. Only three-fifths as many women are called upon to turn up for work in the winter quarter as are used at harvest time; for men it is 86 per cent. Those that do turn out, however, work almost as many days in the first quarter (fifty-seven and fifty-one for men and women respectively) as they do in the third (sixty-three and fifty-six for the two sexes).

These figures are consistent with the following labour force structure: there exists a permanent kolkhoz labour force that is primarily male and, in addition, each kolkhoz contains among its members a pool of underemployed labour that can be called upon when production needs require it. Each kolkhoz has its own reserve army, as it were. And this reserve army is primarily female. This sex structure is partly dictated by patterns of occupational specialisation that result from cultural tradition and, in part, patterns of occupational specialisation (and the skill structures that accompany them) are the result of a need to ensure rather more permanent employment for male kolkhozniki. Finally, the figures in the last two rows of Table 6.6 suggest that sex-linked differences in seasonal demand for labour are not the only cause of differential participation in collective work. In each quarter, the number of days worked by those women who actually took part in collective work was less than those worked by men.

Although available data do not permit a formal analysis, the comments of Soviet economists indicate that the averages for the USSR as a whole, with which we have been concerned so far, conceal substantial regional variations. Fedorova, for example, claims that up to half the women in Azerbaijan, Tadjikistan, Armenia and Georgia who work in July do not turn out at all in December (Fedorova, 1975, p. 62). Rusanov, on the other hand, singles out Byelorussia, Uzbekistan and the western oblasti of the Ukraine, Moldavia and the Transcaucasus as the regions of rural underemployment (Rusanov, 1971, p. 139). I suspect that both are right. In addition one might wish to add parts of the RSFSR – particularly some of the ethnic minority areas.

The figures in Table 6.6 refer only to 'able-bodied' kolkhozniki, that is, those below retirement age. But in addition kolkhozy make use of the old and the young (and also the halt and the lame), particularly at harvest-time. According to the 1967 survey, some 11 to 18 per cent of the labour supplied in different quarters of the year can be attributed to this group. And, of course, given differences in life expectancy, a majority of the aged will be women. Although the figures are not unambiguous, it also appears that women predominate among those non-members recruited on a temporary basis – or at least among those that reside in rural areas. (See, for example, Kostakov and Litvyakov, 1970, p. 88.) And this is not implausible. It has been argued (Manevich, 1974, pp. 4–6) that enterprise managers, aware of the possibility that they might be called upon to supply labour to help with getting in the harvest, have shown a tendency to hoard unskilled labour. Since the bulk of unskilled labour in Soviet industry is female, it is to be expected that the bulk of urban workers dispatched to the countryside for seasonal work will also be women.

So far analysis has concentrated upon the use of labour by kolkhozy and sex-specific data are far more ample for this sector. But some figures do exist that relate to seasonal variations in employment on sovkhozy and it is to this topic that I now turn. It is to be expected that since sovkhozniki are counted as workers for legal purposes they will enjoy greater stability of employment. And that is what the following figures (calculated from Rusanov, 1971, p. 133) show:

*Quarterly Sovkhoz Employment*
*(as % of Qu. III)*

|  | *Qu. I* | *Qu. II* | *Qu. III* | *Qu. IV* |
|---|---|---|---|---|
| Permanent workers | 92 | 98 | 100 | 96 |
| Temporary and seasonal workers | 21 | 64 | 100 | 57 |
| Other (managerial) | 100 | 100 | 100 | 100 |
| All | 82 | 93 | 100 | 90 |

The figures relate to 1968, but, as with those for kolkhozniki, I do not believe that the situation will have changed much in the last decade or so. Unfortunately Rusanov does not provide sex-specific data on seasonal variations in sovkhoz employment, but given the character of the jobs typically done by men and women on state farms I do not believe that the picture will differ substantially from that on kolkhozy. Here also there will be a core of permanent workers, more often male than female, supplemented by a smaller but frequently female seasonal labour force.

It is not only the state and co-operative sectors of agriculture that experience seasonal variations in their demand for labour. Seasonal variations are in large measure the result of the climate and the private sector is also subject to this. Some indication of the demand this makes upon the time of

Table 6.7    *Labour Inputs and Private Agriculture: Kolkhoz Sector, RSFSR, 1967–8*

|  |  |  | *Of which:* | | |
|---|---|---|---|---|---|
|  | *All* | *Able-bodied* | *Men* | *Women* | *Others* |
| Proportion of labour on private plot in 1967 (%) | 100 | 64·4 | 12·7 | 51·7 | 35·6 |
| Increase in hours worked in Qu. III over Qu. I in 1968 (hours per kolkhoznik): |  |  |  |  |  |
| Total |  |  | 101·1 | 150·3 |  |
| Collective work |  |  | 93·2 | 103·0 |  |
| Private plots |  |  | 7·9 | 47·3 |  |

*Sources:* Row (1) Churakov, 1972, p. 223; Rows (2) to (4) ibid., p. 210.

women in the USSR is given by the figures in Table 6.7. Incidentally, the first row of the table shows that in the RSFSR in the mid-1960s 'able-bodied' women supplied more than a half of all the labour put in on kolkhozniks' private plots; men supplied little more than an eighth. Again, although one might expect some regional variations (both within the RSFSR itself and between the Russian republic and the remainder of the USSR), it is unlikely that the picture is radically different anywhere. Similarly, although there may have been marginal changes in the last decade and a half, it is unlikely that the picture is radically different at the present time.

The remainder of the table shows that while both men and women work longer hours in the summer than in the winter, men's work is much more heavily concentrated in the collective sector and also is not subject to such wide seasonal variations. This should not be taken to mean that men work fewer hours in total than women, but rather that they work substantially more hours in the winter months.

The analysis of this section has shown that in both the collective farm and the private sectors of Soviet agriculture, women's work is concentrated in the summer months. It seems plausible to assume that this is also true of sovkhoznitsy (although perhaps to a lesser extent). Female agricultural employment, then, is subject to substantial seasonal variations. This suggests that, to a considerable extent, women in the USSR are regarded as marginal workers; it is they who make up the bulk of the reserve army. While this is not the only factor resulting in differential participation by the two sexes, it is clearly an important one. It must therefore contribute to existing disparities in gross earnings. This situation is in part occasioned by the sorts of agricultural activities most commonly done by women in the Soviet Union. And it will also affect the extent to which women acquire relevant agricultural skills. Occupational segregation constitutes a third factor that has a bearing on gross differentials in earnings. This is taken up below.

### Horizontal and Vertical Segregation in Agriculture

The analysis of Chapter 5 has already shown that, among white-collar workers, while women make up a substantial proportion of technical specialists like agronomists or veterinarians, they are seriously under-represented in line-management positions. Consequently attention here will be focused upon manual agricultural occupations. Also, since I have been unable to locate All-Union data on this topic, the analysis will be based on the results of various sample surveys. These data refer almost exclusively to the kolkhoz sector but what information there is suggests that the position on sovkhozy is more or less the same.

Table 6.8 shows the structure of skills and specialities in the Gorodetskii and Savchenko sample drawn from kolkhozy in Stavropolskii krai. It shows that, at best, women made up a third of the low-level specialist groups and in most cases they accounted for considerably less. Only 7·8 per cent of turners, electricians, and so on, were women, and only 14 per cent of brigadiers. (A brigadier is roughly equivalent to a foreman in Soviet terminology.) Of

Table 6.8    *Occupational Differentiation in Kolkhoz Agriculture: RSFSR,*
*1967-8*

| | Proportion of the Occupational Group that Is (%): | | Average Monthly Earnings (rubles) |
|---|---|---|---|
| | Male | Female | |
| Brigadiers | 84·9 | 13·7 | 124·75 |
| Farm managers[a] | 72·6 | 27·5 | 112·50 |
| Workshop supervisors, garage chiefs | 67·0 | 31·8 | n.a. |
| Engineer-mechanics, technicians-mechanics | 89·4 | 10·5 | 112·27 |
| Section heads,[b] storemen, etc. | 79·6 | 20·4 | n.a. |
| Drivers, tractor-drivers, machine operators | 97·6 | 1·6 | 100·32 |
| Turners, electricians, smiths, etc. | 91·8 | 7·8 | 80·70 |
| Rank-and-file kolkhozniki | 33·8 | 65·8 | 72·30 |

*Notes:* a *Zaveduyushchie fermami*, i.e. those in charge of livestock units.
   b *Zavkhozy, kladovshchiki, ekspeditory, zaveduyushchie skladami*, etc.
*Sources:* Gorodetskii and Savchenko, 1974, pp. 96-8 and 122-4.

particular note is the derisory proportion of women tractor-drivers – less than
2 per cent.

This sample is not untypical. Labzin reports that, according to the 1959
Census, more than 80 per cent of women employed in agriculture possessed
no permanent speciality (Labzin, 1965, p. 99; if I have understood his
calculation aright, the analogous figure for 1970 was 72 per cent). In the
sample drawn from the rural population of the Tatar ASSR women made up
71 per cent of general labourers, *raznorabochie*, and two-thirds of the semi-
skilled; they accounted for only a quarter of the skilled workers and 1·5 per
cent of tractor-drivers, *mekhanizatory* and so on, (Arutyunyan *et al.*, 1973,
p. 329). In a sample of kolkhozniki drawn from the Kabardino-Balakharskaya
ASSR, 79 per cent of the women were unskilled field hands and 13 per cent
were milkmaids, and so on; only 0·1 per cent were classified as *mekhanizatory*
and there were no female drivers or women repair mechanics (Umetova, 1975,
p. 67). One Soviet sociologist has commented:

in the Smolensk region some 60 per cent of those who work in agriculture
are women. But if every second or third man is a tractor-driver, an
electrician, a mechanic, a combine-operator, a driver, an excavator-
operator, a mechaniser in animal husbandry, then, among women, even on
the most optimistic assumptions, only one in a thousand is in charge of a
machine. (Mikhailyuk, 1970, p. 86)

Another way of looking at occupational segregation in Soviet agriculture
is to consider the extent to which particular operations are mechanised.
Rather than use the fivefold classification adopted for industry, Soviet
statisticians identify three: mechanised, manual with the aid of horses,

*konno-ruchnoi*, and manual, *ruchnoi*. The following figures show the sex-composition of these three categories for the Stavropol sample (Gorodetskii and Savchenko, 1974, p. 123):

|                      | *Men (%)* | *Women (%)* |
|----------------------|-----------|-------------|
| Mechanised           | 96·5      | 3·5         |
| Manual, using horses | 39·3      | 60·7        |
| Manual               | 39·9      | 60·7        |

Unfortunately, the authors do not give figures that would allow us to calculate what proportion of women's work is manual or manual-with-horses. But another study claims that among women who work on sovkhozy only 11·3 per cent are engaged in mechanised work; a further 3 per cent work manually with the aid of machines while the remaining 85·7 per cent perform their work wholly manually (Fedorova, 1975, p. 57; the data relate to 1972). In some republics, Uzbekistan, for example, the proportion of women in agriculture engaged on purely manual work is as high as 99 per cent. (Fedorova, 1974, p. 57; Akademii Nauk UzSSR, 1976, p. 66).

Some Soviet authors explain this state of affairs by reference to the age and educational structure of the agricultural labour force. They point out that a relatively high proportion of the latter, both in kolkhozy and sovkhozy, is made up of relatively elderly and uneducated women (in 1970 women aged 40–54 years made up 44 per cent of female kolkhozniki and 42 per cent of sovkhoznitsy; Fedorova, 1975, p. 56). They suggest that these women are unsuited for if not incapable of, acquiring the skills necessary to operate machines; they are condemned therefore to back-breaking physical labour. (See, for example, Gorodetskii and Savchenko, 1974, p. 122; see also Fedorova, 1975, p. 56.)

The occupational segregation that has been detailed in the preceding paragraphs has a number of implications both for levels of inequality in rural areas of the Soviet Union at the present time and for the future viability of Soviet agriculture. Dealing first with inequality: although the data published by Gorodetskii and Savchenko do not permit a formal or quantitative assessment of the contribution to the gross differential in male–female earnings that can be attributed to differences in skill, the figures in the last column of Table 6.8 are suggestive. They show that men predominate in the better-paid job categories and they imply that even among unskilled workers men earn more than women.

Although the Stavropol kolkhozniki were relatively well paid, the differentials reported in Table 6.8 are not out of the ordinary for Soviet agriculture, as the following figures show (Tarasov and Romanchenko, 1974, Table 8):

| | *RSFSR (average monthly earnings, rubles)* | | | |
|---|---|---|---|---|
| | *Kolkhozy* | | *Sovkhozy* | |
| | *1966* | *1970* | *1966* | *1970* |
| Tractor-drivers, machine-operators | 85·5 | 107·6 | 102·4 | 124·1 |
| Drivers | 83·3 | 97·6 | 91·8 | 106·1 |
| Manual-with-horse work | 36·8 | 48·5 | 76·0 | 79·5 |

In both the state and the collective farm sectors the wages paid for field work are substantially lower than those for work involving the use of machines.

The failure of Soviet women to penetrate mechanised occupations in agriculture has other longer-term consequences. As agriculture becomes increasingly mechanised, it means that women will be condemned to low-paid auxiliary status or, as appears to be happening in many parts of the country, will leave the industry altogether and migrate to the towns. This is facilitated by increasing levels of education among the younger age-groups. In so far as this happens, social factors will accelerate the drift of men from the land. This may adversely affect the growth of both output and productivity.

In an attempt to widen the choice of careers open to young women in rural areas, the Soviet authorities made some attempt to increase female recruitment into rural trade schools in the late 1950s and early 1960s. But this policy appears to have failed. In 1961, for example, about a fifth of those enrolled in courses designed to train agricultural mechanisers in Uzbekistan were women; by 1965 this proportion had fallen to 2·9 per cent (Akademii Nauk UzSSR, 1970, p. 218). Nor is the experience in Uzbekistan unique. Fedorova suggests that part of the blame for this must be placed on the quality of the machines themselves. She claims that in many cases these are heavy to maintain and handle and subject to levels of vibration that medical specialists consider damaging to women's health (Fedorova, 1975, p. 58).

In a new attempt to make mechanised occupations in agriculture more attractive to women, in the early 1970s the Soviet authorities passed regulations sanctioning a 10 per cent reduction in output norms as compared with those set for men, for those women who become tractor-drivers, combine-harvester-operators, and so on. They are also to be given six extra days holiday per year, to receive preferential treatment in the allocation of housing and, starting in 1975, those who have worked as tractor-drivers, and so on, for a period of fifteen years will be entitled to a pension at the age of 50 (instead of 55) provided that they have worked for at least twenty years. As far as I can tell, none of these privileges is to be extended to men. The regulations also call for women to be given the preference over men in the use of newer, more developed machines. I cannot believe that this policy will be conducive to social harmony on the farm and, if Fedorova's account of the shortcomings of the most recent models of Soviet agricultural machinery is accurate, it is not likely to be substantially more successful than its predecessor. (For more discussion of this policy see Fedorova, 1975, pp. 58-9 and 63-4.)

## Educational Attainment of the Agricultural Labour Force

The relationship between education and employment in the USSR is explored at length in Chapter 8 and the discussion here is not intended to pre-empt what is said there. But some of the samples with which we have been dealing contain information about the educational attainments of the kolkhozniki they surveyed. This casts some light on the relationship between education and earnings in agriculture and that is the main topic of this section.

In point of fact Soviet investigators have provided information on education broken down by sex for two of the samples for which occupational details

Table 6.9   *Educational Attainment of the Agricultural Labour Force: USSR and Sub-Regions, 1967–70*

| | | | Proportion of the Labour Force Group with: | | |
|---|---|---|---|---|---|
| | | *Average No. of Years Schooling* | *Post-Secondary Education* | *Post-Primary Education* | *Primary Education or Less* |
| USSR: Rural population – Russian nationality, 1970 | | | | | |
| employed | Men | 6·4 | 8·4 | 40·4 | 51·2 |
| employed | Women | 6·7 | 13·5 | 37·1 | 49·4 |
| Stavropol krai: kolkhozniki, 1967 | | | | | |
| | Men | 5·6 | 4·8 | 54·1 | 41·0 |
| | Women | 5·4 | 3·4 | 53·8 | 42·8 |
| KBA.SSR rural population – Balkartsy, 1970 | | | | | |
| employed | Men | 6·8 | 10·6 | 38·5 | 49·9 |
| employed | Women | 6·0 | 9·6 | 29·3 | 61·1 |
| KBA.SSR: kolkhozniki, 1968 | | | | | |
| | Men | 6·8 | 6·7 | 55·3 | 38·0 |
| | Women | 6·2 | 1·5 | 55·3 | 43·2 |

*Notes:* Post-secondary education is defined to include the following Soviet categories (with the hypothetical years of schooling assumed): higher (16), incomplete higher (14), secondary specialist (12). Post-primary education includes the following Soviet categories: general secondary (10), incomplete secondary (8). Primary education or less consists of: primary (4) and the residual (3).

*Sources:* Rows (1) to (2) and (5) to (6) *Itogi* . . . , 1970, Vol. IV, Tables 57 and 58; Rows (3) to (4) Gorodetskii and Savchenko, 1974, pp. 115, 122; Rows (7) to (8) Umetova, 1975, p. 66.

are also given. This is reproduced in Table 6.9 in a somewhat abbreviated form together with analogous information about the parent populations from which, it is presumed, the samples were drawn. The sharp differences in the occupational affiliations of men and women contrast strangely with the similar levels of education reported in Table 6.9. Either one must assume that crucial information has been lost in the process of aggregation, or some factor other than the number of years of schooling must play an important role in occupational selection.

The figures in Table 6.9 show that the women included in the Stavropol sample were, on average, less educated than the men. But differences do not seem to be large. Also, both men and women appear to have had relatively little schooling: more than two-fifths of the persons of each sex in the sample had had four years or less in school and under 5 per cent had received any training beyond a general secondary education. In both of these respects they differ markedly from the general pattern for rural inhabitants of Russian nationality as recorded in the 1970 Census. As other figures in Table 6.9 show, the Stavropol sample (and, possibly, kolkhozniki in general) were, on average, less well educated than the rural population; they had had five and a half years in school as opposed to six and a half. But this difference is misleading. It can be attributed almost exclusively to the fact that the Stavropol sample contained a smaller proportion of highly educated specialists than the population as a whole. A significantly lower proportion of the kolkhozniki in Stavropol had had four years schooling or less than in the rural population as a whole. Among rural Russians in 1970 almost half the population was in this category.

The pattern among kolkhozniki included in the sample drawn from the KB.ASSR was similar, although here the differences in educational attainment between men and women were more marked. Particularly striking is the difference in post-secondary education between the sexes. Also worth noting is the fact that the Balakhartsy were, on average, more educated than the Russian kolkhozniki in the Stavropolskii krai. But, again, the sample of kolkhozniki was scarcely typical of the rural ethnic population of the ASSR as a whole. And again it diverged in the same way: the sample contained a smaller proportion of 'high-level' manpower and it also contained a much smaller 'tail'. Among rural Balakhartsy as a whole, half the men and three-fifths of the women had had four years or less in school. It must be of such people as these that Umetova is thinking when she writes (1975, p. 72):

Persons with little education cannot be thought of as good prospective workers in the sense of further increases in their skills. Insufficient general education among women hinders their effective, *glubokii*, acquisition of specialisms and does not permit them to acquire a facility in the handling of machines.

But her complaint is misplaced in two senses: first, the women in her sample were rather more educated than the average rural Balakhartsy; and secondly, the absence of general education does not appear to have inhibited male kolkhozniki from acquiring these skills. After all, only 35 per cent of the men in her sample were engaged in manual and horse-assisted work.

The figures on the educational attainment of the rural populations of the RSFSR as a whole (Russians) and the KB.ASSR suggest the existence of a small educated upper crust together with a solid core of literate workers and a more or less extensive tail of functionally illiterates. Some of these latter will be elderly, but they are too numerous to be made up entirely of those over 45 or 50 years of age. The relative under-representation of the 'upper crust' in the kolkhoznik samples is to be expected. After all, these people make up what Russians call the rural intelligentsia and they are not members of collective farms.

Finally, in relation to Table 6.9, it is noteworthy that a higher proportion of both rural Russian women and male and female Balakhartsy have had post-secondary education than rural Russian men. In the case of Russian women this is possibly a reflection of their search for a better future than that promised by arduous unskilled labour in fields or cowsheds. For men there is a chance of advancement to a managerial or supervisory position; but, as we have seen, few kolkhoznitsy make it that high. Education and the acquisition of special training offers some chance of improvement in pay and working conditions. But the possibilities are still not very great (Umetova, 1975, pp. 73–4):

> The range of occupational choice facing girls and women in the countryside is still very narrow. What sort of work or profession might a school-leaver count on getting if she decides to stay in the kolkhoz or sovkhoz? A milkmaid or auxiliary worker in the livestock section, *na ferme*, an unskilled field hand or a worker in the services sector that is still so under-developed in the village – a cook or dishwasher, and so on. These, perhaps, are all the opportunities that are open to her. And they are not very attractive . . .

It is small wonder that the drift from the land continues.

The higher levels of general (and specialist) education achieved by Russian women may have allowed a limited number of them to escape from what Marx referred to as the idiocy of rural life but, at least on the information available, it has not resulted in their obtaining substantially better pay. Gorodetskii and Savchenko give details of the earnings of those with different levels of education in their sample (not broken down by sex) and it is possible to use these to calculate what women might have earned had they been paid as well as men with similar levels of education. First, it is noteworthy that there is no smooth progression of earnings with education; indeed there is very little differentiation among those with a general secondary education or less (monthly earnings range from 75 rubles to 82 rubles with the highest figures being earned by those with only 5–6 years schooling); it is only the possession of secondary specialist or, even more, higher education that confers a substantial monetary advantage. Those with higher education received, on average, twice as much as those with secondary education or less. Applying the earnings figures calculated in this way to the distribution of men and women by educational attainment, one obtains a ratio of female and male earnings of 98 per cent (Gorodetskii and Savchenko, 1974, pp. 94–5, 115 and 122). Clearly factors other than education must account for observed differences in the pay of men and women in Stavropolskii krai – and, one would suspect, more generally in Soviet agriculture.

## Conclusion

The gross earnings of women in Soviet agriculture have been shown to be substantially less than those of men. In part, these disparities can be attributed to the fact that women work shorter hours than do men and also to the fact that they are more heavily concentrated in less skilled occupations. But it is doubtful how far either of these phenomena can be considered rational in any but the shortest of perspectives. Rather, they would seem to be further examples of a pervasive sexual inequality on the rural labour market. Low pay, lack of skills and high seasonal variability in employment are intertwined in a way that is difficult to disentangle.

The position of women in agriculture is in many ways analogous to the position of manual non-agricultural women workers elsewhere in the economy - except, perhaps, that they suffer from the additional disability of seasonal variations in employment. In the next chapter, recent Soviet explanations of this state of affairs are examined as an introduction to the analysis of those social forces that might have been responsible for it.

### Notes: Chapter 6

1  That the division of labour in agriculture is the product of cultural convention and not biology is strongly suggested by its geographical inconsistency. A number of anthropologists have pointed out that tasks which are clearly associated with men in one culture are undertaken by women routinely in another. (See, for example, Boserup, 1970.) Some insight into the nature and persistence of cultural tradition in the sexual division of labour in Russian (as opposed to Soviet agriculture) is given in Benet, 1970, especially pp. 95–6 and 255–6.

2  Kozachenko, 1971, p. 24, Table 16; sex-specific rates and earnings are not given explicitly. The figures given above were derived on the assumption that 'primary' workers were all male while 'secondary' workers were female. In so far as unmarried male workers living in families are classified as secondary earners, women's wages will be overstated.

*Chapter 7*

# The Sources of Sexual Inequality in the Labour Market: Soviet Views

The last five chapters have been devoted to a description of the position of women in the Soviet labour market. In summary, they have shown that as early as 1940 female participation rates were high and that in the last thirty or forty years participation has risen to unprecedented heights. In parts of the country it may now be excessive. But the widespread employment of women has not yet resulted in the achievement of sexual equality in other respects.

Women still earn less than men. Although the statistics are inadequate, they suggest that the disparity between men's and women's earnings in the USSR is of the same order of magnitude as that to be found in the more industrialised economies of Western Europe. Nor is there much indication that the gap has closed appreciably in the last twenty years or so. That is, increasing participation does not appear to be associated with a narrowing of sex-linked differentials.

Also, women still do substantially different jobs from men, although here, perhaps, one should distinguish between white-collar work on the one hand and blue-collar or manual agricultural work on the other. In agriculture women are concentrated in seasonal field work, in livestock care, in vegetable-growing. For the most part, they lack formal skills; their work is done, more often than not, without the benefit of mechanisation. In industry, the traditional sectors of textiles, garment-manufacture and food-processing are dominated by women; there are substantial numbers of women assembly-workers in engineering; auxiliary work like loading and packing is done by women in all sectors. The services sector is predominantly female. Women are less skilled and less likely to work with machines than men. Although the range of occupational choice may have expanded since 1940, increased participation does not appear to have led to a reduction in segregation; indeed, segregation may have increased with development, with the emergence of a more balanced industrial structure since the death of Stalin.

It is only among white-collar workers that significant progress towards equality has been made. For much of the Soviet period women have made up a majority of those in the medical professions. They now also dominate teaching and many areas of administration. Increasingly, since the Second World War, women have penetrated previously male preserves. Most professional occupations now have a sizeable minority (or a majority) of women in them; the number of female engineers is particularly striking. However, even here there are shortcomings: increased education and participation have not yet led to women assuming managerial responsibility in proportion to their representation in the labour force as a whole. Women are still largely excluded from positions in which they might exercise control over other people.

Thus one may conclude that in so far as the Soviet authorities have been pursuing the goal of sexual equality in employment as in other areas of social life, their policies have not been wholly successful. Why? Why has the extensive if not universal employment of women not led to the attainment of sexual equality? Is it a consequence of specific features of the Soviet system of economic and social organisation or might one expect a similar outcome from attempts to increase female participation in other countries? This and the next three chapters are devoted to an analysis of these questions. In summary, I argue that the relatively low earnings of women in the USSR can be attributed to the persistence of occupational segregation. This in turn is the result of constraints on occupational choice for women. These constraints are partly legal and in part derived from the wider social environment within which economic decisions are made. They reflect social attitudes, the operation of the educational system and the fact that women still bear primary responsibility for the maintenance of the home and family.

## Participation and Sexual Equality: Soviet Views

The status of women, in the labour market and in society as a whole, has not been an issue of as great political concern in the USSR as in some Western countries, but it has attracted the attention of a number of Soviet economists and sociologists. A few have taken a Panglossian view of the position of women:

> The basic task of socialism is the liberation of humanity – women as well as men – from all forms of exploitation and inequality. As far as women are concerned, this task has been successfully completed through their attraction into social production, their participation in the administration of the state, their work in all spheres of social activity. (Tatarinova, 1964, p. 26)

And the expression of such opinions has increased recently with the expanded output of official propaganda in connection with International Women's Year in 1975; indeed, some usually reputable scholars appear to have joined this bandwagon (e.g. Yankova in Novikova *et al.*, 1978). But, for the most part, those Soviet academics who have written about the status of women in the USSR have adopted a more critical attitude towards the achievements of the Soviet system. They have shown genuine concern, at times verging on outrage, over the persistence of sexual inequality; they have attempted to show the shortcomings of official policy – and to suggest ways in which it could be improved. One of them has even taken Mandel to task for being too uncritical, for neglecting to detail the darker side of the position of women in his book *Soviet Women* (Ryurikov, 1977, p. 118).

There are two strands to this academic critique of the status of women in the USSR. First, it is argued that official policy is based on too simple minded an analysis of social processes. This has the consequence that certain measures, though undoubtedly well intentioned, have the effect of reinforcing the social and economic inferiority of women. It may also lead to conflicts between sexual equality and other social goals. Secondly, it is generally accepted that the unequal position of women derives in large part from occupational segregation and a number of studies have attempted to identify the particular features of the Soviet system (or its level of development) that operate to circumscribe women's occupational choices. These are discussed at greater length below.

In the past decade or so a number of economists and sociologists have pointed out that high levels of participation will not, in themselves, achieve sexual equality, will not necessarily lead to social and personal development. And excessive emphasis upon female employment may lead to conflict with other social goals. Perhaps the clearest exponent of this view is Kotlyar:

> In and of itself a high level of female employment cannot serve as a criterion of the rational utilisation of female labour resources if it is not associated with the socially necessary level of fertility and rate of population growth. (Kotlyar and Turchaninova, 1975, p. 8)

If a policy of 'universal' female employment is to lead to the attainment of sexual equality, it should be accompanied by more extensive (and more flexible) assistance for women in the discharge of their biological (social) roles than the Soviet authorities have provided hitherto;[1] it also requires a more sophisticated approach to the question of protective legislation. Not only should certain occupations be forbidden to women, but others should be reserved for them (Kotlyar, 1973, pp. 414–15). Whether or not such a policy would reduce disparities in earnings and otherwise contribute to a lessening of sexual inequality would depend upon the criteria used to select 'women's jobs'. In so far as tradition and social convention played an important role, such a policy would probably be a retrograde step.

More generally, it is pointed out that 'full' employment for women imposes demands upon location policy if it is to result in the rational use of female labour. Towns and regions should be developed in such a way as to provide adequate employment opportunities for workers of both sexes (Kotlyar and Turchaninova, 1975, p. 9). Certainly the existing sectoral distribution of employed women cannot be attributed to the operation of any rational allocative process. Rather it is to be explained in terms of the country's historical development. That is, implicitly, pressure on real wages in the 1930s forced women on to the labour market in large numbers; the peculiarities of Soviet development resulted in their finding unskilled jobs as auxiliary workers in heavy industry, in construction, and so on, where conditions were unpleasant and the work often unsuitable, as well as in traditional female employment sectors. These distortions have not yet been fully overcome (Kotlyar and Turchaninova, 1975, p. 9; see also Litvyakov, 1969, p. 134; Mailybaeva, 1975, p. 36).

It is recognised, then, that the existing state of affairs in the USSR is unsatisfactory in many respects. Although most women are now in gainful employment, too many of them are doing the wrong jobs. Much of the academic effort of the past decade or so has been devoted to ascertaining the reasons for this, to identifying the features of the Soviet system that channel women into unrewarding occupations. At the risk of some oversimplification, it is possible to group the various suggestions that have been made into four categories: social attitudes, physiology, education and domestic responsibilities. These are examined below.

### Constraints on Occupational Choice: Social Attitudes

Women are too often employed in unrewarding and unsatisfying jobs in the Soviet Union because this is regarded as part of the natural order of things. These attitudes are to be found among the political leadership, among managers at all levels, among male workers - and even among women themselves.

As far as the social ethos is concerned:

> [working women] as a whole still earn less than their husbands. This is in accordance with the demands of the law of distribution according to labour and in no way signifies [the existence of] any sort of discrimination. (Shishkan, 1976, p. 55)

That is (if this view put forward by Shishkan is widely shared), the fact that women generally earn less than men is in accord with socialist principles since, at the present stage of development, the work that they do involves less skill or is carried out in less important sectors of the economy. In fact, elsewhere in her work, Shishkan displays a great deal less equanimity towards occupational segregation; perhaps one can infer that at this point she is voicing a generally held opinion.

It is argued that there is a tendency to regard manual work (that is, *ruchnoi trud*, work done by hand) as synonymous with women's work - both in industry and in agriculture. When particular processes are mechanised, too often, apparently, the female labour force is replaced by men (Shishkan, 1976, pp. 138-9). This results in the continued concentration of women in low-paid, frequently physically demanding jobs, despite increases in mechanisation. In agriculture, indeed, it is suggested that little attempt is made to make use of the skills and qualifications that women possess; as a result, women are moving, in increasing numbers, into the services sector in rural areas, or into other branches of the economy. As one specialist has remarked, 'the existing situation can scarcely be considered rational, *pravomernym*, either socially or economically' (Fedorova, 1975, p. 56). Again, it is suggested that there exists bias, if not discrimination, in promotion - especially that those in positions of authority are unwilling to appoint women to management posts (Shishkan, 1976, pp. 143-4). Thus, in these specific ways managerial decisions contribute to the continuing economic inferiority of women.

Managerial attitudes are reinforced by a more general tendency on the part of men (and perhaps women too) to undervalue women's capacities, to impute to them characteristics derived from the work that they do – and thus confine them to subsidiary economic roles:

> It would be premature, at the present stage of development of socialist society, to consider that the specific place of female labour in production is determined solely by physiology . . . The continued use of small-scale, *melkii*, technology and manual, *ruchnoi*, production methods results in the qualitative differentiation of labour . . . and the natural sexual division of labour (being interwoven with the general division of labour which is characterised by socio-economic differentiation of different forms of productive activity and the identification of these latter with particular groups of people) inevitably acquires a specific socio-economic hue. This process has the result that some proportion of women do not enjoy real opportunities for participation in social production. (Mikhailyuk, 1970, pp. 7–8)

The phrasing in this quotation may be obscure (and has not been helped by the inadequacy of my translation) but the idea, I think, is clear. It is not only biology that explains the jobs that women do in the USSR. Rather, because in the past women have been employed in occupations characterised by low productivity of labour, social attitudes have developed that regard women as relatively unproductive; the existence of these attitudes now acts to constrain women, to channel them into certain sorts of unrewarding activity. They are denied real opportunities to pursue worthwhile or satisfying careers.

Some indication of the extent to which, in practice, job opportunities for women are constrained can be gained from sociological surveys which inquire into worker attitudes and job satisfaction:

> Women rate the occupation of automatic machine-operator, *avtomatchik-metalist*, highest of all, from the point of view of job content, opportunities for raising their qualifications and for the wages it pays. Female lathe-operators, *stanochnitsy*, also rate their work highly from the point of view of pay. It is well known that men in these occupations consider themselves poorly paid. Obviously, this situation is connected with the fact that as a rule women are employed in low-paid work and thus the wages of machinists and lathe-operators seems fairly high to them. (Mikhailyuk, 1970, p. 72)

Many other examples could be cited that make the same point.

It is the low pay and generally poor conditions associated with traditional 'women's work' that have led some Soviet women to choose to work in physically exacting jobs, for example, in the construction industry. Shishkan reports on interviews with a number of them:

> A significant proportion of women are still not interested in restrictions on the use of their labour [i.e. an extension of the ambit of protective legislation, a policy that Shishkan herself favours – A.M.] since heavy and

harmful job-slots usually pay better. In the majority of them annual holidays are longer, the retirement age is lower, profilactic foodstuffs are provided. The absence of nightshifts in construction and the provision of accommodation for a substantial proportion of the labour force are potent factors explaining female employment in this sector. (Shishkan, 1976, p. 116)

In spite of the fact that women in construction are largely confined to the lowest skill grades and that many of them have difficulty in fulfilling their output norms, the women interviewed by Shishkan were in no doubt that they were better off than they would have been in more 'appropriately feminine' occupations. From the style in which the whole passage is written, I think that Nina Shishkan was surprised by the vehemence with which these women put their point of view.

Some women may have voluntarily chosen to do heavy manual labour, but Shishkan also suggests that much female employment in what she regards as unsuitable jobs is to be explained in terms of local imbalances in industrial development (that is, the absence of appropriate work) or the consequences of the Second World War on population structure.

The shortcomings of working conditions in the traditional women's employment sector in the USSR, low pay, awkward hours, and so on, are a reflection, I believe, of the low valuation put upon female labour – often unthinkingly. But these general social attitudes are built upon a basis of more specific beliefs – about differences in male and female psychology, physiology, and so on – and the interaction of these beliefs with the wider social system. It is to these issues and their impact upon job opportunities for women that I now turn.

## Constraints on Occupational Choice: Psycho-Physiology

That there are biological differences between men and women is indisputable, but there is considerable uncertainty, in the Soviet Union as in Western Europe and North America, about how these differences should condition occupational choice – and, indeed, about how far the existing occupational structure among women corresponds to the dictates of biology.

It is still possible to find Soviet sociologists who argue that women are the weaker sex, that they are less productive than men and that these differences justify, implicitly, their lower earnings: 'As a result of the psycho-physiological characteristics, *osobennosti*, of her organism, a woman will undertake directly social labour of less productivity, of less quantity, for a shorter time than will a man' (Yuk, 1975, p. 125). But Yuk is in a minority; most academics would reject her analysis as too simplistic – whatever may be the attitudes of policy-makers or the population at large. Rather, the ideas of a majority of Soviet scholars who have written about female employment correspond in broad outline to those found in non-Soviet writing. But, because Soviet authors appear to think in terms of averages, because they neglect intra-sex variability, their analyses are, on the whole, cruder than those to be found in recent Western work.

It is recognised that women are not as strong as men[2] and that this will put them at a disadvantage in any occupation that requires physical strength. It is suggested that this may explain part of the observed difference in earnings between the two sexes. But even here, it is not only a question of differences in physiology; differences in performance are also attributable in part to 'the special functions that [women] perform in the family and in society, above all to the function of motherhood' (Mikhailyuk, 1970, p. 87). It is also suggested, however, that women can outperform men in many precise operations requiring attention to detail, concentration and manual dexterity (loc. cit.; see also Sonin, 1973, p. 362; Kasimovskii, 1975, p. 133; Mailybaeva, 1975, p. 59). And the idea that there is any difference in intellectual abilities (capacity) is rejected with something close to indignation (Shishkan, 1976, p. 13).

These points are frequently made in Western literature too (see, for example, Mackie and Patullo, 1977, p. 28) where it is also pointed out that in most categories of skill (e.g. verbal tasks, rote memory, manual dexterity, mechanical tasks, and so on) there is substantial overlap between the sexes. For instance, in a recent test boys were on average better than girls at mathematics but 45 per cent of the girls scored higher than half the boys (King, 1973, p. 10; this pamphlet contains an extensive review of recent psychological work on sex differences in aptitudes and abilities).

Soviet academics, then, reject the notion that women are the 'weaker sex' in favour of a more sophisticated version of sex-linked differences in specific abilities.[3] But this can only be the first step in the argument. If one is to explain observed differences in earnings or existing patterns of occupational specialisation in terms of biology, it is also necessary to show that these abilities (and differences in them) are relevant in market opportunities. On this there is much less clarity in Soviet writing.

There seem to be two issues here. It is implicit in much that has recently been written in the USSR that these presumed biological differences can and should serve as a rational basis for the sexual division of labour. First, then, one may ask whether, if men and women were allocated to jobs in accordance with these principles, there would be differences in their earnings? That is, given the present stage of development of the Soviet economy, is women's work subsidiary to that done by men? Secondly, one may ask how far the existing pattern of male and female employment is in accord with these 'rational' principles. Or is it the case that women earn less than men because they are too often in the wrong jobs? If the answer to this last question is in the affirmative, one could go on to ask why.

As pointed out above, the extent to which the sexes overlap in abilities together with the scale of intra-sex variability undermines the implicit premiss of this recent Soviet work. It is doubtful whether one can formulate 'rational' criteria for a sexual division of labour in a modern industrial (or any other) economy. This proposition is one that Soviet academics fail to appreciate because they concentrate too much on mean values of various indicators of performance. Some authors have suggested that the existing pattern of female employment corresponds to the 'rational' division of labour referred to above (see, for example, Litvyakov, 1969, p. 100).

Or, alternatively, it is assumed that traditional areas of female employment, like the services sector, are in accord with the requirements of a 'scientific' allocation of female labour (Sonin, 1973, p. 357; Kuprienko, 1976, p. 39). But, as mentioned above, these views have been criticised for neglecting the distortions introduced by the specifically Soviet path of development (Kotlyar and Turchaninova, 1975, p. 9). Further, the discussion of Chapters 5 and 6 suggested that the existing structure of female employment was some way from the ideal postulated above.

This is not to say that the widespread employment of women cannot cause problems for management – and that these problems are not in some sense attributable to differences in physiology (or to women's biological role). The possibility of such problems may well give rise to a certain reluctance on the part of managers to hire women for specific jobs, that is, it may give rise to discrimination against female labour:

It is possible, in individual enterprises, that as a result of the specific physiological functions of women and their obligation to care for children outside working hours (maternity leave, transfers to lighter work during pregnancy, loss of working time due to illness of children, and so on) it is economically more expedient to employ male labour. And for this reason, obviously, one still encounters frequent instances of illegal dismissal of women, their transfer to other sections, and so on ... (Mikhailyuk, 1970, pp. 89–90)

But these difficulties are only partly ascribable to physiology. Both social attitudes (in placing the onus for child care so heavily upon women) and the state (in requiring both maximum output and the observance of various pieces of protective legislation) contribute their quota.

Incidentally, added strain upon remaining male employees was one of the consequences of the widespread employment of women in British industry during the First World War reported on by a special committee set up to examine the question in 1919 (see Chiplin and Sloane, 1976, p. 19, for more details). Also, Soviet commentators have noted that provisions which excuse pregnant women and mothers with small children from nightwork, for example, place an extra burden on unmarried women in the textile industry – and that this is the source of some resentment.

In summary then, Soviet academics posit the existence of sex-linked differences in mental and physical abilities. They suggest that these differences may serve as a rational basis for the sexual division of labour, but are not explicit about how such a programme might be implemented. Rather, the more or less objective analysis of aptitudes is too often embedded in a wider framework of social convention and this, as often as not, is used to bolster current prejudice rather than to form the basis of a critique of existing recruitment and promotion practices.

### Constraints on Occupational Choice: Education

In many societies the amount and type of education received by girls has differed from that given to boys, with the consequence that the former have been less well equipped to find and keep satisfying jobs, to acquire skills, to make a career for themselves. This was the case in Russia before the revolution and, *a fortiori*, it was true of most other parts of the present-day Soviet Union. It has been suggested by a number of Soviet academics that these practices continued for a time after the revolution and that this in turn can explain part (if not all) of the remaining inequality between the sexes in the labour market:

> The relatively low educational level of women in the middle and upper age-groups lowers their interest in the content of their work and together with the historically determined attitudes towards women's earnings as a secondary source of family income, lowers the need that they feel to raise their qualifications. (Litvyakov, 1969, p. 129)

This failure to ensure equal access to education immediately after the revolution, so the argument goes, was due not only to the fact that in a relatively backward and war-torn society resources were not available, but also to the fact that the education of children depends upon collaboration between the family and the school system – and it takes time to change popular attitudes. But attitudes have been changed, the Soviet educational system now offers identical opportunities to children of both sexes and, as a result, among the younger age-groups, lack of education does not constitute an impediment to women making for themselves rewarding and satisfying careers.

In this respect, as in much of their other work on socialisation, Soviet sociologists place what appears to me to be undue weight upon the influence of formal education – and thus upon the direct role of the state. They undervalue the contribution of the family, the community and the culture in forming social and political attitudes. This is strange because, at the same time, some emphasis is placed upon the role of the mother in the inculcation of moral values (not only among pre-school age children but throughout childhood). Still, as will be shown in Chapter 8, the Soviet authorities have invested heavily in education – for girls as well as boys – and in parts of the USSR where the contrast between traditional folk ways and the precepts of 'modern' knowledge are most marked perhaps this conclusion is valid.

More to the point, however, the quiet self-satisfaction with which some academics view the undoubted achievements of the Soviet government in women's education has been challenged in the past decade or so. Some economists and sociologists have questioned whether guarantees of equal access to formal education are enough to overcome female inferiority, whether, in time, current policies will lead to the attainment of sexual equality. On the contrary, it has been suggested that current practice, in conjunction with wider social attitudes and the demands of the environment, may act to reinforce the inferior status of women in employment.

There seem to be two grounds for this scepticism. First, it is argued that official policy places too great an emphasis on formal education and pays insufficient attention to vocational training; secondly, there is some discussion of the content of formal education and of the tendency for girls and boys to specialise in different subjects in the upper classes. This is linked, by some authors, to sex-related differences in psychology, to differences in motivation, to wider social attitudes. But, again, little formal analysis of the importance of social convention in sex-typing and sex-role assignment is attempted.

It is argued that the vast majority of women workers receive little more than on-the-job training: 'This permits them to acquire no more than a few simple skills, *navyki*, without sufficient theoretical preparation; this reduces [their] ability to employ the achievements of science and technology' (Shishkan, 1976, p. 143). But even this comment cannot account for the inferior position of women in Soviet industry. It presents too static a picture of the process of skill acquisition and therefore fails to capture the complexity of the processes that lead to the relegation of too many Soviet women to dead-end jobs. Shishkan, for example, argues that, in modern conditions, technical progress does not so much demand high levels of formal education (which, as we shall see, Soviet women increasingly have) but a willingness to go on learning, to undergo continuing training, to re-qualify at several points in one's working life. Both interruptions in work due to pregnancies and the burden of child care or domestic responsibility make this pattern of behaviour a hard one for Soviet women to adopt (Shishkan, 1976, p. 142; see also Kotlyar and Turchaninova, 1975, p. 80).

But even this does not exhaust the interactions. Because women have less time available for study, they tend to be less well qualified than men; because they are less well qualified, they tend to be employed on less satisfying, *soderzhatelnye*, jobs; lack of stimulation at work tends to undermine the will to study, to raise qualifications, and so on (Shishkan, 1976, p. 139). The heavy involvement of women in monotonous and repetitive work tends to encourage high levels of turnover – at least in certain plants and sectors. This reinforces managerial prejudices and makes managers less willing to promote women to positions of greater responsibility or to provide them with facilities for raising their qualifications. Thus the vicious circle is complete (Filipov *et al.*, 1975, p. 77).

Recent Soviet reflections on the educational system, then, provide conjectures about several mechanisms that could result in observed levels of occupational segregation. For occupations where formal education is enough (basically white-collar job categories) the undoubted successes of the Soviet government in increasing the enrolment of girls in the upper classes of secondary schools and further educational establishments could well have resulted in diminishing segregation through time. But where vocational training is concerned, discriminatory recruitment, the impact of protective legislation and social prejudice may well have interacted to produce a situation of substantial occupational segregation: a situation that is maintained, if not intensified, by the motivations of women themselves and the conflicting demands that society places upon them.

### Constraints on Occupational Choice: Domestic Responsibilities

Traditionally, social convention has ascribed to women primary responsibility for the care of children and management of the home. And these attitudes add substantially to the burden borne by women in gainful employment. In recent years feminists have questioned the logical (or, possibly, the physiological) basis of this convention, pointing out that biology only requires that women should give birth to children and, perhaps, assume exclusive responsibility for their nurture until they are weaned. Similarly, although the tone of the discussion has been more muted, Soviet academics have underlined the extra burden that domestic responsibilities place upon the shoulders of working women, a burden made heavier by the inadequacies of the Soviet services sector and the attitudes of Soviet men. They have suggested that this 'double shift' may in part be responsible for the apparent inferiority of women in social production.

There are two slightly different arguments advanced in the Soviet literature. Almost all those who raise the issue agree that the time and energy spent by most women on domestic work adversely affects their productivity while in gainful employment, discourages them from undertaking the study necessary to raise their qualifications, tends to encourage women to choose jobs that are convenient rather than satisfying, and so on (see, for example, Labzin, 1965, p. 100; Sonin, 1973, p. 355). And it is frequently pointed out that these adverse consequences are reinforced by the attitudes of their husbands and families and by the failure of men to undertake a proportionate share of domestic chores (Labzin, 1965, p. 100).

Soviet authors are more ambivalent, however, about the role of women in maternity and child care:

> The function of motherhood imposes upon women great and complex responsibilities. The mother is the natural choice of person to be responsible for the child's upbringing, *estestvennaya vospitatelnitsa*, early in life when the basic outlines of its personality are being formed. (Danilova, 1972, p. 43)

It is not clear what interpretation Danilova places upon the word *natural*. Does she mean to imply a physiological or merely a social relationship? In strict logic, the word implies the former; but in context, perhaps only the latter is involved. It is this natural affinity between mother and child that is used to justify the provision of state support, of special working conditions for women with young children; and it is this 'natural affinity' that results in these privileges being restricted to working mothers rather than their being extended to fathers as well. However, privilege implies obligation and it is women who are expected (by the state and by the population at large) to take charge of both the physical and moral welfare of their children. And greater awareness of what this involves, higher standards, and so forth, are in large part responsible for the fact that

there is a tendency for the domestic responsibilities of women to grow with time. At the beginning of the 1930s . . . the time spent by women on domestic affairs was [on average] four hours per day, but at the present time, according to our sample survey, it is from four to six hours per day. (Yankova, 1970, p. 43)

But Soviet sociologists have not advocated with any great heat that these responsibilities be shared more equally by husbands and fathers.

In the view of Soviet academics, then, the greater domestic responsibilities of women go far in explaining their subordinate status in the labour market. In part this is a consequence of social attitudes, of the unwillingness of men to undertake domestic chores like cooking and cleaning. And these social attitudes are reinforced by various provisions in the legislation which place women in a privileged position. The difficulties faced by women are made worse by the rudimentary nature of the Soviet services sector in many parts of the country and for much of the period since the revolution. But, implicit in much Soviet writing, there is recognition of a more fundamental conflict of interest. The population must reproduce itself, children will be born, must be cared for, brought up, fed, and all of this takes time and effort. Within the context of the nuclear family, Soviet sociologists see primary responsibility for these tasks as devolving upon women. (It is this that explained early bolshevik enthusiasm for communal living, an enthusiasm that one can still find echoes of today.) Until and unless the family can be replaced by alternative arrangements for care of the young (and, even, today's workers) this conflict of roles will remain.

## Conclusion

It is not possible, or even desirable, to produce a synthetic statement of Soviet views on the causes of the continuing inequality of women in the labour market and in society at large. There are clearly wide differences of opinion, even among those who are dissatisfied with the status quo. But certain themes emerge from the discussions of this chapter and these will guide the analysis to be found in the remainder of this book.

First, on the whole, Soviet economists and sociologists see the problem as lying with the factors that influence or determine women's choices of job or career. That is, sexual inequality is seen as different from the more general question of income distribution and the appropriate scale of earnings differentiation. Attention is therefore concentrated upon recruitment mechanisms and promotion procedures.

Within this general framework, the importance of social attitudes is recognised and particular examples of prejudice have been alluded to. But the issue has not been subjected to any very systematic analysis. Similarly, it is suggested that psychological and physiological differences might provide the basis for a rational sexual division of labour. But again no very systematic formal statement of how this might be implemented has been provided. Rather, there has been a tendency to view the existing allocation as conforming, in broad outline, to what is required. Soviet discussion of this topic as often reinforces popular prejudice as criticises it. In any case, neglect of intra-sex variations in aptitudes and abilities probably undermines the logic of the Soviet argument.

Both social attitudes and biological differences, however, have received relatively little attention in the work of Soviet economists and sociologists. Much more emphasis has been placed upon education and domestic responsibilities, what the Russians call *byt*, in accounting for continuing sexual inequality. As far as education is concerned, it is possible to formulate a number of conjectures that can be tested against available data. On the one hand, there are those who argue that inadequate formal education has in the past acted as a brake on the employment of women in satisfying (and lucrative) careers. Indeed, regional and ethnic differences in the access to educational facilities by girls continue to act as impediments to the attainment of sexual equality in employment. But great strides have been made in the education of women in the Soviet Union and, in time, these will show their effects. That is, current policies are appropriate and their adequacy will shortly be demonstrable.

But this view has been challenged. It has been suggested that, for the mass of women, it is not so much formal education as access to vocational training facilities that is decisive in determining their choice of occupation – and, consequently, whether or not sexual equality in the labour market will be achieved. And it is pointed out that current policy results in the exclusion of women from those channels of training that have the better prospects. Protective legislation and social convention act to confine women to a relatively narrow range of occupations. And the effects of this are reinforced by women's own motivation. Too often the burden of family responsibility undermines the willingness to invest in further training.

Again, it has been suggested that too great an emphasis on the amount of formal education received by girls could be misleading. It is not only the quantity of education but also its content that affect career choice and career prospects. For a variety of reasons, in the upper classes of the secondary school girls are often to be found studying those subjects that lead to careers with fewer opportunities for advancement.

Finally, some have claimed that education is not a panacea, that formal education of itself will not enable women to overcome social prejudice or social inertia. It does not allow them to resolve the conflict of roles that their sex and society's goals force upon them.

The Soviet strategy for the attainment of sexual equality recognises the existence of this role conflict; indeed, it constitutes the justification for the provision of specific assistance and protection. The second strand of Soviet analysis of the continuing inferiority of women in employment is concerned with the adequacy with which that assistance has been provided. There are two levels on which current policy has been criticised. First, it has been pointed out that, in spite of considerable achievements, in spite of the fact that the state devotes substantial resources to the provision of social service facilities, not enough is provided. The relative underdevelopment of the services sector broadly understood, in conjunction with wider social attitudes, places a heavy, even intolerable, burden upon women. This has the result that women's employment often appears inexpedient to the managers of state enterprises. Secondly, it is suggested that present policies are often formulated in too simplistic a manner and may, in consequence, aggravate the problems they were intended to alleviate.

These questions are taken up in the next three chapters. Chapter 8 is devoted to an analysis of the educational attainments of Soviet women and their relationship to the pattern of female employment. In Chapters 9 and 10 I examine the Soviet record on protective legislation and the provision of state support for working women.

## Notes: Chapter 7

1   Kotlyar and Turchaninova, 1975, p. 9. Kotlyar and Turchaninova, in common with most Soviet economists and sociologists, believe that as a matter of biology women are more suited than men not only to the production but also to the rearing of children. Many Western feminists would dispute this; they would argue that social convention and not biology places the onus of child care upon the female sex. For further discussion of Soviet attitudes – and the policy implications derived from them – see below, Chapter 9.

2   Soviet estimates of sex differences in physical strength vary. One recent work, drawing upon both Soviet and French research, suggests that women are 70 per cent as strong as men when the gap is smallest (at age 20) and only 54 per cent as strong when the gap is at its widest (at age 55). It also claims that male musculature is much more responsive to training (Shishkan, 1976, pp. 12-13). This is somewhat less than the 80 to 85 per cent implied in a recent Western source (Mackie and Patullo, 1977, pp. 145-6). But since this was written by journalists, I suspect that the Soviet figures are the more accurate.

3   There is little, if any, discussion in the Soviet Union of the extent to which measured differences in aptitudes, like those reported by King, are the product of differential socialisation. Rather, they are automatically ascribed to biology.

*Chapter 8*

# Education and Employment

It is sometimes suggested that differences in the earnings of men and women can be explained by differences in their education. This, in essence, is the implication of human capital theory; it also forms part of the analysis advanced by Soviet sociologists and economists, as was pointed out in the last chapter. In this chapter I review the evidence that can be brought to bear on this hypothesis and conclude that, at least in its simpler quantitative variants, it fails to account for observed earnings differentials in the USSR.

Human capital theory claims that the remuneration of individuals can be thought of as comprising a reward for simple labour and a return on human capital. Earnings differences, then, are attributable to the fact that different individuals embody different amounts of human capital. This in itself is unobservable but the theory is rendered non-vacuous by the assertion that human capital accumulation is effected through the educational process. Thus, earnings should be positively correlated with educational attainment. Further, a narrowing of differences in educational experience between population groups (say, between men and women) should be associated with a reduction in earnings differentiation. There are certain problems associated with the measurement of educational attainment in the USSR but the available evidence is presented in the next section. In summary this shows that although in the past women in the USSR were less well educated than men, the gap had largely disappeared by 1970; indeed, among younger age-groups women had more formal education than men. But, as has been shown in earlier chapters, the narrowing of educational differences over the past thirty or forty years has been associated with an increase in occupational segregation and the maintenance of significant earnings differentials.

This result suggests that perhaps the emphasis on the number of years of formal education is misplaced. Education, after all, is only the process through which human capital is created; it is not in itself that human capital. That is, perhaps there are systematic differences in the type of schooling received by boys and girls and these have not changed in the last four decades or so. There are two aspects of this question that can be investigated on the basis of available data: first, one can examine the type of educational establishment attended by the two sexes and, secondly, one can explore differences in the subjects that they study. These issues are taken up on pages 148–53. The evidence presented there suggests that systematic differences between the sexes exist in both these respects and that these differences have persisted for much of the period under review. That is, the Soviet educational system, broadly defined, appears to result in boys acquiring more market-relevant skills than do girls.

But the fact that the educational experience of boys in the USSR differs from that of girls can only serve as a proximate explanation of occupational segregation and earnings differentiation. In turn, the factors leading to differences in education require elucidation. This issue is taken up on pages 153-61. On the basis of recent sociological work into the career aspirations of school leavers, it is suggested that at the age of 16 or 18 the sexes are already differentiated. That is, even with a common secondary educational curriculum, girls and boys have developed divergent career goals in response to (presumably differentiated) socialisation pressures from school, family and society at large. Secondly, some attempt is made to determine whether or not the aspirations of female secondary school leavers are frustrated more frequently than those of their male contemporaries. Finally, it is suggested that differences in career orientations between men and women are accentuated in the fifteen years or so after girls leave school as a result of the so-called dual burden. That is, responsibility for home and family conflicts with the process of continuing education and vocational training on which career advancement in the USSR depends to a large extent. The discussion of this topic leads naturally into a wider consideration of possible conflicts between family and job. These are taken up in Chapters 9 and 10.

## The Educational Attainments of Men and Women, 1939-76

There are no published statistics which relate the educational attainments of Soviet men and women to their earnings and consequently any formal test of hypotheses inspired by human capital theory is difficult if not impossible. But statistics on educational achievement and the way that it has changed in the last forty years or so are available - most conveniently in successive population censuses - and these, together with the material already presented on increasing occupational segregation and continuing earnings differentials, make it seem unlikely that differences in the amount of schooling received by the two sexes can account for the continued inferiority of women in the USSR.

In this section I describe the format in which Soviet statistics on education are usually presented and suggest a way in which they can be transformed into an indicator more suited to the purposes of this chapter on the basis of an outline knowledge of Soviet educational institutions. I then present figures which demonstrate the growth of educational attainment for both sexes in the past forty years or so and finally attempt to relate education to attributes that might plausibly be assumed to be correlated with earnings.

Soviet statistics on education are presented in terms of the number of persons in specified population groups who have attained particular educational standards. Two standard hierarchies are commonly employed: first, the conventional tripartite structure of primary, secondary and higher education is used (and sometimes contracted into the proportion of the population group with at least some secondary education). Secondly, each of the elements in the tripartite structure is subdivided into completed and incomplete sub-

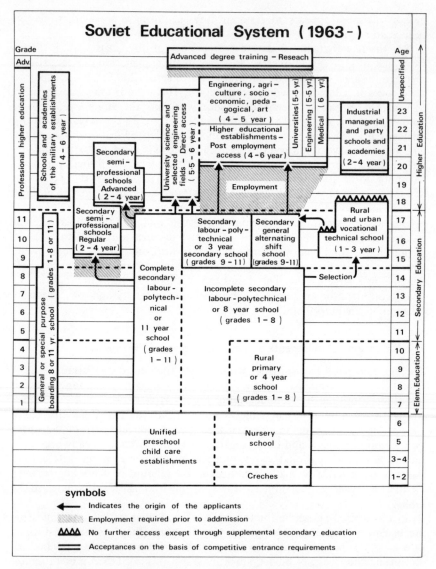

Figure 8.1   *The Structure of Soviet Educational Institutions.*
*Source:* Reproduced with permission from N. de Witt, *Education and Professional Employment in the USSR* (NSF 61–40), Washington DC, 1961.

categories and a seventh category, secondary specialist education, is also identified separately. That is, rather than report simply the number of persons with, say, secondary education, the census tabulations list the numbers with incomplete secondary education, with completed secondary education and with secondary specialist education separately. The categories of primary and higher education are treated analogously (although, for those who might wish to consult Soviet data themselves, it should be pointed out that the category of incomplete primary education is almost invariably given only implicitly, as a residual).

Although I do not propose to describe the structure of Soviet educational institutions in any detail, a few words are in order if these various categories are to convey more than the crudest impression of the educational attainments of the Soviet population.[1] Such a description will also help to justify the procedure used below to convert distributions of the population by educational attainment into estimates of the average number of years of schooling possessed. Figure 8.1 provides an overview of the structure and interrelationships between the various educational establishments and levels of education in the USSR in the period between 1963 and the early 1970s. I will take this as the paradigm and later will add a comment about the structure that preceded it and about the way that it has evolved in the last decade or so.

Although kindergartens, *detskie sady*, are administered by the ministries of education in individual republics in the USSR, the services they provide are not considered to be part of formal education. Primary education starts at the age of 7 - and it is only from this age that parents are obliged by law to send their children to school. (Equally, the state is only obliged to provide places for children from this age; access to pre-school child care facilities is subject to availability.) Further, although increasingly in urban areas children attend eight-year or ten–eleven-year schools, primary education is defined to comprise the first four classes. Secondary education starts at the age of 11. All children are then required to remain in school for a further four years. On graduating from the eighth class (or on reaching the age of 15 in the case of those who have had to repeat one or more years) children are faced with their first choice: they can leave school and go to work, they can transfer to one of a range of professional or vocational training institutions, or they can remain at their general educational school. Those who leave school after eighth grade are deemed to have an incomplete secondary education. Students who transfer to a professional training institution (either at 15 or after tenth–eleventh grade) and complete the appropriate programme, for example, in nursing, are classified as having secondary specialist education. Those who remain at school until the age of 17 or 18 and successfully graduate from tenth–eleventh grade are deemed to have a completed secondary education. At this stage they can either get a job, enter a professional training institution, or attempt to be selected for higher education. Those who enter universities or analogous institutions of higher education (what the Russians call *VUZy*) will graduate some four to six years later with a completed higher education. (The category of incomplete higher education comprises those who, at the time of the census, were still registered at a *VUZ* or had satisfactorily completed part of a recognised higher-level course.)

The description given in the previous paragraph refers to the Soviet educational system after 1963. There were three main changes introduced in that year. First, incomplete secondary education was increased from seven to eight years; that is, effectively, the school-leaving age was raised from 14 to 15. Secondly, completed secondary education was extended from ten to eleven years. There has been a tendency since the late 1960s to revert to the ten-year school programme and this is now (1980) much more common than the eleven-year school. For most of the period 1963–75, to which statistics given below refer, both types of programme coexisted in the USSR. Finally, an attempt was made to impose a requirement that applicants for secondary specialist and higher educational establishments should acquire some work experience before being deemed eligible for admission. This last was 'more honoured in the breach than in the observance' and has now been largely abandoned. Further, although it has not resulted in any formal institutional change, a new policy has been adopted in the 1970s designed ultimately to achieve universal completed secondary education. This involves the teaching of the general secondary educational syllabus for grades nine to ten–eleven to students at vocational and professional educational institutions.

The format in which Soviet statisticians present information about the educational attainments of the population can be used to derive a general impression of educational standards; but it is not very suitable for explicit measurement of changes or of differences in the level attained by different sub-populations. The information contained in Figure 8.1, however, permits one to specify an aggregation procedure that generates a more appropriate indicator. One can postulate that the attainment of specified educational standards involves a certain number of years of schooling (explicit values for which can be extracted from the figure) and thus for any distribution of a population between standards one can calculate the average number of years of schooling that members of that population have. As the proportion of the population with higher standards rises, so will their average number of years of schooling, and vice versa.

Clearly such a conversion procedure can only be approximate. There are, I think, two main sources of error or bias. First, there are differences in the length of courses classified as equivalent by Soviet statisticians. Secondly, even where, in a given year, the length of a course is unique, differences in the date at which individuals received their education may involve differences in the number of years of schooling implied by a particular standard. I have made no attempt to allow for the effects of increases in the school-leaving age in 1963 or for more recent changes in the length of the secondary school syllabus in the calculations used in this chapter. Rather, for all distributions the following conversion factors have been used:

| Educational Standard | Equivalent Years |
|---|---|
| Incomplete Primary | 2·5 |
| Completed Primary | 4·0 |
| Incomplete Secondary | 8·0 |
| Completed Secondary | 11·0 |
| Secondary Specialist | 13·0 |
| Incomplete Higher | 14·5 |
| Completed Higher | 16·0 |

It is not clear what sort of bias this procedure will introduce into the calculations given below. First, however, one can suggest that it will result in an understatement of the improvement over time since, for example, those who left school with an incomplete secondary education before 1963 will be classified as having had eight years of schooling whereas in fact they only received seven. By the same reasoning it will result in a flattening of age-education profiles since the average number of years schooling of the older age-groups will be overstated. Finally, in so far as older men are more likely to have received a secondary education than older women, it will overstate men's education relative to that of women; on the other hand, if older women are more likely to have had a secondary education than men, the bias will be in the opposite direction. But given the crudity of the comparisons attempted here, I do not think that these biases are likely to be significant.

There is one final topic that should be mentioned before I present some of the available information on the educational attainments of men and women in the USSR. In addition to the normal breakdowns (male-female, rural-urban and by union republic) the Soviet censuses provide tabulations of education both in terms of the total population (aged 10 years and over) and the occupied population. For men, this distinction involves little more than the exclusion of the oldest age-groups, given the high and stable rates of participation achieved. For women, however, the difference is more significant – and its significance has changed over time with increases in female participation. Nor is it immediately clear which tabulation is the more appropriate in the context of hypotheses drawn from human capital theory. On the one hand, if one is concerned to establish relationships between earnings and education one should perhaps concentrate only on the employed population. However, if the decision to participate is affected by educational attainment and if earnings are sensitive to changes in participation (both plausible propositions), perhaps total population is the relevant category. Although below I place somewhat greater emphasis on tabulations relating to the occupied population, rather than resolve this issue on theoretical grounds I adopt an agnostic attitude and present estimates of educational achievement based on both tabulations.

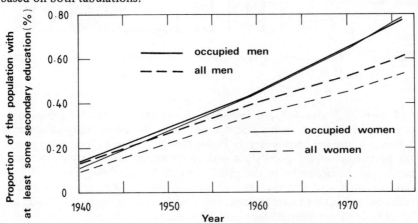

Figure 8.2  *The Growth of Secondary Education in the USSR: 1939–76.*
  *Sources:* Derived from *Zhenshchiny* (1975), p. 61, and *Vestnik Statistiki*, no. 1, 1977, p. 84.

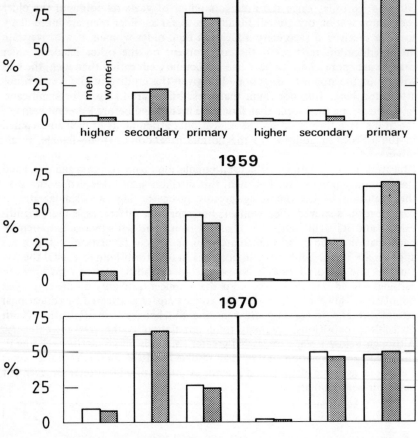

Figure 8.3    *Educational Attainment of the Occupied Population: USSR, 1939–70.*

Figures 8.2 and 8.3 are intended to convey a general impression of educational standards in the USSR in 1939 and the substantial improvement achieved in the last forty years. In Figure 8.2 the crudest of indicators is used, the proportion of the population with an incomplete secondary education or better. At the beginning of the period covered by the figure a mere 12·7 per cent of men and 9·0 per cent of women could claim even this meagre educational level. But over the next two decades improvement was steady and in 1959 39·2 per cent of men and 33·8 per cent of women could boast at least an incomplete secondary education. According to the figure, progress was maintained at about the same rate for the next decade or so and at the 1970 Census 52·2 per cent of men and 45·2 per cent of women had some secondary education. Finally, over the last decade, improvement has been more rapid (due in large measure to the death of an increasing proportion of those born before or immediately after the revolution) and by the mid-1970s 61·4 per cent of men and 53·2 per cent of women had incomplete secondary education or better. Throughout the period, on this indicator, women remained less well educated than men. Indeed, the gap between the sexes widened; in 1939 only 3·7 per cent more men than women could claim an incomplete secondary education (or better) while in 1976 the figure was 8·2 per cent – more than twice as large. But this conclusion is misleading. The indicator itself is not sensitive to changes in the amount of schooling above the cut-off point; it relates to total and not to the occupied population; it is not clear that the difference in percentages (as opposed, for example, to their ratio) is the appropriate measure of differences in educational standards.

Figure 8.2 also provides information about the educational attainment of the occupied population – again using the same indicator. In 1939 some 13·6 per cent of occupied men and 10·4 per cent of occupied women had incomplete secondary education; that is, the occupied population was little better educated than the population as a whole. Over the next two decades the educational level of the occupied male population increased at about the same rate as that of the male population as a whole and in 1959 some 43·4 per cent of employed men could claim some secondary education. Over this same period the educational standards of employed women rose to a level almost equal to that of men; in 1959 as many as 43·1 per cent of occupied women had an incomplete secondary education. In the following decade the educational improvement among employed women mirrored that of employed men and diverged from that of the population as a whole. This divergence was a reflection of the retirement of many of those born and brought up before the revolution. Finally, by the mid-1970s occupied women overtook men in educational attainments; in 1977 some 78·1 per cent of occupied women and only 77·9 per cent of occupied men could claim incomplete secondary education or better. But, again, I must stress that the indicator used here is not particularly sensitive.

Figure 8.3 attempts to provide more detail on the educational standards of occupied men and women over the period 1939–70. It presents histograms of educational achievement for the occupied population for the three census years. Distributions are given for the rural and urban populations separately and the conventional tripartite standard hierarchy is used (that is, incomplete primary education is included as primary education, both incomplete and secondary specialist education are included with secondary education, and so on).

The figure shows generally that the urban population has been better educated than the rural population. Even in 1970 some 47 to 50 per cent of the latter could claim no more than a primary education – in 1939 the proportion was between 92 and 96 per cent. In urban areas, in contrast, approximately three-quarters of the population in 1939 had no more than a primary education and, by 1970, only a quarter were still so badly educated. Secondly, as implied by Figure 8.2, Figure 8.3 shows the growth of secondary education. In 1939 approximately a fifth of the urban occupied population could claim some secondary education; by 1959 the proportion had grown to a half and in 1970 to about two-thirds. Over the same period the proportion of the rural population with some secondary education increased from about 5 per cent to almost half. Finally we see, not unexpectedly, that those with higher education are still to be found almost exclusively in urban areas. Even in 1970 only 2 or 3 per cent of the rural population could claim incomplete or complete higher education. In the Soviet countryside the educated elite is spread very thinly.

Figure 8.3 also casts some further light on the relative educational attainments of occupied men and women in the Soviet Union. In urban areas in all three years fewer women than men had only a primary education. Similarly, in urban areas in all three years more women than men had some form of secondary education. But in both 1939 and 1970 more urban men than women had some higher education. In 1959, on the other hand, almost certainly as a result of population losses and educational disruption during the Second World War, a higher proportion of urban women than men had higher education. (But the difference was small – 6·0 as opposed to 5·8 per cent.) In rural areas of the Soviet Union, however, a more traditional picture emerges: in all three census years a higher proportion of occupied men than women had secondary or further education. Changes in the degree of urbanisation, then, account for apparent inconsistencies in the lessons to be drawn from Figures 8.2 and 8.3. In urban areas, on the indicator used in the earlier chart, women have been better educated than men at least since 1939. But this was not so for the country as a whole since in that year (and for some time thereafter) the urban sector was small relative to the population as a whole.

The information provided in Figures 8.2 and 8.3 is still very aggregated; the category secondary education in particular covers a wide range of actual schooling (from eight years for incomplete to thirteen years for specialist, according to the estimates given earlier in this chapter). But it is possible to transform the tabulations of educational attainment given in Soviet censuses into estimates of average schooling to give a clearer idea of differences in educational standards for the two sexes. This is done in Table 8.1 for the last two census years. (Unfortunately it proved impossible to obtain suitable figures relating to 1939.)

The figures in Table 8.1 confirm the conclusions reached on the basis of Figures 8.2 and 8.3. Taking the occupied population definition first: in 1959 occupied urban women had on average 7·6 years of schooling whereas occupied urban men had only 7·2 years. By 1970, however, the gap had virtually disappeared – although women were still fractionally the better educated. In rural areas, by contrast, occupied men had, on average, 5·4 years of schooling in 1959 while women had only 5·0 years. In 1970 educational levels had risen, but men were still better educated than women. But, again, the gap had narrowed.

Turning to the total population figures: they show that in both rural and urban areas men are better educated than women. Indeed, they suggest that the gap in educational attainment remained constant over the decade 1959–70 or even increased slightly. In 1959 urban men had 0·4 more years of schooling than women; in 1970 this had increased to 0·5 years. For the rural population the figures were 0·67 and 0·69 years respectively.

Table 8.1  *Average Number of Years Schooling: Men and Women, 1959-70*

|  | Urban | | Rural | |
|---|---|---|---|---|
|  | *Men* | *Women* | *Men* | *Women* |
| Population (aged 10 and over) | | | | |
| 1959 | 6·8 | 6·4 | 5·1 | 4·4 |
| 1970 | 7·9 | 7·5 | 5·8 | 5·1 |
| Occupied population | | | | |
| 1959 | 7·2 | 7·6 | 5·4 | 5·0 |
| 1970 | 8·9 | 9·0 | 6·7 | 6·5 |

*Source:* Calculated from *Itogi* . . . , 1970, Vol. III, Tables 1 and 6, using weights given on page 138 above.

The statistics given so far refer to the population as a whole – and thus fail, perhaps, to reveal the nature of the changes in educational attainment in the Soviet Union that have been taking place over the past twenty years or so. Some further insight into these changes is given in Figure 8.4 which contains age-education profiles for rural and urban men and women for the last two population censuses. The statistics on which the figure was based were calculated by the same methods as those given in Table 8.1. Unfortunately, profiles could be constructed only for the population as a whole; published sources do not contain a cross-tabulation of age and education for the occupied population.

According to Figure 8.4 urban women in both the 20-29 and 30-39 year age-groups were better educated than urban men in both 1959 and 1970. Among older age-groups, on the other hand, there was a substantial difference in the other direction. Three inferences at least can be made from these age-education profiles. First, in so far as elite managerial and professional positions in Soviet society are held by those in their fifties (or older), the substantial difference in educational attainment between the sexes for these age-groups might be held to account for differences in the frequency with which men and women are to be found in positions of power and authority. If this were the case, however, since there is little difference in the educational attainments of those aged 45-49 years in 1970, the next population census (in fact held in 1979) should reveal a substantial increase in the number of women to be found in what might be called 'top jobs.' But, as pointed out in Chapter 5, current statistics have contained little hint of any radical change in the sex-composition of status hierarchies.

Secondly, the relationship between the age-education profiles for both men and women for the two years suggests that the acquisition of education in the USSR, far from being completed by the age of 18 or 20, continues until perhaps the age of 40. To put it crudely, in the absence of migration and mortality the age-group that was 20-29 years old in 1959 should correspond

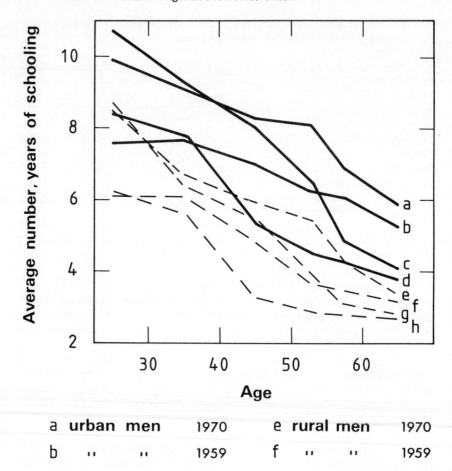

| a | **urban men** | 1970 | e | **rural men** | 1970 |
|---|---|---|---|---|---|
| b | " " | 1959 | f | " " | 1959 |
| c | " **women** | 1970 | g | " **women** | 1970 |
| d | " " | 1959 | h | " " | 1959 |

Figure 8.4    *Average Number of Years of Schooling, by Sex, Age and Place of Residence: USSR, 1959–70.*

*Source:* Calculated from *Itogi* . . . , 1959, Table 20, and *Itogi* . . . , 1970, vol. III, Table 1.

more or less to the one that was 30–39 years old in 1970. If education had ceased by the age of 20, the average number of years of schooling should have remained constant over the intervening decade. Further, since the rural population is less well educated than the urban one, other things being equal substantial rural–urban migration should result in a *fall* in average educational attainment. In fact, for both sexes, between 1959 and 1970 the two youngest age-groups in the earlier year recorded a substantial increase in average schooling. There was even an increase in the average educational level of the youngest rural age-group in 1959 in the intercensal period. This suggests that the recorded increase cannot be attributed solely (or mainly) to differential rural–urban migration rates.

Thirdly, the effect described in the last paragraph was much more marked for men than for women. For example, in 1959 the average amount of schooling among urban men and women aged 20–29 years was 7·56 years and 8·37 years respectively. That is, women in this age-group on average had 0·81 years more schooling than men. In 1970, among those aged 30–39 years (basically the same group) women had on average 9·29 years of schooling and men as much as 9·12 years. On average, then, women in this age-group now had only 0·17 years more schooling than men. To put it another way: between 1959 and 1970, urban males who were aged 20–29 years in 1959 improved their average educational level by 1·56 years while over the same period their female contemporaries managed only a 0·92-year improvement. That this is not only a consequence of interruptions in boys' education due to military service obligations is suggested by the fact that in all other age-groups (except the highest) the change in male educational attainment is larger than that for females. In fact, although in other age-groups the absolute improvement is not as large as for those aged 20–29 years, the ratio of male and female changes is often greater. This differential improvement in measured educational attainment of the two sexes reflects differences in their social situation and I return to it at greater length below (pages 256–9).

The age-education profiles for the rural population, also given in Figure 8.4, merit less comment. First, one can see that in both 1959 and 1970 in the youngest age-group women were better educated than men. But by the age of 30–39 years male superiority had been established – and was increasingly dominant among the older age-groups. Secondly, the fact that for a given cohort average education falls between 1959 and 1970 (for groups other than those aged 20–29 in the earlier year) suggests that some differential rural–urban migration did take place. That is, it appears that the better educated were disproportionately represented among those who migrated from country to town. This is plausible in itself but may mask ethnic differences in migration patterns since the rural population in Central Asia, for example, is largely non-Russian and both less well educated and more immobile. (As an aside, I am not aware of any work that has established whether it is nationality or lack of education that contributes more to Central Asian immobility.)

The figures presented so far have been derived from various population censuses and have referred to men and women irrespective of the sectors in which they were employed. Soviet sociologists and economists have published other data, based for the most part on sample surveys, which suggest that, by the early 1970s at least, the position among industrial workers was essentially the same as among the population as a whole. For example, using the methodology described above to calculate average schooling, it can be estimated that in 1973 male industrial workers had, on average, 7·89 years of education while among female industrial workers the figure was 8·04 years. For workers under 30 years of age the analogous figures were 9·31 years and 9·76 years for men and women respectively.[2] That is, in the youngest age-group female superiority in formal education was, as usual, greater than that for the population as a whole. Given the extent to which the skill ratings of male industrial workers exceeded those of women (see pages 80-1), and given the relationship between skill rating and earnings, these figures make it unlikely that variations in education can explain any substantial proportion of the difference in male and female earnings.

Nor should it be thought that the results reported so far are a consequence of inadequacies in the way in which educational attainment has been calculated. Kotlyar and Turchaninova report the average number of years of schooling for male and female workers by age for five industrial branches and in all five women workers are better educated than men in the age-groups 'under 25' and '25-44'. It is only in the highest age-group that men's schooling exceeds that for women.[3] Now, it is possible that male workers in male-dominated and relatively well-paid branches like ferrous or non-ferrous metallurgy are better educated than those in the branches listed above; they may even be better educated than the women in these branches. But the educational gap cannot be large in view of the figures derived from Stepanyan. These figures must, therefore, undermine the plausibility of explanations of the difference in the earnings of men and women industrial workers that rely upon differences in educational attainment.

Finally, the relative educational standards of men and women workers in the early 1970s differ strikingly from those for the 1930s. In 1936 among young workers (presumably those under 30 years of age) some 43 per cent of males had incomplete secondary education or more while only 29 per cent of females came into this category. In machinebuilding the gap was narrower, although men were still markedly better educated than women - 50 per cent with some secondary education as opposed to 41 per cent. (Shkaratan, 1970, p. 294). Yet in spite of the striking improvement in women's formal education implied by these figures, the results of earlier chapters suggest that there has been no comparable reduction in occupational segregation or earnings differentiation.

Two further survey results reinforce the conclusion that there is little connection between earnings and education in the USSR - or rather that differences in the earnings of men and women cannot be attributed to differences in their formal education. (For each sex taken separately there may well be a reasonably close correlation between earnings and education.) First, from a sample of workers with secondary specialist or higher education (drawn from Taganrog in 1967-70) it was reported that they had the following skill ratings (Gruzdeva, 1975, p. 94):

|                | *Men (%)* | *Women (%)* |
| -------------- | --------- | ----------- |
| Highly skilled | 46        | 10          |
| Semi-skilled   | 48        | 50          |
| Unskilled      | 6         | 40          |
|                | 100       | 100         |

Thus two-fifths of the women in this sample were classified as unskilled even though they had at least a secondary specialist education; only 6 per cent of men in the sample were so classified. The relationship between skill and earnings previously alluded to and results like the one given here suggest that educational attainment has little effect on the earnings of female industrial workers.

The second sample, also drawn in 1967, relates to male and female employees in a single factory – the Urals Heavy Chemical Machinebuilding Factory. One has the following figures on education and earnings for two classes of employee (Kamovich and Kozlovskaya, 1969, pp. 102–4):

| | *Education (years)* | *Earnings (R per month)* |
|---|---|---|
| Office staff | 9·5 | 97·0 |
| Workers | 9·1 | 152·5 |

Given the name of the factory, it is plausible to assume that a majority of the workers in the sample would have been men. We are told, however, that the category office staff (which excludes managerial and supervisory personnel, *ITR*) was 96 per cent female. Thus, in spite of being better educated, the women employed at this factory were earning less than two-thirds as much as male workers. There is surely some basis for asserting that differences in education between the sexes in the USSR can account for little of the observed difference in their earnings.

So far in this chapter I have been concerned almost exclusively with educational standards among the Soviet population as a whole. But, as has been made clear in previous chapters, there is substantial regional diversity in economic structure in the USSR and it is to be expected that educational standards in the different regions would exhibit a similar variability. The population censuses provide data that would permit a detailed analysis of regional variations in education in the Soviet Union. I do not report figures for individual republics here but, in general, they suggest that there is in fact relatively little variation in standards between republics. All the same, one can show that, as the educational standards of women rise relative to those of men, the concentration of women in relatively low-wage sectors of the economy increases. That is, at least on a geographical cross-section basis, these figures constitute a weak refutation of an implication of human capital theory. In Chapter 5 I introduced an index of administrative segregation, $R_k$, which measured the extent to which women were concentrated in low-wage sectors. (The index was available for thirteen of the fifteen republics, suitable primary data for Turkmenistan and Kazakhstan being unobtainable for 1970.) If values of this index are regressed against the ratio of female to male educational attainment, the following result is obtained:

$$R_k = 1·2852 - 0·3847E_k \qquad R^2 : 0·7642$$
$$(20·7) \qquad (5·7) \qquad\quad DF : 10$$

where $E_k$ is the ratio of the average number of years schooling of women and men in the $k$th republic in 1970.[4] This equation suggests that, at least in Soviet conditions, as the educational standards of women rise relative to those of men, they increasingly come to occupy positions in particular service sectors to the exclusion of men (e.g. education, administration, and so forth) that are or become relatively low-paid. Thus increased education tends to reinforce administrative segregation and, consequently, sex differentials in earnings. Not too much weight can be placed on this result, but it is consistent with the analysis of the rest of this section.

In summary, then, analysis of available information on the educational standards of the Soviet population has shown the following: there has been a substantial increase in the amount of schooling possessed by both sexes in the past forty years or so. The urban population is and always has been better educated than those who live in rural areas. Even in 1939 a higher proportion of occupied women than men in urban areas had some secondary education (though fewer had higher education); since that date, the superiority of occupied women in terms of formal education has become more firmly established. The same superiority existed in the early 1970s among industrial workers – although women workers were certainly the less well educated in the 1930s. In the light of material presented in earlier chapters, these results suggest that the amount of formal education an individual possesses cannot, by itself, explain his or her skill grading. Differences in formal educational achievement will account for little of the observed occupational segregation or earnings differentiation. This, in turn, suggests that emphasis on the *amount* of education received by individuals is misplaced. Perhaps occupational affiliation depends not so much on the number of years of schooling that an individual has received as upon the subjects studied in school (or, rather, in post-secondary school training establishments, upon the formal qualification awarded by the educational institution). These topics are discussed in the next section.

### Sex-Specific Differences in Vocational Training

There is much less quantitative information available about the content of education in the Soviet Union than about its amount, but the material produced in this section does suggest that, at least after they have left their secondary schools, the educational experience of boys and girls diverges. First, it appears that boys are more likely than girls to receive some form of vocational or professional training. Secondly, the training received by boys is more likely to equip them to pursue careers in industry or, more generally, in what the Soviets call the productive sphere. Finally, it appears that some forms of market-relevant vocational training are not included in the statistics on education that have been presented in the previous section; this introduces an element of bias into sex-linked education data.

In the secondary school pupils follow a common curriculum with little scope for choice between subjects until fairly late in their careers. It seems plausible to assume, then, that there is virtually no difference in the subjects studied by boys and girls in the USSR before the end of eighth grade. The search for evidence of divergent educational experience can therefore concentrate on post-secondary vocational and professional training establishments. In this context, two sets of statistics appear to be relevant: first, those that relate to sex differences in channels of vocational training and secondly, those relating to differences in subject specialisms within a given class of institution. Each is discussed below.

On leaving one's secondary school in the USSR, there are five channels by which a person can effect the transition into full-time employment (see Figure 8.1). First, he or she can proceed to a *VUZ*; alternatively, he or she can proceed to an institution providing a secondary specialist education (at the age of 15 or 18); or, again, he or she can enter a so-called *PTU* (*professionalno-tekhnicheskie uchilishcha*) at the age of 15; finally, he or she can enter the labour market directly, without any special training. Within this framework, the first important distinction is between the *PTU* network and those establishments that provide a secondary specialist education.

There are two channels for the training of skilled workers in industry and, presumably, in other sectors of the productive sphere. First, there is on-the-job training, *individualno-brigadnoe uchenichestvo*; this is used to provide relatively short periods of training that equip workers with basic skills. Secondly, workers can attend a vocational training establishment for a period of between six months and two years where, in addition to practical expertise, they are given some formal or theoretical instruction in the principles under-lying the technology of the industry for which they are being trained. For the most part, these vocational training establishments are the so-called *professionalno-tekhnicheskie uchilishcha* (*PTU*), although some industrial training schemes are run by *tekhnikums* and establishments that offer a secondary specialist educational qualification. Soviet authors frequently assert that it is difficult if not impossible for workers with only a *BIU* back-ground to attain highly-skilled status; for this, it is felt, attendance at a *PTU* is desirable if not essential. Secondary specialist educational establishments provide courses in industrial training. They also offer preparation for a wide variety of non-industrial careers, for example, nursing, book-keeping, some pre-school child care training, primary school teaching, and so on. Although the position is not wholly clear, it appears that those who successfully complete a course of training at a secondary specialist establishment (even if only in book-keeping) will have the fact recorded in the statistics on education whereas those who complete a course of training in an industrial skill at a *PTU* may well not figure in the statistics as having more than incomplete secondary education. That is, perhaps for bureaucratic reasons (the *PTU* are not part of the Ministry of Education hierarchy), *PTU* courses are not counted as education.[5]

It is difficult to provide accurate figures on the relative importance of these different channels of access into the labour market, but some orders of magnitude can be estimated. It is reported that in 1972 some 2·1 million young people entered *PTU* and that this constituted 39 per cent of the relevant age-cohort. A further 40 per cent of the cohort 'entered work directly, bypassing the system of professional-technical education'. Thus an estimated 21 per cent of the cohort entered upon secondary specialist or further educational training courses (Korchagin, 1974, p. 151). The actual enrolments at these latter educational establishments given in statistical handbooks are somewhat higher than those implied by Korchagin – but these may well include some mature students. Taking Korchagin's figures at face value, and assuming that the proportions of males and females in the overall student bodies of the various educational establishments also apply to the cohort to which his figures refer, one can calculate the following distribution of post-school experience for the two sexes:

|  |  | Boys (%) | Girls (%) |
|---|---|---|---|
| Transfer to: | VUZ | 8 | 8 |
|  | Secondary specialist institutions | 11 | 14 |
|  | PTU | 57 | 19 |
|  | Work | 24 | 58 |
|  | Total | 100 | 100 |

Thus in the early 1970s apparently about a quarter of all boys and three-fifths of all girls went directly from school to work. Somewhat less than a fifth of boys and slightly more than a fifth of girls went on to a secondary specialist or higher educational establishment. Almost three-fifths of boys and only a fifth of girls went to *PTU*. It is this difference in *PTU* recruitment that constitutes the first major divergence in educational experience between the sexes. And, as the figures in Table 8.2 show, it is a divergence that has existed at least since the end of the Second World War.[6]

Table 8.2  *Admissions to Post-School Professional-Vocational Training Establishments: USSR, 1940–75*

|  | VUZy | | Secondary Specialist Establishments | | PTU | |
|---|---|---|---|---|---|---|
|  | Total (thousands) | % Female | Total (thousands) | % Female | Total (thousands) | % Female |
| 1940 | 263 | 58 | 383 | 55 | 602 | – |
| 1950 | 349 | 53 | 426 | 54 | 385 | 8 |
| 1960 | 593 | 43 | 769 | 47 | 810 | 17 |
| 1965 | 854 | 44 | 1100 | 50 | 1151 | 20 |
| 1970 | 912 | 49 | 1338 | 54 | 1837 | 26 |
| 1975 | 994 | 50 | 1404 | 54 | 2323 | n.a. |

*Sources:* Cols (1) and (2) *Narodnoye obrazovanie, nauka i kultura v SSSR*, Moscow, 1977, p. 246; Cols (3) and (4) ibid., p. 174. (Proportion of women in the student body in 1965 from *NK. SSSR*, 1977, p. 506.) Cols (5) and (6) calculated from *Trud v SSSR*, Moscow, 1968, pp. 306–7, and *NK SSSR*, 1970, p. 528.

A number of reasons have been advanced by Soviet specialists to account for the under-representation of women among *PTU* students. First, it is claimed that women are precluded through the operation of protective legislation from admission to nine-tenths of the occupations for which training is provided in these establishments (Rogovskii, 1976, p. 54). But it is also alleged that women are in fact employed in a number of these supposedly prohibited occupations (Kotlyar, 1973, p. 399). This probably reflects in part inadequacies in the system of vocational training. It has been argued, for example, that both the number of places provided and the curricula followed for a number of training schemes are inadequate. Enterprises employing labour with the skills in question have been forced to supplement *PTU* courses with on-the-job training and even to prepare their own skilled workers. It is at least possible, in these circumstances, that some plants have recruited and trained women for occupations that, formally at least, they are prohibited by law from undertaking. Alternatively, the fact that some women are employed in these occupations may be a consequence of the fact that certain sections of the code (for example, that which precluded the employment of women in underground mining) were suspended during the Second World War and the later Stalin period.

Secondly, another shortcoming of the system of vocational training operated through the *PTU*: it is alleged that both the type of training provided and the relative availability of places frequently does not correspond to the demands of industry. Too few places are provided for newer industrial occupations. In so far as these occupations are available to women, these inadequacies will reduce the number of them trained through this system.

Finally, it is claimed that the under-representation of women in the *PTU* system is a reflection of managerial prejudice if not discrimination. It is apparently the case that many if not all *PTU* recruit their students in accordance with projections of labour demand submitted by plants within their areas. In these projections, enterprises specify the sex of the future workers they require and the *PTU* admit accordingly. If enterprise managers want male rather than female workers, this will be reflected in the sex-composition of the *PTU* student body, whether such preferences are rational or not (Mikhailyuk, 1970, p. 80).

It is not only the fact that fewer girls than boys attend *PTU* that results in a divergence in the career paths of men and women in the Soviet Union. Soviet statistical sources provide some limited information on the subjects studied by the two sexes while enrolled in secondary specialist or higher educational establishments and this suggests that the divergence already commented upon is reinforced. In fact, the statistics classify educational establishments (or, possibly, faculties) by the branch of the economy for which they provide training. Five areas are identified – which exhaustively classify the student body. These are: industry, construction, transport and communications; agriculture; economics and law; medicine and physical education; education, art and cinematography. In Figure 8.5 the proportion of males and females registered in the first two of these areas has been plotted for the period since 1940. That is, the figure shows the proportion of the two sexes enrolled in courses that formally qualify them for careers in the productive sphere at the secondary specialist and higher levels.

On the basis of the chart, one can infer that secondary specialist education, for both sexes, is more 'practical' than higher education. Also, the education of men, in both types of institution, is more heavily weighted towards the productive sector than that of women. Finally, although the proportion of women studying subjects that would lead to careers in industry, and so on, has increased since the late 1930s, the most rapid growth occurred between

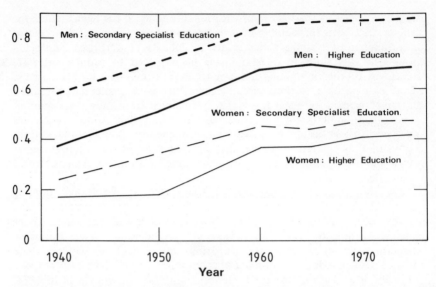

Figure 8.5   *Proportion of Those Studying for 'Productive Sphere' Careers in Secondary Specialist and Higher Educational Establishments in the USSR: 1940–75.*

*Source:* Calculated from *Narodnoye obrazovanie*, 1971, pp. 186–8, and *Narodnoye obrazovanie*, 1977, pp. 174–5, 246–7.

1940 and 1960; since then, numbers have increased only slowly. That is, for the past twenty years or so, between a half and three-fifths of the women admitted to secondary specialist or higher educational establishments have been enrolled on courses that would channel them into the (lower-paid) service sectors of the economy; only one-sixth to one-third of men have been in this category.

Thus, one can conclude that Soviet educational institutions, at least at the post-secondary school level, are operated in a fashion that results in men and women following broadly different career patterns. Girls are much more likely than boys to go straight from school into full-time employment. Among those who do receive some vocational or professional training, boys are more likely than girls to be admitted to an institution or a course that will prepare them for a job in the productive sector of the economy.

There are two further points that may be made at this stage. First, it is possible that girls have reacted to the relative scarcity of places for them in the *PTU* system by differentially remaining on at the general secondary school. This will explain, in part, the predominance of women in terms of formal education reported in the first section of this chapter. That is, it is a statistical anomaly, a result of past Soviet failure to classify *PTU* training as formal education. But, secondly, continued attendance at the secondary school has in fact raised the educational level of women in the USSR; as their education has increased relative to that of men, they have come to dominate particular sectors. For example, in 1940 some 52·5 per cent of men enrolled in institutions of higher education were on courses that prepared them for careers in education; in 1975 the proportion of men students on these courses was less than a fifth. Among women, on the other hand, the proportion enrolled in these courses only fell from 67 per cent to 40 per cent and the actual number of students doubled. The emergence of an educated elite in the female labour force has encouraged occupational segregation. Given the sectoral pattern of earnings relativities, this segregation has resulted in the maintenance of, if not the increase in, sex-related earnings differentials.

Even if the role of the educational system in the generation and maintenance of occupational segregation is as set out in the previous paragraph, one should still ask what factors influence career choices by boys and girls. Is choice determined exclusively by the availability of places in vocational training establishments or do the aspirations of the sexes differ? Does subsequent labour force experience depend only on differences in access to training, or does the conflict in social roles also affect the Soviet woman's achievement? These topics are taken up in the next section.

## Education, Socialisation and Social Roles

In previous sections I have identified two principal ways in which the educational experience of men and women in the USSR differs, ways which, I suggest, contribute to occupational segregation and consequent earnings differentiation. First, men and women receive different amounts and types of professional or vocational training. Women are less likely than men to attend a post-secondary school training establishment; of those who are admitted to such institutions, women are less likely than men to pursue courses leading to careers in industry or other branches of the productive sphere. This tendency towards separateness in types of training appears to be more marked in the more developed regions of the country and also to have become more pronounced in the past twenty years or so.

Secondly, the time profile of education for women differs from that for men. Women are less likely than men to continue to study in their twenties and thirties. While at the age of 20 it appears that women, particularly urban women, have on average more formal education than men, much of their superiority has been eroded by the age of 30; it has probably disappeared by the age of 40.

In this section I examine these two features of Soviet society in somewhat more detail. First, some attempt is made to determine how far differences in access to post-school training facilities can be attributed to the recruitment policies operated by various secondary specialist, vocational and further educational establishments; or do they, at least in part, reflect differences in the aspirations of boys and girls? Secondly, it is suggested that differences in the frequency with which men and women pursue courses of further education in their twenties and thirties can be attributed to differences in their responsibilities for family formation and the running of the household. This argument leads on to a wider consideration of the impact that women's conflicting roles has upon their career prospects. This is taken up in Chapter 9.

One reason for the divergence in the educational experience of boys and girls after the age of 15 is the recruitment policy of the *PTU*. Girls are not eligible for many of the training programmes they offer due to the operation of the USSR's protective legislation. Similar factors may also affect admissions to secondary specialist and even some further educational institutions. But the sources of differentiation may not all be on the demand side, as it were, may not only be the result of official discrimination. In the past two decades a number of Soviet sociologists have investigated the problem of career choice and their work suggests that by the time they graduate from eighth grade Soviet boys and girls have formulated preferences about their future careers – and that the preferences of the two sexes differ. That is, there is evidence to suggest that part of the impetus for educational differentiation after incomplete secondary education comes from the supply side, from the children themselves (or their families).

There is an extensive Soviet literature on the problem of career choice and it is not possible to review it here comprehensively. Rather, I shall concentrate on the findings of one recent investigation, with an occasional reference to earlier work. The study to which I shall refer most frequently was based on interviews (questionnaires) with eighth graders and tenth (eleventh) graders in five West Siberian oblasts in 1973–5. It has the advantage that some attempt was made to follow up the children questioned and it therefore gives information about the extent to which the plans of school leavers were realised. Further, although in principle Konstantinovskii's results are applicable only to Siberia, in general terms at least they appear to conform to the findings of earlier investigators working in other parts of the RSFSR. Similar studies are available for the Baltic states but I am aware of little that relates to the Transcaucasus or Central Asia.

The core of Konstantinovskii's study consisted of presenting school leavers with detailed lists of occupations and asking them to indicate which they regarded as the most and least attractive or, to be more precise, to award them notional scores. Children were also asked about their plans for the next year and, as mentioned above, some attempt was made to ascertain how far these plans were realised. In presenting his results, Konstantinovskii casts light on three dimensions of the transition from school to work: first, he reveals something of the preferences of girls and boys for careers in different branches of the economy; secondly, he indicates differences in attitude towards specific occupations; finally, he deals with attitudes towards different channels of post-school training. On the first two topics he presents his findings in graphical form. This does not lend itself to a precise quantification of differences between the sexes and, no doubt with some degree of error, I have attempted to convert his histograms into numerical measures. The results are given in Tables 8.3 and 8.4.

Table 8.3 shows the distribution of preferences among branches of the economy for eighth grade children in rural and urban areas. Even at this level of aggregation, differences in the attitudes of boys and girls are apparent. First, considering those occupations that require no more than an incomplete secondary education: boys in both urban and rural areas rank such occupations in heavy industry more highly than girls. The same pattern appears to apply to jobs in construction too. Only rural boys think highly of jobs in

Table 8.3    *Percentage of Eighth Graders Expressing First Preferences for Various Occupations: Siberia, 1973*

| Branch/Sector | Urban | | Rural | |
|---|---|---|---|---|
| | Boys | Girls | Boys | Girls |
| Occupations requiring only incomplete secondary education: | | | | |
| Heavy industry | 5·2 | 1·9 | 4·4 | 1·3 |
| Construction | 4·0 | 1·8 | 4·6 | 1·8 |
| Agriculture | 3·9 | 1·1 | 10·7 | 3·1 |
| Communications | 0·8 | 2·0 | 3·2 | 6·0 |
| Light industry | 1·0 | 3·7 | 1·5 | 5·2 |
| Transport | 17·9 | 5·2 | 19·9 | 6·6 |
| Trade and catering | 2·5 | 4·9 | 2·3 | 7·3 |
| Occupations requiring secondary specialist or further education: | | | | |
| Heavy industry | 11·0 | 6·3 | 8·7 | 4·3 |
| Construction | 12·4 | 13·7 | 11·9 | 12·0 |
| Agriculture | 6·0 | 3·9 | 7·6 | 4·5 |
| Light industry | 1·5 | 5·9 | 2·0 | 5·0 |
| Transport | 9·9 | 3·3 | 7·4 | 2·2 |
| Education, etc. | 10·4 | 20·2 | 4·6 | 14·1 |
| Medicine | 13·3 | 26·2 | 11·2 | 26·6 |

*Source:* Derived from Konstantinovskii, 1977, Figures 3 and 5. Entries were obtained by measuring the heights of histogram columns for each of the five areas identified in the source, summing across population groups and averaging; column totals were then adjusted to sum to 100 per cent.

agriculture; rural girls are similar to urban boys in their regard for such jobs. Interestingly, more eighth grade rural boys expressed a preference for agricultural jobs not requiring special education than for those that did require further training. Presumably, if one is going to invest in further education, one might as well move to an urban area altogether. Boys are more scornful than girls of jobs in light industry; the sexes also differ in their attitudes towards trade and catering. Finally, transport was the most popular sector with three out of the four population groups – although it appealed to boys much more than to girls.

Turning to occupations requiring secondary specialist or further education: again boys were keener than girls on occupations in heavy industry, but all four groups were similar in their attitudes towards construction. Girls, both rural and urban, were indifferent between heavy and light industry; for boys, on the other hand, light industry came a poor second to heavy. Urban boys thought more highly of jobs in agriculture, even, than those in light industry! Finally, the sexes differed in their attitudes towards education and medicine. Some 40 to 45 per cent of girls preferred occupations in these sectors, whereas only 15 to 25 per cent of boys did so.

The figures in Table 8.3 suggest that by the age of 15 the career aspirations of boys and girls in the Soviet Union have diverged. But it is difficult to determine, from the data given, how different they are. For example, do the preferences of urban boys differ more from those of urban girls or rural boys?

Table 8.4  *Root-Mean-Squared Error in Post-Secondary School Allocation: Siberia, 1973–5*

|  | Boys: Plans and Realisation | Girls: Plans and Realisation | Plans: Boys and Girls | Realisation: Boys and Girls |
|---|---|---|---|---|
| Eighth Graders: |  |  |  |  |
| All | 9·6 | 13·3 | 14·3 | 10·7 |
| Urban | 10·9 | 10·4 | 14·6 | 10·5 |
| Rural | 10·6 | 15·4 | 17·1 | 12·1 |
| Tenth Graders: |  |  |  |  |
| All | 23·1 | 23·7 | 10·4 | 9·8 |
| Urban | 22·7 | 25·7 | 12·5 | 9·2 |
| Rural | 24·6 | 24·9 | 13·4 | 13·3 |

*Note:* Each entry is calculated according to the formula:

$$U = \left( \frac{1}{n} \sum_j \sum_i (x_{ij} - y_{ij})^2 \right)^{\frac{1}{2}}$$

where $x_{ij}$, for example, is the percentage of boys indicating an intention to enter the $i$th channel in area $j$ and $y_{ij}$ is the percentage that actually do so. The index $i$ ranges, for eighth graders, over work, *PTU*, secondary specialist and secondary school; for tenth graders, the last category is replaced by *VUZ*. The index $j$ ranges over the five regions used by the source.
*Source:* Derived from Konstantinovskii, 1977, Tables 1–6 and 8–13.

One way of measuring the extent of difference in the distributions given in the table is to compute the root-mean-squared error between them; that is, one sums the squares of differences between entries in any two columns, divides by the number of entries and takes the square root of the result. The RMS error is a measure of the average difference between entries in different columns. Proceeding in this way, one obtains:

|  | Urban Boys | Urban Girls | Rural Boys | Rural Girls |
|---|---|---|---|---|
| Urban Boys | – | 6·3 | 2·8 | 6·1 |
| Urban Girls |  | – | 7·8 | 2·3 |
| Rural Boys |  |  | – | 7·0 |

Thus, one can infer that, at the age of 15 at least, gender is more important than residence in determining occupational preferences. That is, the attitudes of urban girls are closer to those of rural girls than they are to those of urban boys and, similarly, the attitudes of urban boys are closer to those of rural boys than they are to those of urban girls. It is impossible to say whether the differences between urban and rural children of the same sex are significant in a statistical sense without some idea of the scaling of the indicator; this I am unable to provide.

Konstantinovskii also provides information on the attitudes of tenth graders towards occupations in different branches of the economy. I have not attempted to use it to generate an analogue to Table 8.3, since enough has been said to demonstrate the existence of sex-specific preferences in the

USSR. Casual inspection suggests that differences among 17-year-olds are not as marked as among eighth graders.

In addition to the analysis in terms of sectors, Konstantinovskii also provides information on the attitudes of boys and girls towards specific occupations (Konstantinovskii, 1977, Figures 4 and 6). The form in which he presents his data makes them hard to interpret, but in the light of the analysis of occupations undertaken by men and women in Chapters 4 and 5 above the following comments are of interest. There was a marked difference in the attitudes of rural boys and girls towards the occupation of tractor-driver: some 21 per cent of boys and only 2·5 per cent of girls were attracted by it. Similarly, by far the most popular profession among boys, both rural and urban, was that of driver, *shofer*, with some 42 per cent and 28 per cent of the two groups opting for it; girls on the whole did not find it appealing – only 6 per cent in urban areas and 12 per cent in the countryside ranked it highly. These differences are reflected in the occupational classifications given in various population censuses. They are similar to the patterns that have been reported by other scholars. (See, for example, Rekunov and Shlapak, 1969, p. 105.)

The third dimension of the transition from school to work on which Konstantinovskii's study casts some light involves the immediate plans of school leavers for further training and their realisation. All those who filled in his questionnaires were asked to indicate what they intended to do in the following year; the investigators attempted subsequently to find out what in fact happened to their respondents. Konstantinovskii gives the percentage of boys and girls in each of his ten population sub-groups intending to enter one of four transition channels: work, *PTU*, secondary specialist institution or secondary school for eighth graders, and the first three plus *VUZ* for tenth graders. He also gives the actual distributions that resulted. This material has been compressed into a set of RMS errors which are intended to measure how different the various distributions are from one another. These are given in Table 8.4.

Before turning to a discussion of these figures, however, I should like to make one or two comments about the distributions on which they are based. These suggest, for instance, that boys are about twice as likely as girls to opt for a *PTU* at the age of 15; girls are somewhat more likely than boys to want to go on to a secondary specialist institution. Girls are also more likely than boys to want to stay on at school: about half the girls and two-fifths of the boys were in this category. Only half of the girls who expressed a preference for secondary specialist education were in fact admitted to such programmes; fewer boys were admitted to *PTU* than wanted to go there too, but the divergence was not so marked. In fact, about half the boys in the sample and between two-thirds and three-quarters of the girls stayed on at school for another year or two. In general terms, these results conform to the allocations derived in previous sections; but Konstantinovskii suggests that a higher proportion of the cohort stays on in some form of education than do Korchagin's data. In part this may reflect the narrowness of the geographical base from which the sample is drawn, but it is also probably a result of Konstantinovskii's not discussing the fate of those who leave at the end of ninth grade. (For a discussion of this group, see Ksenofonteva, 1969, especially pp. 50–1.)

Turning to the figures in Table 8.4: although I would be hesitant about the verbal interpretation to be placed on these numbers, substantial differences do, I believe, reflect real differences in the degree of consonance between distributions. What inferences, then, can one make about the plans of boys and girls for the transition from school to work – and their realisation? First, it would seem that the plans of eighth graders, both boys and girls, are closer to reality than those of tenth graders. This is largely the result of frustrated aspirations for higher education among the latter group.

Secondly, among 15-year-olds, it seems that the plans of boys are more likely to be fulfilled than those of girls; this is largely due to a higher incidence of disappointments among rural girls than boys. In urban areas and among tenth graders there is little to choose between the sexes. On the whole, then, it does not seem that girls are less well adapted to their environment than boys. It is not the case that the aspirations of the two sexes are similar and that those of boys are achieved while those of girls are frustrated through the operation of a discriminatory admissions policy on the part of post-school training establishments. This is confirmed by the third and fourth columns of the table.

Among 15-year-olds there is at least as much dissonance between the plans of boys and girls as between the plans of either and their actual achievements. Further, the actual distribution of the two sexes among channels of transition is more similar than were initial plans. Among tenth graders the position is slightly different. The plans of boys and girls are markedly more similar to each other than are either to their actual achievements. That is, both sexes are alike in their excessive aspirations for higher education. Again, the actual distribution of the sexes is relatively similar.

The results derived from Konstantinovskii's data are similar in character to those that emerge from other studies of the career plans of youth in the Soviet Union. (See, for example, Petrov, 1969, p. 44; Ksenofonteva, 1969, p. 50.) Petrov, although he uses a different measure, also suggests that among eighth graders girls are slightly more likely to be frustrated in their aspirations than are boys.

Two conclusions emerge, I think, from this brief survey of sociological work on the aspirations of school leavers. First, differences in the type and amount of professional training acquired by men and women cannot be attributed solely to the recruitment policies operated by the various professional and vocational educational establishments. By the age of 15 boys and girls have themselves developed differing attitudes towards particular occupations and careers. This may be due to innate differences between the sexes; but it can more probably be attributed to sex-specific differences in socialisation.

The question of socialisation and sex-role typing is difficult and will not be pursued here. Clearly, family attitudes will play a part in developing perceptions of male and female among children and the jobs that are suited to such self-identifications. So will attitudes in society at large. It is also possible that the content of formal education contributes to the development of differing sex-role perceptions, in spite of the fact that boys and girls follow an essentially common curriculum up to the age of 15. A recent study claimed to have identified significant differences in the attributes commonly associated with men and women in Soviet first grade readers (Rosenhan, 1977) but this is suggestive rather than conclusive. It is important that material studied later in the school career also be examined.

This leads on to the second conclusion. It is interesting that, on the level of aggregation dealt with here, differences between the aspirations of boys and girls are more marked at the age of 15 than at the age of 17. In part, this is a reflection of the fact that those with the least ambition for an academic career (or whose families can least afford it - see Ksenofonteva, 1969, p. 51.) have selected themselves out of the sample base by the end of tenth grade. But one might also infer that the educational system (and society at large) has implanted a broadly similar appreciation of formal education among the children of both sexes who remain with it. This, at least, is consistent with data presented in earlier chapters: occupational segregation is more marked among manual workers than among those whom Soviet statisticians classify as engaged in primarily mental labour. But these similarities in outlook should not be overstated. In the upper classes of the Soviet school the child has some scope for subject specialisation and a broadly similar respect for education can conceal substantial differences in subjects studied. Already by the age of 15 sex-specific differences in attitude towards the sciences and the humanities are evident (Petrov, 1969, p. 42; Rekunov and Shlapak, 1969, p. 107). And these are mirrored in the subsequent careers of professional men and women, as we have seen.

So far in this section I have been concerned with differences in the attitudes of boys and girls towards education, vocational training and a variety of occupations. All of the material presented has dealt with individuals who had not yet become full-time members of the labour force. But a number of Soviet analysts have suggested that, in modern industrial conditions, what is required of the worker is not so much a high standard of initial general education as a willingness and an ability to continue studying for some years after he or she embarks on a career. Whether or not this behaviour pattern is in fact dictated by the character of modern technology, there can be little doubt that it is encouraged by Soviet institutional practice. And it is a pattern that accords badly with the other demands put upon the time of women.

In various studies in the past ten or twenty years Soviet sociologists and labour economists have recorded the proportion of workers in their samples who are attempting to combine paid employment with some form of study. The numbers are often substantial but, of more significance in this context, almost invariably a far higher proportion of men than women report that they are engaged in an attempt to raise their qualifications. Further, many of the women who report that they are engaged in extra-curricular study, are in fact doing little more than pursuing a general course of self-improvement or satisfying their general cultural interests (this at least is the interpretation that I place upon the last entry in the tabulation given below). In one sample of working women from Leningrad, the following proportions were reported to be engaged in various forms of educational activity (Kharchev and Golod, 1971, p. 54):

| General education | 1·04 |
|---|---|
| Specialist education | 2·76 |
| Courses for raising qualifications | 1·18 |
| Political education | 7·02 |
| All those engaged in study | 12·60 |

And these results are typical.

The same point is made by a rather different statistic. In 1974 the proportion of graduate students who were women was 27·9 per cent; this was virtually the same as in 1965 – 27·3 per cent (Shishkan, 1976, p. 137).

Soviet sociologists and labour economists also point to what they regard as the main reason why the behaviour of the sexes differs so markedly – the greater obligations incurred by women in caring for the home and raising children. This is brought out by the following figures. In one sample of working women in the Moldavian SSR, more than a quarter of those without children claimed to be continuing with their studies; this dropped to 13 per cent among women with one child, 9 per cent among those with two and 0·6 per cent among those with four or more (Shishkan, 1976, p. 143). These figures are high when compared with those reported by most other investigators. More typical are the following, taken from Kotlyar and Turchaninova, 1975, p. 126):

| *No. of children* | *% of women studying* |
|:---:|:---:|
| 0 | 11·8 |
| 1 | 4·5 |
| 2 | 3·0 |
| 3+ | — |

The same source also reports that whereas 17·9 per cent of single women claimed to be pursuing some course of study, only 3·8 per cent of married women and 2·8 per cent of widows and divorcees made a similar claim.

Among manual workers, certainly, and also possibly among professional groups, the accepted procedures for career advancement in the Soviet Union operate to the detriment of women as a sex. The initial acquisition of a technical skill involves attendance at a *PTU* or a *tekhnikum* and relatively few women are accepted at the former. Although girls make up more than half of all students at secondary specialist training facilities, their numerical superiority in these institutions does not compensate for their lack of numbers at the *PTU*. A majority of women in industry have had to make do with the training offered by the *BIU* system; in other sectors women too often have to rely upon their general secondary education.

Further advancement in industry involves the acquisition of higher skill grades. This involves the worker in demonstrating knowledge as well as practical competence. Too often it also requires attendance at courses 'for the raising of qualifications'. And these frequently take place out of working hours. Not only is it the case that the material covered in these courses is assimilated more easily by those who have had the benefit of a *PTU* training, but also the key initial steps in this procedure are taken between the ages of 20 and 30 which for women 'coincides with the time when their children are being born and need to be looked after, when they are involved in setting up home and looking after their families' (Kotlyar, 1973, p. 398). By the time the children are able to look after themselves, when women have time to devote to their careers, it is often too late. They have been outdistanced by their male contemporaries. Although this procedure is most clear-cut in the case of industrial and other workers, essentially similar factors affect the promotion prospects of women in the professions and the services sector. This no doubt accounts in part for the male-dominated status hierarchies observed in education, in medicine, in the universities, and so on.

There is some suggestion, too, that the real difficulties that women's double burden places in the way of their long-term career advancement are compounded by an unwillingness of managers (or superiors) to invest in women. Knowing that, often, women's domestic responsibilities adversely affect their performance on 'improvement courses', managers are sometimes reluctant to put them forward. This then develops into a vicious circle: sensing that they have few prospects for advancement, women are less willing to make the considerable effort necessary to improve their qualifications; because few women study, managers are confirmed in their belief that further training for women is a bad investment, and so on:

> for many women workers at the enterprises studied, there is little to be gained from combining work and study; this undoubtedly reduces the attractiveness of such a course to women. The undervaluation by enterprise managers of the significance of raising women workers' qualifications and even, sometimes, the deliberate downgrading of women acts as a factor that inhibits the growth of skills among this section of the labour force. (Kotlyar and Turchaninova, 1975, p. 82)

The domestic responsibilities of women, to which I have referred in the last few paragraphs, affect their performance in employment in more ways than through impeding the acquisition of qualifications. Just what these are and how women are affected by the services provided by the Soviet government is the subject of Chapters 9 and 10. But first I describe the way in which protective legislation and the provision of particular services have affected women's employment.

## Notes: Chapter 8

1  Those readers who would like a more detailed account of the Soviet educational structure should consult De Witt, 1961; Jacoby, 1975, is an excellent journalist's account that provides a flavour of the reality that lies behind the formal structures described in more academic sources.
2  These estimates were derived from distributions given in Stepanyan, 1975, p. 191. The top three categories (higher, incomplete higher and secondary specialist) were combined into one in the source and a weight of 14·5 years was used in the calculations reported in the text.
3  These results were based on a survey of 11,000 persons at twenty-two industrial

plants of which two-thirds were located in the RSFSR. The branches covered were machinebuilding, textiles, garments, meat-processing and baking. Kotlyar and Turchaninova, 1975, p. 62.

4   The equation given in the test was estimated excluding the entry for Tadjikistan which, from the scattergram, appeared to be anomalous. The equation was also estimated using data on the relative educational attainments of the occupied population. Results were broadly similar but the coefficient of determination was not as high:

$$R_k = 1 \cdot 1451 - 0 \cdot 2174 E_k^* \qquad R^2 : 0 \cdot 494 \qquad DF: 10$$
$$\phantom{R_k = } (16 \cdot 8) \qquad (3 \cdot 13)$$

where $E_k^*$ is the ratio of the average years schooling of occupied women to occupied men in the $k$ th republic in 1970.

5   Although in so far as the new policy of ensuring that all those who attend a *PTU* also complete the secondary educational syllabus is successful, this fact will surely be acknowledged in the statistics.

6   Since 1970, the Soviet statistical handbooks have ceased to publish figures relating to the sex-composition of those admitted to *PTU*. It is reported, however, that in 1972 girls made up 22·9 per cent of those studying in these establishments (Starodub, 1975, p. 62). A figure of 22·7 per cent for 1974–5 is implied by Rogovskii, 1976, p. 54.

*Chapter 9*

# Protective Legislation and Other Services for Women

In both socialist theory and Soviet official thinking, sexual equality must be predicated upon the fullest possible participation of women in the social economy and the political life of the state. The analysis of Chapter 3 showed that the goal of full employment for women had been largely achieved by 1970 and that even as early as 1940 female participation rates were extremely high by international standards. The very high levels of female employment achieved in the USSR in the past forty years or so have emphasised the possibility of conflict between the roles of woman-as-worker and woman-as-mother or woman-as-wife. In this chapter I explore the ways in which the Soviet authorities have attempted to alleviate this conflict and to assist women in reconciling their divergent obligations. I also try to assess how far short-comings in the support and assistance provided by the state may be responsible for the continued occupational segregation described in previous chapters or, indeed, whether the policies pursued by the Soviet government have accentuated the unequal position of women in the Soviet labour market.

There are four facets to the assistance that the Soviet authorities provide to help women combine the roles of worker and mother. First, there are more or less elaborate regulations governing the terms and conditions of women's employment and restrictions on the range of occupations in which they can be hired; these are discussed on pages 164–73. Secondly, the Soviet social security system provides a number of financial benefits for women (and others are made available on special terms). Thirdly, the state and many Soviet enterprises provide subsidised pre-school child care facilities. These so-called welfare benefits are described on pages 173–82. Finally, official statements even in the 1920s have recognised the contribution that the development of the services sector can make to alleviating the burden of housework. This is dealt with on pages 182–8. In the next chapter, an attempt is made to assess the efficacy of these various policies in making it possible for the ordinary Soviet woman to combine motherhood with paid employment.

In fact, the analysis of this chapter suggests that these various Soviet policies have not achieved their aim. It is possible that the legislation regulating the terms and conditions of women's employment may have contributed to occupational segregation – at least among manual non-agricultural workers. More certainly, inadequacies in the support provided for mothers have adversely affected the continuity of women's employment, thus damaging promotion prospects. Similarly, the burden of housework, due in part to shortcomings in the services sector, has undermined women's commitment to their jobs, their willingness and ability to acquire skills. The problem of the so-called double burden may well have contributed to ill-health and declining birth rates. Indeed, it may not be too far-fetched to suggest that the nexus of problems that has emerged in the past ten or fifteen years is associated with the very high female participation rates achieved over this period, and that these problems have forced a reconsideration of the assumptions on which policy has been based since the revolution.

### Protective Legislation and Women's Employment

The widespread employment of women, upon which, as we have seen, the Soviet drive for sexual equality is based, immediately raises an issue of principle: should there be special laws regulating the terms and conditions of their employment or should they be hired on the same terms as men? This is not a problem unique to the Soviet Union; indeed, it was debated in the nineteenth century when the state first accepted a responsibility for regulating conditions in industry. Some feminist groups argue that the existence of special regulations applying only to women puts them at a disadvantage relative to men in hiring and promotion decisions and that they are thus discriminatory. Recent developments in the USA and the United Kingdom suggest that official policy is coming to share this opinion. But socialists in Eastern Europe and the USSR do not agree with this argument; they remain firmly convinced of the desirability of protective legislation and cite Marx's support for the Ten Hours Act in England as evidence of the orthodoxy of their position. The ILO also believes that special regulations for women are desirable. (For more details see Scott, 1976, pp. 17–20.)

The fact that women's terms and conditions of employment should be governed by different principles than those of men has long been an issue of socialist principle and has two consequences. First, there is no discussion of its desirability or otherwise in recent Soviet sociological or legal writing; there is even very little analysis of the premises on which regulations should be based. Secondly, the USSR has a long history of such regulation, dating back, in fact, to the first RSFSR Labour Code of 1922. Further, since in general the Soviets have shown a predilection for the introduction of law into industrial relations, some indication of changing official intentions can be gained by tracing changes in the legislation. (This, of course, raises the question of how far the law is obeyed in the USSR and of variations in the incidence of illegality at different periods. Some attempt will be made to comment on this question at various points below.)

The corpus of Soviet labour law contains provisions relating to four categories of women: there are regulations governing the conditions of employment of all women and restrictions on the jobs that they may do; in addition, there are supplementary provisions that relate to pregnant women, nursing mothers and those with young children. Changes in the nature and extent of protection offered to each of these groups since the early 1920s are examined below. But first, it is worth pointing out that none of the provisions of the Labour Code applies to collective farmers – and therefore kolkhoznitsy have only enjoyed the benefits of those protective elements included in kolkhoz law; these have been few (*Kommentarii* . . . , 1975, p. 13).

### All Women

There are three sorts of restrictions applying to women's employment to be found in Soviet labour law, although one of them has not been enforced since the 1920s – if it was then. There are restrictions on the weights that women can lift, the hours that they can work and the jobs that they can do. In 1932 the Soviet government issued a detailed set of regulations governing the maximum weights that women could be required to lift: on level surfaces a woman should not lift and carry more than 20 kilos (44 lb), nor should she be required to shift more than 115 kilos (253 lb) with the aid of a barrow (*Sbornik Zakonodatelnykh Aktov o Trude*, hereafter *SZAT*, 1961, p. 413). In the context of Soviet industry, both in the 1930s and even today, with its heavy reliance on manual labour in auxiliary occupations (see above, pages 83–6), some limit on the amount that women can be asked to lift is probably desirable. The actual limits specified in the 1932 regulation appear on the low side in terms of industrial requirements, even if the average woman might find them taxing. If they had been rigorously adhered to, they would surely have disadvantaged women in competition for loading and unloading jobs. Since many of these jobs are in fact done by women, one can but wonder whether these limits are adhered to. In any case, during the 1960s a number of commentators suggested that they were inadequate, first because the limits for single lifts were too high and secondly because the regulations imposed no limits on the weight that women could be asked to move in the course of a shift. As yet, however, there has been no official response to these suggestions for reform.

The RSFSR Labour Code of 1922 prohibited the employment of women on nightwork (defined as work between the hours of 10 p.m. and 6 a.m.) (*SZAT*, p. 756) but this restriction had been eroded before the end of the decade. In 1926 nightwork for women was permitted among seasonal workers (*SZAT*, 1961, p. 472) and in the next twenty years or so this clause in the law was widely ignored. In the RSFSR Labour Code of 1971 postwar practice has been codified: Article 161 states: 'The employment of women on nightwork is not allowed with the exception of those branches of the economy where this is called for by special need; in such cases it is permitted as a temporary measure' (*Kommentarii* . . . , 1975, p. 542). This is taken to sanction the widespread use of women on nightshifts in the textile industry and other branches employing a high proportion of female labour. Indeed, Article 161 constitutes so small a deterrent to the employment of women on nightwork that an attempt not to hire women for work on the railways because the job involved working at night was declared illegal under this Article (loc. cit.). Thus, as far as one can tell, Soviet enterprises face virtually no restrictions on the employment of ordinary women at night. The case of pregnant women, nursing mothers and those with small children is dealt with below.

Neither of the restrictions considered so far, however, is as important as those relating to the range of occupations open to women. It is these that form the core of Soviet protective legislation. The 1922 Code prohibited the employment of women in all exceptionally heavy and harmful occupations[1] and in underground mining. Exceptions were permitted only with the consent of the VTsSPS (the All-Union Council of Trade Unions) (*SZAT*, 1961, p. 403). This blanket prohibition was modified in 1932 when the *Narkom trud*, in consultation with the *VTsSPS*, produced a list of specified occupations in which the employment of women was prohibited. This list, with various amendments to be described below, governed the employment of women until 1978 when the State Committee on Labour and Social Questions promulgated a new one (*Byulleten Gosudarstvennogo Komiteta-SSSR po trudu i sotsialnymi voprosami*, 1978, pp. 3–23).

The list of occupations published in 1932 was detailed and little purpose would be served by reproducing it here. (The complete text can be found in *Byulleten finansovogo i khozyaistvennogo zakonodatelstva*, 1933, no. 47, pp. 29–30). In summary, however, it appears to have excluded the employment of women underground, in occupations involving molten metal, in occupations requiring the handling of some dangerous chemicals, in jobs involving exceptional hazards (like firemen) or continued heavy lifting (such as stokers on the railways or in the mercantile marine). The impression one gets from reading the decree is that the 1932 Regulations cover more occupations than did the blanket prohibition in the 1922 Code. But this may be misleading; the decree made no mention of provisions for retraining or relocating those displaced by the new law (and this was a feature of both subsequent substantive changes in the extent of protective legislation); and, certainly, a relaxation of the terms and conditions of women's employment would be more in keeping with the spirit of the times than would the imposition of greater restrictions.

In any case, the issue is somewhat academic if the position with regard to the employment of women underground is typical. Even before the publication of the decree, *Pravda* had advocated allowing women to work down the mines in 1930; and this position had been supported in a report published early in 1933 by the National Conference of Research Institutes on Female Labour. Throughout the decade the provisions of the law were widely disregarded and finally, in 1940, that section of the decree was repealed. (For details, see Schwartz, 1952, pp. 288–90.) Similarly, in 1938, the prohibition on employing women as stokers on the railways was lifted and in 1940 women were permitted to work as dockers (*SZAT*, 1961, pp. 410–11). Thus, by the beginning of the war, there was no legal prohibition on the employment of women in a number of jobs (some of them well paid) requiring considerable physical strength. And the press reports, cited by Schwartz, suggest that the law was being disregarded on a considerable scale in the previous decade. The war itself led to a substantial expansion of female employment in both prohibited and permitted jobs. Indeed, it seems that the most important effect of the 1932 decree, at least until the early 1950s, was to inhibit the training of women for skilled jobs in heavy industry – although the evidence even for this conclusion is not substantial.

But the 1932 decree remained on the statute books and, from the early

1950s, was certainly used to restrict access to industrial training facilities, as was shown in the previous chapter. Further, in 1957, the employment of women underground was again restricted; after that date women could work only in certain managerial or auxiliary positions in the mines (*SZAT*, 1970, pp. 760-2). More generally, the period since 1956 has been characterised by a concerted attempt to enforce the legal regulation of industrial relations. (For details up to 1965 see McAuley, 1969, *passim*.) It is to be expected that this will have had the effect of making the restrictions in the 1932 decree more operational.

In the later 1960s a number of commentators suggested that the list of prohibited occupations contained in the 1932 decree was outmoded; changes in industrial technology had rendered some listed occupations 'safe' for women while new techniques and new materials had made other non-listed jobs undesirable. In 1978 the authorities responded to these suggestions by publishing a revised list of occupations in which the employment of women was prohibited. In general terms, the new list is constructed on the same principles as the old one: women are excluded from occupations involving molten metal and many noxious chemicals, they are banned from jobs involving exceptional risks (e.g. fire-fighting, test pilots) or continuous heavy lifting. (In this last category, however, only some 'heavy' jobs are included.) But there are differences. First, the 1932 decree was drawn up in terms of activities, the 1978 one specifies occupations; this reflects, I think, the greater bureaucratic elaboration of industrial relations in the later period. Further, the 1978 list is more precisely specified. Secondly, the 1978 list covers a far wider range of industries than did that of 1932 - thirty-seven as opposed to twelve. In part this is no more than a reflection of the greater complexity of Soviet industrial structure after fifty years of rapid industrialisation, but there are substantive additions. Protection is extended to women working in agriculture (but not kolkhoznitsy) and some other non-manufacturing sectors. Finally, within individual branches, a wider range of occupations are now closed to women; changes are particularly marked within the chemicals industry.[2]

The 1932 and 1978 decrees deal with activities or occupations; they give no indication of the number of women actually or potentially employed in these jobs. I can think of no way of quantifying the restrictions that they impose. In general terms, however, given the apparent frequency with which the law was disregarded under Stalin, I suspect that the 1932 decree had little direct impact on women's employment before the mid-1950s. From that time on, in view of the greater attention paid to labour law, the 1932 decree may have contributed to the increased horizontal segregation recorded above. Throughout the period 1932-78 I believe that the 1932 decree has operated to restrict women's access to certain forms of industrial training; it may thus have contributed to the vertical segregation described in Chapter 5. Although the 1978 decree allows women to undertake some previously prohibited occupations, it is my impression that the relaxations are relatively minor and that the net effect of the new law will be to close off further areas of activity to women. If this is the case, one might expect an intensification of occupational segregation - at least among manual non-agricultural employees.

(This may not be evident in the 1979 Census, since that was probably taken before the effects of the 1978 decree had had time to show themselves.)


*Pregnant Women*

The RSFSR Labour Code of 1922 contained three articles that gave extra protection to pregnant women: it was forbidden to ask them to work overtime (or, of course, to employ them on nightwork), they could not be sent on trips, *kommandirovki*, after the fifth month without their consent and they were entitled to eight weeks maternity leave before the birth of their child (*SZAT*, 1961, p. 403; Dewar, 1956, p. 232). In subsequent years the first and third of these privileges were substantially eroded before being gradually reinstated along with certain other benefits. Since the course of events is complicated, I will deal with regulations governing overtime and maternity leave before dealing chronologically with the introduction of other provisions.

With the onset of full-scale industrialisation, during the First Five-Year Plan, there was a general disregard for the limitations on hours of work built into the labour legislation; this applied to all workers, men as well as women, and to both pregnant women and those with small children. (For details see Schwartz, 1953, pp. 278-9.) The trend towards compulsory overtime for pregnant women continued, or rather was intensified, during the 1930s, although there was no change in the law until 1941. At that date overtime was prohibited only after the sixth month (Schwartz, 1953, p. 287). In 1944 this was reduced to the fifth month; subsequently it was lowered to the fourth month (*SZAT*, 1961, p. 414) and in 1971 it was again established that pregnant women could not be required to work overtime (or be employed on nightwork or sent on *kommandirovski*). This prohibition operates from the date that pregnancy is established (*Kommentarii* . . . , 1975, p. 543).

The 1922 Code guaranteed pregnant women eight weeks maternity leave before the birth of a child (six weeks for those employed in non-manual occupations). It also provided for eight weeks post-partum leave but this will be dealt with below in the section dealing with nursing mothers. According to the 1922 Code maternity leave was available to all employed women, but in 1927 this privilege was restricted to those who had worked for at least six months in the year preceding the year of the pregnancy. (This restriction was of more importance in determining eligibility for maternity benefits; Schwartz, 1953, p. 318.) In 1936, when abortion was made illegal, maternity leave was increased to eight weeks prior to the birth for all women; in 1938, however, this was reduced to five weeks where it stayed until 1956 when it was again raised to eight weeks (ibid., pp. 319-20; *SZAT*, 1961, p. 404). This is still the position today.

In addition to the three privileges set out in the 1922 Labour Code, there have been two further legislative benefits extended to pregnant women in the past half-century or so. In 1937, it was enacted that managers must transfer pregnant women to lighter work, without loss of pay, if the medical authorities deemed it desirable (*SZAT*, 1961, p. 403). This requirement is still in force. In 1949 women were given the right to transfer to work nearer their homes during pregnancy while preserving a continuous employment record, *nepreryvnyi stazh*; this was important for social security purposes, but was probably not a concession that many women availed themselves of. If such jobs were available, it is likely that women would have moved anyway – in so far as the Stalinist law allowed. In any case, this provision has disappeared from the 1971 Labour Code (*SZAT*, 1961, p. 404).

### Nursing Mothers

The 1922 Code prohibited the employment of nursing mothers on nightwork and overtime, it guaranteed them breaks for feeding their children (with pay and in addition to meal-breaks) and it provided for eight weeks post-partum leave. As with the concessions given to pregnant women, these privileges were seriously eroded during the 1930s and 1940s, but since then they have been reinstated and, indeed, nursing mothers (and those with small children) have been given further substantial concessions. Again, because the timing of various changes is complex, I shall deal with the three categories of concession sequentially rather than attempt to provide a chronological account for all three taken together.

First, nightwork and overtime: when the Soviet authorities introduced legislation governing the terms and conditions of those employed in seasonal work in 1926, nursing mothers continued to be exempt from nightwork (*SZAT*, 1961, p. 472). But they suffered along with the rest of the labour force from the general disregard for the laws governing hours of work during the 1930s; in 1941, women were exempted from overtime only for the first six months after delivery (Schwartz, 1953, p. 300). In 1944 they were again explicitly exempted from nightwork and this exemption is repeated in the 1971 Code. In fact, in the new code, the exemption lasts for as long as the mother continues to breast-feed her child; there is no chronological limit imposed (*SZAT*, 1961, p. 414; *Komentarii* . . . , 1975, p. 543).

In 1956 the concession relating to feeding-breaks was extended by giving women the right to take one of these breaks at the end of their shift on days preceding public holidays or rest-days. In effect, this reduced the time that nursing mothers had to spend at work on these days by half an hour without loss of pay (*SZAT*, 1961, p. 293).

In the 1922 Code post-partum maternity leave was set at eight weeks for manual workers and six weeks for those in non-manual jobs (Schwartz, 1953, p. 318). In 1936, when abortion was made illegal, this was raised to eight weeks for all women. In 1938, however, this was reduced by half to four weeks; it was raised again to six weeks in 1944 and finally eight weeks post-partum maternity leave was reintroduced in 1956 (ibid., p. 320; *SZAT*, 1961, p. 404). At the same time women became eligible for three months unpaid leave after the termination of their maternity leave (ibid., p. 406). That is, they could remain at home for up to five months after the birth of a child without losing their job. Further, at the same date, women who left their jobs in connection with a birth were entitled to preserve an uninterrupted employment record for social security purposes if they returned to paid employment before the child's first birthday (loc. cit.). Finally, in 1968 these two concessions were elided: after that date, women were entitled to take unpaid leave until the child's first birthday without losing either job or uninterrupted employment record. In this respect at least, recent Soviet practice is more liberal than the 1922 Code.

### Women with Small Children

For the most part, the Labour Code of 1922 and subsequent legislation only recognised two categories of women entitled to special concessions: those who were pregnant and nursing mothers. But there are scattered references to those with small children, whether or not they are being breast-fed, and in recent years the trend has been to extend concessions to women with progressively older children. In 1925, for example, it was laid down that single mothers with children under 1 year old could be dismissed only with the consent of a labour inspector (*SZAT*, 1961, p. 111). In 1949 the privilege of transferring to work nearer home without loss of uninterrupted employment record was extended to all mothers with children under 1 year old (ibid., p. 404). In 1966 the privilege of up to one year's unpaid leave without loss of *stazh* was extended to women adopting babies directly from a maternity home (*SZAT*, 1970, p. 758). In the 1971 RSFSR Labour Code, women with children between the ages of 1 and 8 years can only be called upon for overtime or sent on *kommandirovki* with their consent (*Kommentarii . . .*, 1975, p. 543).[3]

The protection offered by Soviet labour law to pregnant women, nursing mothers and those with small children, in formal terms at least, is substantial. By the late 1960s or early 1970s the law had re-established or extended the concessions embodied in the codes adopted immediately after the revolution. And there is reason to suppose that, for the most part, the law is observed. In an attempt to force managers to pay more attention to the law, in 1960 it was made a criminal offence to refuse to hire a woman, to dismiss her, or to lower her wages simply because she was pregnant or because she was a nursing mother (*SZAT*, 1961, p. 404). The courts have shown themselves reluctant to initiate proceedings under this Article, so probably it should be seen more as a declaration of intent than a real threat. But in subsequent years accounts of cases in which enterprises have attempted to infringe upon the rights of pregnant women and nursing mothers have continued to appear. (It is not clear whether these cases represent isolated aberrations or are symptomatic of a more widespread disregard for the law, the tip of an iceberg most of which never gets as far as litigation.) My feeling is that existing Soviet law goes a considerable way towards helping women cope with the demands of pregnancy and paid employment; it also now alleviates the conflicts faced by those with children under 1 year old. It does little, however, for those with older children. By the same token, since it does make real concessions, it tends to make women less attractive as potential employees to managers and those responsible for hiring and promotion decisions. This may help to explain the continued vertical segregation in Soviet employment described in Chapter 5.

In addition to the general regulations covering the terms and conditions of women's employment discussed so far, there are two additional pieces of legislation that apply to women in particular occupations, specifically those who drive tractors and trucks. In 1931 a law was passed requiring managers to give women preference in access to caterpillar tractors, tractors with starters, and so on. At the same time, on presentation of a medical certificate, women were entitled to be transferred to other work for three days during menstruation (*SZAT*, 1970, p. 760). Thirty-eight years later, in 1969, another law was passed which entitled women operators of mechanical equipment in agriculture to twelve days extra holiday per year (as opposed to six extra days for men) and a reduction of 10 per cent in their daily output norms. Again, managers were enjoined to allocate women to equipment with the most up-to-date seating, with cabins, with starter motors, and so on (ibid., p. 759). In view of the very small numbers of women employed as drivers, tractor-drivers, and so forth, in the USSR, it is not worth spending more time on the details of these pieces of legislation.

In assessing the contribution of law to the reconciliation of the conflicting demands that paid employment and motherhood impose upon the Soviet woman, I believe that there are three issues to be discussed. First, how effective have the various provisions been? How well has the law operated to protect the interests of mother and child? From the various comments given above, it will be seen that for much of the period covered by this book, legal protection has been limited and that which was given has often been ignored. The present position, however, is reasonably satisfactory. But the law should not be considered in isolation and further discussion of this issue will be deferred until Soviet assistance through the social security system has been discussed.

Secondly, how well does existing legislation protect the interests of women as workers? Again, this has been raised already and a final assessment will have to wait until other aspects of state policy have been reviewed. But it is my belief that the law has acted to restrict the range of occupational choice open to women and thus increased the supply of labour to recognised 'women's work'. This, in turn, may have contributed to the continuing differences in average earnings accruing to the two sexes. But I have been unable to derive a quantitative estimate of the significance of this factor.

In view of these conclusions, the third issue is that of the propriety of special regulations governing the employment of women. Is such paternalism justified or should individual women be permitted to decide for themselves what they want to work at? The existence of precise legal regulations governing the employment of pregnant women and those with small children can ensure uniformity of treatment and are, it seems to me, essential for equity. Further, if one wishes to encourage female participation, these regulations should be generous. Such a legal framework can protect the interests of the individual who, through ignorance, immobility, or lack of suitable alternative employment, is liable to be exploited by enterprises. (This is as true of a socialist state like the USSR as it is of a market economy like the United Kingdom.)

But the desirability of regulations governing the employment of women in other circumstances is less clear-cut. Again, perhaps one can distinguish between regulations that limit the employment of women in heavy manual work, as stokers on steam trains, for example, and those that restrict their employment in a polluted atmosphere – in the chemicals industry, for instance. As far as the first category is concerned: for the most part the health hazards associated with these jobs are well understood and derive from attempts to work beyond the limits of one's physical capacity. The appropriate policy in such cases would seem to be to set upper limits on the physical exertion that can be required of a worker without regard for sex and allow self-selection to determine who in fact will do the job. This would make the appropriate allowance for intra-sex variations in physical capacity (that is, strong women could do the jobs and weak men would have to look elsewhere). Setting the limits on physical exertion at a reasonably high level would enable the authorities to minimise the labour cost of particular operations; it is to be expected that such jobs would continue to be done primarily by men, but competent women would not be precluded. Exploitation of the weak and defenceless in such circumstances would best be avoided by the maintenance of a buoyant demand for labour and the provision of a variety of job opportunities in different locations. On this argument, for example, the Soviet prohibition on the employment of women at the coal-face would be misguided. Women who think that they can fulfil the existing output norms in the Soviet coal industry should be permitted to sign on as miners.

But the assumptions underlying the argument of the last paragraph can be challenged. Perhaps the risks associated with such manual jobs are not well understood; perhaps individual women do not have a clear idea of their own capacities; perhaps individuals are sufficiently shortsighted to undertake such jobs for the high current rewards they offer – even though they recognise that this will seriously damage their health. In a pure market economy, in which the individual himself or herself paid for the medical services consumed as a result of such shortsightedness, this would not matter. The decision to ruin one's health for current gain would be a self-regarding action in Mill's terms. But ignorance, the presence of dependants and the existence of a state medical system imply that such decisions have external effects. They impose costs on other members of society. It is at least possible that, when these are internalised, the most appropriate policy is to exclude women from certain categories of employment. This may be inequitable in individual cases but probably involves the expenditure of fewer resources than would a system in which applications for employment were dealt with on a person-to-person basis.

Where the risks to health come, not from actions involved in the job itself, but from the long-term effects of atmospheric or other pollution on the body, the second category identified above, the emphasis is slightly different. Since individual workers are more likely to be ignorant of the long-term effects in question, there is a strong case for the introduction of legal controls on working conditions and official monitoring of emission standards, and so forth. But even if one accepts the principle of public control, one still has to resolve the issue of discrimination between the sexes. If one decides on common standards, since the ill-effects of many substances depend upon body weight and since in general men are heavier than women, standards will have to be set on the low side. Since control of emissions involves a real cost, this will result in higher production costs than in other circumstances. This suggests that there is a *prima facie* case for discrimination. In so far as prolonged exposure to noxious substances leads to accumulations in the body of the worker that might result in foetal damage, the case for discrimination is strengthened. This is an external effect that is usually much stronger in the case of women than of men. On balance, then, I would suggest that there is some scope for differential restrictions on the employment of men and women. This is not to say, however, that all the occupations actually included in either the Soviet 1932 or 1978 decrees can be justified on these grounds – or that there are not others that should have been included. I do not possess enough knowledge to pass judgement on this question. But I do not think that one can claim that the Soviet approach to the regulation of the terms and conditions of employment of women is wrong in principle.

So far, this chapter has concentrated on the rights and privileges enjoyed by Soviet working women under various provisions of the labour law. But legal protection does not exhaust the assistance to women provided by the Soviet state. They also derive welfare benefits from the social security system. These are described in the next section.

## Social Security Benefits for Women

The Soviet government's assistance to women in combining the roles of worker and mother or wife is not limited to legal protection under the labour code. In addition, working women are entitled to a variety of financial benefits under the Soviet social security system on somewhat different terms than men and the state also subsidises the provision of pre-school child care facilities. In this section I describe the terms on which various cash benefits have been made available over the past half-century or so; the development of day-nurseries and kindergartens is discussed on pages 178–82.

The three major cash benefits to which both men and women in the Soviet Union are entitled are old age pensions, disability pensions and sickness benefits. In addition, working women are entitled to maternity pay. Secondly, women are entitled to a number of grants and payments, either as a result of their own employment or on their husband's account. Finally, certain benefits are payable to women with children, whether they work or not. The development of each of these categories of benefit is described briefly below. (More detail can be found in McAuley, 1979, ch. 11.)

### Old Age Pensions

Pensions and social security were among the first areas to be legislated for by the new Soviet government after the revolution. The system introduced at that date conformed in most respects to the programme set out by Lenin at the Prague Party Congress in 1912; but economic disruption and shortage of resources generally meant that many of the provisions in the law were only partially implemented or were neglected altogether. After 1931 the legal framework itself became more restrictive in terms of entitlement and benefit levels tended to fall behind levels of real wages – which themselves were low enough in the Stalin years. But the system as a whole was reorganised in 1955 and the bewildering variety of industrially based pension schemes was unified into a single programme covering the vast majority of state employees. (Teachers, doctors and certain other categories of white-collar personnel continue to enjoy their own scheme in which entitlement depends on length of service rather than age; although both schemes use both criteria, as will be seen below.) Kolkhozniki had to wait until 1965 before a national scheme was set up for them. Prior to that year collective farmers were dependent upon payments from their kolkhoz in sickness, old age or infirmity; in fact, most received little or nothing from this source.

Under the 1955 scheme, women are entitled to an old age pension at the age of 55 if they have worked for at least twenty years; men can retire at 60 if they have a twenty-five year employment record (Zakharov and Piskov, 1972, p. 180). When pensions were introduced for collective farmers, kolkhoznitsy could retire at 60 (given an employment record of twenty-five years) but two years later these entitlement limits were reduced to those used for state employees (ibid., p. 270). Women who have been employed underground, in hot shops, in heavy conditions or in certain specified textile occupations are entitled to a pension at the age of 50 – given a twenty-year employment record. The same concession applies to women disabled in the Second World War and to kolkhoznitsy who live in the Far North (ibid., pp. 180 and 270). Women who have given birth to five children and raised them to the age of 8 are also entitled to a pension at the age of 50; for these women only fifteen years' employment is necessary. (This applies to both state employees and kolkhoznitsy; ibid., pp. 181 and 270.)

The value of the pension received depends upon earnings in the twelve months preceding retirement. Although the formula used is complicated, in general terms the pension is set at half one's earnings subject to a minimum of 45 rubles a month and a maximum of 120 rubles. Pensions are lower in rural areas and, initially, a less generous formula was used to calculate kolkhoznik pensions. A more favourable formula is used to calculate the pensions of those entitled to early retirement due to their conditions of work. The same formulae are used for both men and women but, since women's earnings are usually lower than those of men, women receive the smaller pensions on average. When compared with average wages, Soviet pension levels are not generous, but the authorities have, over the past fifteen years or so, progressively removed restrictions on continued employment by those in receipt of a pension.

*Disability Pensions*

The present Soviet social security scheme recognises three levels of disability and two sources of disability. Class I invalids are those incapable of work and in need of attendance; Class II invalids are those incapable of work; and Class III invalids are those whose working capacity has been impaired. Disability can arise either as a result of an industrial accident or of a (specified) occupational disease; or it can result from general illness. If disability is occasioned by an industrial accident or an occupational disease, both men and women are entitled to a disability pension irrespective of the number of years that they have worked. If, however, disability arises as a result of general illness, a pension is paid only to those with a sufficient employment record. The number of years of employment required depends upon one's age at disablement and there are separate scales for men and women. In general terms, men are required to have worked half the years between the age of 20 and the age of disablement while women are only required to have worked a third of them. That is, a man who becomes disabled at the age of 40, for example, will require an employment record of at least ten years if he is to qualify for a pension; a woman needs only seven years (Zakharov and Piskov, 1972, p. 183). Until 1965 kolkhozniki were not entitled to disability pensions; since 1967 Class I and Class II pensions have been available to collective farmers on the same terms as to state employees. Kolkhozniki are still not entitled to Class III pensions (ibid., p. 271).

The value of the disability pension depends upon the cause of disability and one's previous earnings. In the past pensions have been niggardly, especially for those suffering from general illness, but the position was improved somewhat in the 1970s. (For details see McAuley, 1979, ch. 11.) The same formulas are used for men and women.

*Sickness Benefits*
Both men and women suffering from a temporary loss of working capacity, certified by a physician, are entitled to sick pay. Benefits are paid to state employees from the first day of incapacity for as long as the illness lasts (Zakharov and Piskov, 1972, p. 58). Kolkhozniki have only been entitled to sick pay since 1970 and there are restrictions on the length of time for which it can be paid (ibid., p. 108). In addition, both kolkhozniki and state employees are entitled to sick pay if they have to stay at home to care for a sick member of their family. Sick pay is only available in these circumstances if there is no other member of the family able to care for the invalid (with the exception that mothers with a child under 2 years of age are entitled to such a benefit irrespective of the availability of other family members). Until 1974-5 benefits were paid in these circumstances only for three days and to kolkhoznitsy only if they would have been called upon to work for those days (ibid., pp. 58 and 108); in the Ninth Five-Year Plan period, however, the number of days for which benefit would be paid in these circumstances was raised from three to seven (Rzhanitsyna, 1979, p. 63).

The value of the sickness benefit paid depends upon the length of a worker's uninterrupted employment record: those with less than three years in the same job receive 50 per cent of their average earnings and this rises to 100 per cent for those with more than eight years in the same job. Workers who do not belong to a trade union get half the above rates subject to a daily minimum (Zakharov and Piskov, 1972, p. 59). In 1974-5 these restrictions were waived for workers in families with three of more children: these now receive 100 per cent of their average earnings irrespective of their union status or employment record (Rzhanitsyna, 1979, p. 63).

*Maternity Benefits*
According to the 1922 Labour Code, women were entitled to maternity benefits equal to their previous wages for the full sixteen weeks of their maternity leave (Schwartz, 1953, p. 318). Further, this benefit was available to all working women (i.e. state employees, not peasants). In 1931 benefits equal

to one's previous pay were available only to those women who had been members of a union for three years or more and who had been employed at their last job for at least two years. Those who failed to meet these conditions qualified only for reduced benefits (ibid., p. 319). In 1938 the eligibility conditions were tightened even further in that women were then required to have worked for at least seven months in the year preceding the year in which they took their pregnancy leave in order to qualify for benefit at all (ibid., p. 320). This condition was dropped in the 1955 reform, but the dependence of maternity pay on union status and length of uninterrupted employment was retained (Zakharov and Piskov, 1972, pp. 70-1). Kolkhoznitsy became eligible for maternity pay (at a rate equal to two-thirds of their previous average earnings but not less than 40 kopeks a day) only in 1965 (ibid., p. 118). In 1973 all female state employees once again became entitled to maternity benefits equal to previous average earnings (Kotlyar and Shlemin, 1974, p. 118). It is not clear whether this provision also applies to kolkhoznitsy.

In addition to the maternity pay described above, the 1922 Labour Code provided for the payment of a maternity grant (to assist in the purchase of a layette) and a second lump sum payment at the time that the child was weaned. It appears that, even in the 1920s, these were not paid at the rates laid down in the statutes and while provisions for such payments have remained in the law, both the amounts issued and the conditions on which they were paid have become more restrictive. At the present time they are payable only to those with wages very close to the minimum. (For details, see Schwartz, 1953, pp. 318-20, and McAuley, 1979, pp. 279-80.)

*Survivor Pensions*

In the 1920s it was possible for wives (or even husbands) as well as minor children, minor siblings and parents to claim a survivor's pension on the death of the family's breadwinner. But this was early seen to be in conflict with the policy of encouraging female participation and in 1928 this right was restricted to wives (or husbands) who had already reached the age of retirement (Schwartz, 1953, pp. 328-9). This position was reaffirmed in the 1955 Pension Law, although additionally a relative or spouse who is not already employed and who is occupied with the care of children under the age of 8 years is entitled to be treated as a dependant for purposes of calculating the value of the pension payable (Zakharov and Piskov, 1972, p. 185). Since the value of the pension at the time increased little as the number of dependants rose, it is doubtful if this clause allowed many widows the luxury of staying home to look after their families. Indeed, neither old age nor disability pensions make any very substantial allowance for dependants (before 1974 the old age pension, for example, was increased by 10 per cent for one dependant and by 15 per cent for two or more; in 1974 these were changed to fixed (but not very munificent) ruble amounts); rather, the Soviet system is designed to offer personal insurance against loss of earnings; women are thereby encouraged to make provision for themselves and are penalised if they do not do so.

So far in this section, discussion has centred on benefits available to women who are employed – or whose husbands work. In addition, limited assistance is made available to women with children, irrespective of their employment status. First, there are child allowances. Since 1948 a payment of 20 rubles has been made to each woman on the birth of her second child; on the birth of a third child, a woman receives 65 rubles and 4 rubles per month from the child's first to its fifth birthday. The size of both the lump sum payment and the monthly allowance increases until the eleventh child (when they are 250 rubles and 15 rubles per month). Secondly, unmarried mothers receive 5 rubles a month for one child (7·50 rubles for two and 10 rubles for three or more) until the child reaches the age of 12 (or is adopted or placed in a children's home) (ibid., pp. 576–9). The amounts paid under these schemes have remained unchanged since the late 1940s and, with the trend to smaller families, have become increasingly irrelevant – especially in the European part of the country.

Because of this, and also to deal with persisting pockets of poverty, in 1974 the Soviet authorities introduced a so-called family income supplement. This allows for the payment of 12 rubles per child per month to any family whose per capita income is less than 50 rubles per month. Payment continues until the child's eighth birthday (or until the family's income rises above the official poverty level). (For more details see McAuley, 1979, pp. 282–3).

A full assessment of the adequacy of these various welfare payments and of the assistance they provide to women in combining the roles of mother and worker must wait until the next chapter. But three preliminary comments can be made at this stage. First, although the social security system provides for women to retire at an earlier age than men, no very clear justification for this concession has been given. Rather, most commentators make some vague reference to the extra burden that women shoulder in raising a family. This has led one economist at least to suggest that the retirement age for women should be raised and that early retirement should become a privilege extended only to mothers (Shishkan, 1976, p. 73). In principle, given the gerontocratic tendencies that the Soviet system shows, this might make it easier for women to achieve positions of responsibility. In practice, however, the benefits accruing from such a change in the law are likely to be minor. At the present time there is little to stop those state employees who wish to from continuing to work after the official age of retirement. If women continue to retire earlier than men, it is presumably because they recognise that they are unlikely to receive further promotions, even if they remain at their jobs for a further five or ten years.

Secondly, for much of the period covered by this book, the levels of financial assistance provided under the various programmes intended to ease the burdens of motherhood have been low. This is still true of child allowances, although maternity benefits and sick pay have attained more appropriate levels within the last decade. But the periods for which these benefits are payable are still relatively short (however well they may compare with what is available in the market economies of Western Europe and North America). This has had two consequences. Most women have returned to the labour market soon after the birth of their children. Perhaps this was what the system designers intended but it has placed a strain on available pre-school child care facilities, a strain that, until recently, has been relieved by the extended family system. Where, however, day-nurseries have not been available and where there has been no babushka to fall back on, the arrival of children has led to a significant decline in family living standards. This in turn has contributed, I believe, to the substantial postwar decline in the Soviet birth rate. That is, the scale and character of financial assistance provided under the Soviet social security system have not been such as to enable a majority of Soviet women to combine the roles of mother and worker without strain.

## Pre-School Child Care Facilities

If married women are to participate actively in the social economy, arrangements must be made to relieve them of some of the responsibilities that occupy so much of their time in a traditional society. This was clearly recognised by late-nineteenth-century socialist theorists and by Soviet writers in the 1920s. The literature of the period contains a number of descriptions of the new society in which family life has been replaced by communal arrangements for cooking and eating, for the care of children and (although usually implicitly) for cleaning and laundry. At the time, these descriptions were little more than fantasies and little more is heard of most aspects of this dream after the onset of full-scale industrialisation. The only component of the new society to which the Soviet authorities remained committed was the partial socialisation of the rearing of children.

Throughout the period covered by this book, official Soviet government policy has stressed the desirability of pre-school child care facilities. Day-nurseries and kindergartens, it is argued, are good for children in that they help to inculcate collectivist attitudes; they are also good for mothers in that they allow them to return to paid employment sooner than would otherwise be the case. Soviet propaganda also stresses the considerable resources that the state devotes to the provision of such facilities. And, indeed, not only do local authorities provide them, but the day-nursery or kindergarten is one of the services that many enterprises and organisations provide for their workers. The 1971 RSFSR Labour Code requires (or at least sanctions) enterprises employing large numbers of women to set up kindergartens and day-nurseries and this merely codifies an obligation first imposed in 1944 (*Kommentarii* . . . , 1975, pp. 557–8).

In fact, the scale of provision of pre-school child care in the Soviet Union has been rather more modest than official pronouncements and the casual comments of observers would lead one to believe. Some relevant figures are given in Table 9.1. These show that in 1940 some 2 million Soviet children were enrolled in these facilities; over the next thirty-five years the numbers attending have increased sixfold – but much of this growth took place in the 1960s and 1970s. Secondly, the figures show that pre-school child care is largely an urban phenomenon. In 1940 a little more than a quarter of the children attending day-nurseries and kindergartens lived in rural areas; in the next twenty years this proportion declined to a fifth, where it remained throughout the 1960s. It is only in the past decade that the share of rural residents in those attending pre-school child care facilities has started to

Table 9.1    *The Provision of Pre-School Child Care Facilities: USSR, 1940-75*

|  | Children Enrolled (thousands) | | | % of Age-Cohort Enrolled | | |
|---|---|---|---|---|---|---|
|  | All | Urban | Rural | All | Urban | Rural |
| 1940 | 1,953 | 1,422 | 531 | 6·42 | | |
| 1950 | 1,788 | 1,380 | 408 | | | |
| 1959 | 3,886 | 3,122 | 764 | 11·72 | 22·34 | 3·98 |
| 1970 | 9,281 | 7,380 | 1,901 | 30·63 | 50·74 | 12·07 |
| 1975 | 11,523 | 8,980 | 2,543 | | | |

*Note:* For 1939 the age-cohort was calculated as 70 per cent of those aged 0–9; for 1959–70 it was calculated as the sum of the cohort aged 0–4 and 40 per cent of that aged 5–9.

*Sources: Narodnoye obrazovanie*, Moscow, 1977, pp. 119–21; *Itogi* . . . , 1959, p. 49; *Itogi* . . . , 1970, Vol. II, Table 3.

increase; but their share is still less than it was in 1940.

The rates of growth in attendance at day-nurseries and kindergartens implied by the figures in Table 9.1 are impressive, but the base from which the USSR started in 1940 was low. The second panel of the table attempts to provide some further perspective on this question. It contains the results of a rough calculation of the availability of pre-school child care places for various years. The calculation is rough because the Soviet authorities do not publish a breakdown of the population by single ages. Taking the figures as they stand, however, they show that in 1940 little more than 6 per cent of Soviet children under the age of 7 (which, it will be remembered, is the age at which primary schooling starts in the USSR) were enrolled in child care facilities.

In 1959 this proportion had doubled; in that year an eighth of all children in the relevant age-group attended day-nurseries or kindergartens. The figures in Table 9.1 also show how great a disparity there was between urban and rural areas. At this time an urban child was more than five times as likely as a rural child to be enrolled in a child care facility – some 20 per cent of urban children attended kindergartens or similar while less than 4 per cent of rural children did so.

Eleven years later, in 1970, some 30 per cent of the relevant age-group attended pre-school child care facilities;[4] although there were still large differences in the availability of child care places between urban and rural areas, the disparity was less than it had been at the beginning of the previous decade. Urban children were now only four times more likely than those in rural areas to go to a kindergarten. Also, for the first time, in 1970 a majority of the under-7s in urban areas were enrolled at kindergartens or day-nurseries.

From another point of view, it is possible to argue that the scale of effort implied by the Soviet figures for 1970 is of the same order of magnitude as government expenditure on this age-group in a country like Britain – although resources are allocated differently. In the United Kingdom primary education starts at the age of 5 – thus two-sevenths (28·6 per cent) of the relevant age-group will be enrolled in the infant departments of our primary schools.

Although nursery education is not widespread, in 1975 some 5 to 6 per cent of under-5s attended day-nurseries, kindergartens, or playgroups (Heitlinger, 1979, p. 113). This means that about a third of the age-group were involved in some form of child care facility. If this calculation is accepted, then the figures in Table 9.1 imply that for much of the period covered in this book the assistance given to mothers in caring for their children by the Soviet state has been less than that afforded by the British authorities. Before the mid-1960s this was true even of the urban population, since it was only at that date that the proportion of the under-7 age-group attending child care facilities reached 28 to 30 per cent. Further, the greater availability of child care facilities in urban areas since that date has been achieved at the expense of women living in rural areas. The facilities provided in the countryside, even in 1970, were equivalent only to a situation in which primary education started at the age of 6.

The figures in Table 9.1 refer to the USSR as a whole; they conceal a considerable diversity of performance among individual republics. In 1970, for instance, the proportion of children under 7 who were enrolled in day-nurseries and kindergartens ranged from 43 per cent in Estonia to as little as 10 per cent in Tadjikistan. Within this range, the order of republics conforms to one's expectations. Also, for the most part, patterns of enrolment are similar for urban and rural areas; that is, if a high proportion of a republic's urban children attended a kindergarten or day-nursery then so did a high proportion of its rural children and vice versa. The major exceptions to this rule seem to have been Byelorussia, Moldavia and Kirgizia where urban attendance was close to the All-Union average while rural figures were well down.

Table 9.2 highlights another aspect of the provision of pre-school child-care in the Soviet Union - its cost and the scale of state subsidisation (although, unfortunately, figures for 1940 appear to be unavailable.) The figures in the table are in nominal terms; that is, no allowance has been made for changes in the price level. It is not clear what effect this has on the conclusions one draws from the table, since it is not clear what the appropriate deflator should be. But the neglect of price-effects probably overstates the magnitude

Table 9.2    *Expenditures on Pre-School Child Care Facilities: USSR, 1950-70*
              *(rubles per year)*

| | Average State Expenditure per Child | | | Kindergarten | | Nurseries | |
|---|---|---|---|---|---|---|---|
| | All | Urban | Rural | State | Parent | State | Parent |
| 1950 | 283·25 | 341·88 | 199·50 | | | | |
| 1955 | 239·89 | 259·15 | 167·97 | 208·55 | 62·97 | 306·78 | 51·54 |
| 1960 | 238·73 | 243·39 | 219·47 | 211·81 | 86·48 | 302·59 | 71·29 |
| 1965 | 287·57 | 300·23 | 234·59 | 273·01 | 87·30 | 349·18 | 71·01 |
| 1970 | 330·88 | 346·08 | 271·86 | 321·04 | 90·72 | 398·39 | 70·70 |

*Sources: Gosudarstvennyi Byudzhet SSSR: byudzhety soyuznykh respublik*,Moscow, 1966, pp. 33–5 and 62–4; ibid., 1972, pp. 39–41 and 68–70 and Table 9.1.

of the decline in quality of service after 1950 and also overstates the improvement that has occurred since 1965. These at least are the implications of using the recently published unofficial cost-of-living index compiled by Schroeder and Severin. (For details of this see McAuley, 1979, p. 326.) Deflating the figures given in the first column of the table by this index, one obtains the following series (figures from Table 9.2 are given for comparison):

|      | Nominal | Real |
|------|---------|------|
| 1950 | 100     | 100  |
| 1955 | 85      | 102  |
| 1960 | 84      | 97   |
| 1965 | 102     | 109  |
| 1970 | 117     | 117  |

These figures imply, then, that the decline in nominal expenditure per child between 1950 and 1955 was paralleled by a decline in costs, resulting in the maintenance of provision standards. After some decline in the next five years, the early 1960s witnessed an improvement; by 1970 total real (or nominal) expenditure per child was some 17 per cent higher than it had been twenty years previously.

Table 9.2 also shows that not only are fewer rural children enrolled in pre-school child care facilities, but less is spent on rural children than on those who live in urban areas. The disparity was greatest in 1950, when the cost per rural child was approximately three-fifths of the cost for urban residents. Over the next decade the disparity closed considerably and in 1960 total expenditure per rural child was as much as 90 per cent of expenditure on urban children. Since then the gap has widened and in both 1965 and 1970 expenditures per rural child were little more than three-quarters of those per urban child.

The second panel in Table 9.2 attempts to measure the extent of the subsidy provided by the Soviet authorities to those parents whose children are enrolled in pre-school child care facilities. In this panel, for the first time, a distinction is made between day-nurseries (for the under-3s) and kindergartens (for the 3–6 age-group). In recent years the Soviet authorities have introduced a number of combined day-nursery/kindergartens; these have been included with kindergartens in the calculations underlying Table 9.2.

In 1955 the state spent an average of 208 rubles per child per year on those enrolled in kindergartens while parents spent an average of 63 rubles. That is, the authorities met between three-quarters and four-fifths of the cost of kindergarten places. Fifteen years later the state's contribution had increased to 321 rubles per year; that of the parents was now 91 rubles. The state was still meeting between three-quarters and four-fifths of the cost of kindergarten provision. As might be expected, both the total cost and state expenditure per child in day-nurseries was higher than in kindergartens. But again, in both 1955 and 1970 parents met approximately the same proportion of the bill – some 14 or 15 per cent in each year. In the early 1960s, parental contributions formed a higher proportion of total cost for both forms of child care.

In point of fact, pre-school child care fees in the Soviet Union are differentiated according to both the type of facility and parental income. A recent source reported that for day-nurseries parents paid between 3·8 and 10 rubles per month while for kindergartens charges ranged from 5 to 12·5 rubles depending upon income (Mamontova, 1973, p. 79). Mamontova also claims that the income scale according to which fees are assessed has remained unchanged since 1948, with the result that the overwhelming majority of parents pay at the top rate. According to a scale of charges, referring to 1957, a fee of 10 rubles per month was payable where parental income exceeded 120 rubles per month (Conquest, 1967, p. 135).[5] Since this apparently refers to total parental income and since it appears that no allowance is made for family size, this would mean that all complete families with two workers would have paid the top rate after 1968 when the minimum wage was raised to 60 rubles a month. Single women earning between 60 and 80 rubles per month, however, would have continued to pay 6·3 rubles, while those earning more than 80 rubles would have paid 8·1 rubles per child. Whether all these figures are consistent or not depends upon the number of months in the year that children attend these institutions, but the figures in Table 9.2 appear to imply that, on reasonable assumptions, a sizeable minority of parents pay less than the maximum.

Finally, almost as an aside, the figures in the table appear to imply that new higher scales of fees were introduced between 1955 and 1960, although I have come across no statement to this effect. Again, by implication, the increase at this time would appear to have been of the order of 35 or 40 per cent. (A new scale of fees would be consistent with the publication of a scale in 1957 that was cited by Conquest.)

The figures given in this section show that although the Soviet authorities have been committed to the principle of pre-school child care for the past forty or fifty years, it is only recently that as many as half of the relevant urban age-cohort has been enrolled in such establishments. Day-nurseries and kindergartens are still uncommon in rural areas. For most of the period covered by this book, a majority of mothers have had to make their own arrangements to see that their children are cared for. This has either involved them in withdrawing from the labour force themselves, or leaving their offspring with an elderly (and usually female) relative – the ubiquitous babushka.

Secondly, child care facilities are relatively expensive. I suspect that an unwillingness or an inability to meet the costs of expanded pre-school child care provision has been a major factor in explaining why so little was done in this direction until the 1960s. And, as I show below, concern over cost is one of the elements that has prompted specialists to advocate alternative policies for the care of children before they go to school.

## Housework and the Services Sector

The fourth area in which state assistance, according to socialist theoreticians, could help women to reconcile the conflicting demands of home and job, was in the development of a modern services sector. This, it was argued, would alleviate the toil and drudgery associated with housework. The persisting shortcomings of consumer services in the USSR are well known; no attempt will be made here to chart the history of the failure of Soviet policy in this area. Rather, attention will be focused on the impact of that failure upon the lives of working women. This will be achieved by an analysis of the results of a series of time-budget studies undertaken by Soviet economists and sociologists at different times in the last half-century.

In these studies, a sample of individuals (almost invariably from urban areas) is asked to record how much time each spends on a variety of activities. Since the studies used here were undertaken at different times by different individuals a comparison of results clearly raises questions of consistency in the classification of different activities. Also, there is the problem of the extent to which the various samples are representative of the behaviour of Soviet men and women in other parts of the country at the time when the study was conducted. To minimise the distortions introduced by these factors, it was decided to concentrate for the most part on a set of time-budget studies that had been collected and analysed in a recent *Soviet Studies* article (Zuzanek, 1979).

In Table 9.3 an attempt is made to measure the amount of time that men and women have spent on work and housework in the Soviet Union at various

Table 9.3    *Time Spent on Work, Housework and Work-Related Activity: Men and Women, 1923/4–1972/3 (hours per week)*

|  |  | Men | | Women | |
|---|---|---|---|---|---|
|  |  | Work and Work-Related Activity | Work, Housework and Work-Related Activity | Work and Work-Related Activity | Work, Housework and Work-Related Activity |
| (1) | 1923–4 | 53·25 | 66·63 | 51·13 | 88·00 |
| (2) | 1930a | 49·72 | 58·91 | 50·32 | 84·68 |
| (3) | 1930b | 53·41* | 63·36* | 54·74* | 87·31* |
| (4) | 1930c | 47·38* | 56·04* | 48·57* | 83·71* |
| (5) | 1936 | 41·00** | 53·00** | 40·00** | 74·00** |
| (6) | 1959 | 61·04 | 80·46 | 57·44 | 89·69 |
| (7) | 1963a | 55·15 | 72·06 | 52·00 | 87·85 |
| (8) | 1963b | 50·15 | 66·49 | 48·42 | 84·04 |
| (9) | 1965 | 46·30* | 60·96* | 44·39* | 79·44* |
| (10) | 1965–8 | 53·17 | 70·84 | 49·50 | 82·67 |
| (11) | 1967–70 | 41·00** | 51·00** | 38·00** | 65·00** |
| (12) | 1972–3 | 44·69** | 74·59** | 40·66** | 77·78** |

*Notes:* Entries marked with a single asterisk include only travel-time among time expenditures connected with work.

Entries marked with a double asterisk include no explicit allowance for travel-time and other work-related activities (and may not include allowance for overtime, etc.).

Row (2) refers to a sample of trade unionists in the Moscow region; Rows (3) and (4) to samples from selected urban centres in European Russia working an 8-hour and 7-hour day respectively. Row (7) refers to a sample from Krasnoyarsk Krai and Row (8) to a sample drawn from four oblasti in the RSFSR.

*Sources:* Rows (1) to (4) and (6) to (10) Zuzanek, 1979, pp. 208–9; Rows (5) and (11) Gordon *et al.*, 1977, p. 153; Row (12) Kulli, 1975, p. 78.

times in the past fifty years. Rows (1) to (4) and (6) to (10) are probably internally consistent, all having been taken from the same source. Rows (5), (11) and (12) come from two different sources and almost certainly are based on different definitions – both between themselves and between each and the rest of the table. They were included largely to give a more up-to-date reference than could be derived from Zuzanek, but their limitations should be borne in mind when interpreting the table.

The figures in Table 9.3 cast light on two questions: on how the burden of work and housework has changed for each sex taken separately over the past half-century; and on the size of the so-called double burden, on the amount of extra time women spend on work, housework and work-related activities. Let us consider men's experience first: in 1923–4 the average urban male in the USSR spent a little more than fifty-three hours per week at work or on work-related activities (principally travel-time); a quarter of a century later, in 1965–8, he was still spending just over fifty-three hours per week on these activities. There is some suggestion that in the intervening period the amount of time spent on work, and so on, may have increased somewhat, but the evidence is confused. The years 1965–8 are the latest for which Zuzanek provides estimates, but the impression of constancy of workload over the period is reinforced by the figures taken from Gordon *et al.*: they show no change in hours worked between 1936 and 1967–70 (although the level of workload differs between the two series). Kulli's figures even suggest an increase in workload in the 1970s, but this is probably misleading. Gordon *et al.* clearly make no allowance for overtime, for travel-time or for second jobs; it is not clear which, if any, of these are included by Kulli.

In 1923–4 men spent an average of thirteen hours per week on housework; a quarter of a century later this had risen to almost eighteen hours, according to the sources cited by Zuzanek. The evidence relating to changes in men's housework burden in the intervening years is confused. Gordon *et al.* do not confirm this finding of a rising housework burden for men; their figures suggest a decline of two hours between 1936 and 1967–70. Kulli, on the other hand, implies that men spent a total of thirty hours per week on housework in the early 1970s – but this probably includes travel-time and moonlighting.

In 1923–4 women spent an average of fifty-one hours per week on work and work-related activities – that is, slightly less than men. A quarter of a century later, in 1965–8, the number of hours spent on work, and so on, had fallen to forty-nine. According to the figures in Table 9.3, only in 1930 did women work longer hours than men. Gordon *et al.* confirm both the fall in women's hours and the fact that women spend less time in paid employment than do men. Kulli also supports this last point.

In 1923–4 women spent an average of thirty-seven hours per week on housework, almost three times as much as men. A quarter of a century later, in 1965–8, women were still spending more than thirty-three hours per week on housework. It should be noted, however, that the figures taken from Gordon *et al.* imply a more substantial reduction in the burden of housework for women than do those of Zuzanek – from thirty-four hours to twenty-seven hours per week between 1936 and 1967–70. Kulli's figures, on the other hand, imply no change between 1923-4 and 1972-3; the total was thirty-seven in both years.

According to the figures in Table 9.3, in 1923-4 women spent some twenty-one hours per week more than men on work, housework and work-related activities. In 1965-8 the disparity had fallen to twelve hours or so. Gordon *et al.* also suggest that before the Second World War women spent some twenty-one hours per week more than men on these activities but suggest that, at the end of the 1960s, the gap between the sexes was wider – fourteen hours per week as opposed to twelve. These figures are clearly of the same order of magnitude. Only Kulli reaches a divergent conclusion. He suggests a disparity of as little as three hours per week. (Perhaps this is a reflection of a fuller accounting for male moonlighting or it may be a consequence of some shortcoming in his sample selection procedure.)

The figures given above indicate that the lion's share of housework in the Soviet Union, as elsewhere, is done by women and that this involves the average woman in some thirty to forty hours work per week. It is this that Soviet sociologists refer to when they speak of the double burden borne by women. More insight into what it is that Soviet women do during their second shift and how patterns of housework have changed during the past half-century is given by Table 9.4. This provides more detail about time allocation in the studies analysed by Zuzanek.

The figures in Table 9.4 suggest that the only category of activity in which women spent less time in 1965-8 than in 1923-4 was the preparation of food. Time spent on cleaning, on laundry, on shopping and the care of children all increased. In all probability these results can be attributed to the general process of urbanisation and modernisation, since they are paralleled by the experience of other countries, and also Soviet divergences from this

Table 9.4    *Changing Patterns of Housework: Women, USSR 1923-68*

|  | Total Housework | Of which: | | | | |
|---|---|---|---|---|---|---|
|  |  | Cooking | Cleaning | Laundry, etc. | Shopping | Children |
| 1923-4 | 36·7 | 18·8 | 2·7 | 5·0 | 1·5* | 3·8 |
| 1930a | 34·4 | 14·2 | 3·7 | 5·7 | 6·2 | 2·5 |
| 1930b | 32·6 | 16·5 | 3·2 | 4·4 | [5·4] | 3·1* |
| 1930c | 35·1 | 16·1 | 4·4 | 4·5 | [5·6] | 4·5 |
| 1959 | 32·2 | 10·8 | 4·6 | 4·6 | 6·0 | 4·2 |
| 1963a | 35·8 | 10·8 | 3·9 | 4·9 | 6·1 | 5·4 |
| 1963b | 35·6 | 9·7 | 4·8 | 8·3 | 5·7 | 4·0 |
| 1965 | 35·0 | 10·1 | 5·8 | 5·6 | 7·4 | 2·7* |
| 1965-8 | 33·2 | 10·3 | 4·5 | 5·8 | 5·8 | 5·8 |

*Source and Notes:* Zuzanek, 1979, pp. 208-9.

Entries marked with an asterisk refer to activities at which men spent more time than women.

Entries in square brackets refer to items calculated by Zuzanek from more detailed data in original sources.

Row (2) refers to a sample of trade unionists in the Moscow region; Rows (3) and (4) to samples from selected urban centres in European Russia working an 8-hour and 7-hour day respectively; Row (7) refers to a sample from Krasnoyarsk krai and Row (8) to a sample drawn from four oblasti in the RSFSR.

pattern. The reduction in time spent on cooking is in part attributable to the greater prevalence of public catering in the 1960s than in the 1920s (factory canteens, school meals, and so on) and in part due to the availability of more modern cooking facilities - gas stoves, and so on. (For more details see Kostyuchenko, 1967, pp. 81-2.) So far as cleaning, laundry, and so on, are concerned, the greater availability of technical aids has probably been offset by higher standards and larger quantities of personal possessions. Similarly, reductions in family size have probably not led to time-savings on child care since changing social attitudes demand that parents spend more time with each child. The fourfold increase in time spent on shopping must be due at least as much to chronic underinvestment in that sector (leading to queues and shortages) as to the fact that Soviet households in the 1960s had more to spend than did their counterparts in the 1920s.

An implicit assumption in much that has been written about the burden of housework in the USSR is that women are forced to do more than their fair share of the chores because men refuse to occupy themselves with what has traditionally been regarded as women's work. There is a lot of truth in this, as the figures in Table 9.5 show, but it may not be the whole story. (A caveat is in order here: the figures in different columns of the table have been taken from different studies and no attempt has been made to ensure that the activities included as housework in each of them are defined consistently. Thus inferences drawn from reading across individual rows should be made with caution if at all. Within individual columns, of course, definitions are consistent.)

Table 9.5   *Variations in Housework with Family Status: USSR, 1959–73 (hours per week)*

| Family Status | (1) 1959 | (2) 1960 | (3) 1970 | (4) 1973 |
|---|---|---|---|---|
| **Women:** | | | | |
| Single | 29·4 | 13·8 | 18·2 | 17·7 |
| Single with children | | 32·0 | | |
| Married without children | | 31·2 | | |
| Married with 1 child | | 42·0 | 34·3 | 30·4 |
| Married with 2 children | 36·1 | 38·6 | | |
| Married with 3 or more children | | 44·7 | | |
| **Men:** | | | | |
| Single | 16·6 | | 9·8 | 5·7 |
| Married without children | | 8·5 | | |
| Married with 1 child | | 14·8 | 14·0 | 12·2 |
| Married with 2 children | | 14·7 | | |
| Married with 3 or more children | | 22·8 | | |

*Sources:* Col. (1) Prudenskii, 1964, p. 319, refers to workers in Krasnoyarsk Krai. The figure for single women may include those with children. Col. (2) Sazonova, 1963, pp. 18 and 21, refers to workers in various factories in the Urals; figures in the table are calculated as the weighted average of hours spent on work-days and rest-days. Col. (3) Velichkene, 1970, p. 97, refers to workers in one factory in Lithuania. Col. (4) Gruzdeva, 1975, p. 96, refers to workers at (six) factories in Taganrog.

The first thing to note about Table 9.5 is that single women appear to spend about twice as much time on housework as single men. This comes out most clearly in Velichkene's figures for 1970 but is also implied by Prudenskii and Gruzdeva; indeed, Gruzdeva suggests that single women spend more than three times as long as single men on household chores. It is not clear whether this disparity reflects the greater demands that mothers place upon their grown-up daughters than their sons who may be living at home or whether it reflects a difference in habits and interests. Both factors probably play a role.

Secondly, the figures in the second and third row of Column (2) suggest that a husband is almost as much of a burden to a woman as is a child. Sazonova records that a single woman with children (most often, presumably, only one) spends an average of thirty-two hours a week on housework; married women without children in her sample spent thirty-one hours a week in this way! At the same time, in so far as it is legitimate to read across rows, marriage results in a decline in the amount of time that men spend on housework – a substantial decline if one uses Prudenskii's figures, more modest if one relies on Velichkene, but a decline all the same.

Finally, Sazonova suggests that there is little increase in the burden of housework for women with the arrival of the second and subsequent children – although one wonders how sensitive these results are to small-sample variance. She also implies that the burden of housework falling on men increases substantially with the arrival of the third child. In this connection, I would conjecture that the apparent fall in the burden of housework, for both men and women, recorded in Table 9.5 owes as much to changes in sample composition (the trend to smaller families) as it does to any real alleviation in the burden borne by adults of a given family size.

The greater responsibilities for running the home shouldered by Soviet women, and the failure of state assistance (or their husbands) in reducing the amount of time they spend on housework, means that women have less time available for other things. Since the amount of time that individuals require for sleep is more or less physiologically determined and does not differ much between the sexes, the burden of adjustment is borne by the category 'free time'. According to the usual Soviet methodology of time-budget studies this includes time spent on study and reading and time spent participating in voluntary and political activities.

Differences between men and women in the amount and allocation of free time in the studies analysed by Zuzanek are given in Table 9.6. The figures in this table show that in 1923–4 men enjoyed an average of thirty hours per week of free time; this figure changed little in the following half-century. In 1923–4 women, on the other hand, enjoyed only seventeen hours per week of free time; forty-five years later this had risen to nineteen hours – still less than two-thirds of the time enjoyed by men. Out of their more restricted ration of free time, women devoted less to two activities that, in Soviet conditions, have an important bearing on social mobility. They have spent less time than men in activities classified as 'social participation', that is, attendance at political meetings, voluntary work, and so forth. They have also spent less time on study and reading. The results of this have already been remarked upon in the analysis of educational attainments of the two sexes in Chapter 8.

Table 9.6    Utilisation of Free Time by Men and Women: 1923/4-1965/8
(hours per week)

| | | Men | | | Women | |
|---|---|---|---|---|---|---|
| | Total | Social Participation | Study, Reading, etc. | Total | Social Participation | Study, Reading, etc. |
| 1923-4 | 30·1 | 2·4 | 11·9 | 16·9 | 2·0 | 3·9 |
| 1930a | 39·1 | 6·1 | 15·0 | 16·3 | 4·2 | 5·4 |
| 1930b | 33·6 | 6·5 | 11·2 | 15·3 | 4·0 | 4·7 |
| 1930c | 39·2 | 6·9 | 12·8 | 17·6 | 3·5 | 6·2 |
| 1959 | 23·0 | 0·3 | 8·1 | 18·6 | 0·4 | 6·0 |
| 1963a | 33·1 | 1·2 | 12·3 | 20·8 | 0·8 | 7·7 |
| 1963b | 32·5 | 1·5 | 8·2 | 19·0 | 1·5 | 3·8 |
| 1965 | 32·1 | 0·8 | 11·5 | 19·0 | 0·5 | 4·9 |
| 1965-8 | 31·0 | 0·8 | 9·2 | 19·0 | 0·5 | 5·8 |

*Note:* In addition to the activities listed, free time includes sport, cinema and theatre-going, radio and television, social visits and 'idling'. See source for more details.
*Source:* Zuzanek, 1979, pp. 208-9.

Undoubtedly, then, the burden of domestic responsibilities has contributed to the persistence of vertical segregation in the Soviet labour market and to continuing earnings inequality.

The failure of the Soviet authorities to develop the availability of consumer services to a level that would permit women to combine the roles of housewife and worker without strain, together with the failure of men as husbands, sons, or fathers to make compensating adjustments in their behaviour has resulted in a substantial overload on working women in the USSR. These failures have combined with shortcomings in Soviet protective legislation and the social welfare system to affect adversely women's performance both as workers and as mothers. It is to these topics that the next chapter is devoted.

## Notes: Chapter 9

1  These are technical terms in Soviet labour practice. Soviet wage scales provide for higher wages to be paid for 'heavy' and 'exceptionally heavy' occupations. In the 1960s the premium for the first category was 10 to 15 per cent, for the second, it was as high as 20 to 30 per cent. I have been unable to find out what premia were paid for these categories in the 1920s and 1930s. For more details see McAuley, 1979, pp. 192-4.

2  A list of the chemicals in whose production or use the employment of women is restricted in the 1978 Regulation was sent to the Royal Chemical Society. Their consultant commented:

Although many of the substances listed are undoubtedly unpleasant, toxic, or otherwise hazardous chemicals, I cannot identify any particular logical pattern running through them and indeed there are many equally obvious candidates for inclusion if general hazard or toxicity were the criteria.

As you know, the recent philosophy in Britain has been quite the reverse of this apparent Soviet one. (Robert Murray, private communication)

Thus it does not appear that the new regulations confine restrictions on the employment of women to those occupations which might pose an exceptional risk to women's menstrual cycle or childbearing.

3   Finally, a puzzle: according to a recent legal text, in 1968, as a concession, pregnant women and those with children under 1 year old, on completing courses of secondary specialist or higher education, were entitled to be assigned to employment at the permanent place of residence of their husband or family. In 1970 the same privilege was extended to those completing graduate work (*Kommentarii* . . . , 1975, p. 556). In fact, this appears to represent a tightening-up of the law, since previously this privilege was available to all married women – at least this is the explanation usually given for the phenomenon of Moscow wives, marriages entered into to obtain a residence permit. But the whole process of graduate distribution is shot through with anomalies and it is unclear what current or past practice is.

4   For this year, an alternative method of calculating the relevant age-cohort is available, using published birth rates and infantile mortality rates for the early 1960s. This approach, though also approximate, confirms the figure given in the table. It implies that 31·27 per cent of the age-cohort attended day-nurseries or kindergartens in 1970.

5   According to this scale, fees were also differentiated between urban and rural areas and varied according to the length of time the child spent in the day-nursery. See Conquest, 1967, p. 135, for details.

*Chapter 10*

# Women as Workers and Mothers: the Impact of Soviet Policy

Socialist theory and Soviet policy require women to combine two social roles if they are to achieve sexual equality - they are expected to be both workers and mothers (wives). The last chapter was devoted to an account of the assistance they are given by the state in fulfilling their obligations. In this one I attempt an assessment of the way that inadequacies in the character and amount of help provided, together with the influence of social attitudes, adversely affect their performance in these roles.

### Women as Workers

The analysis of earlier chapters has shown that Soviet policy has been success-ful in achieving its first aim: the overwhelming majority of women in the USSR are in paid employment. But high levels of female participation have not led to the attainment of sexual equality in the labour market. Women still earn substantially less than men; they tend to work at different jobs than men; where the two sexes work in the same plants or industries, women tend to occupy the subordinate positions. That is, widespread female employment has not resulted in the equalisation of hiring practices or promotion prospects.

Soviet economists and sociologists have attributed these failures in part to managerial prejudice, to the persistence of outmoded social attitudes, and there is undoubtedly some truth in this claim. But an analysis of work per-formance shows that there are differences between the sexes in a number of dimensions. Given the constraints under which the Soviet enterprise operates, these differences might be sufficient to justify managers in their predilection for male employees. In general terms, available evidence suggests that women are less likely than men to leave their jobs - and the reasons they give for leaving differ too. Women are also less likely to be guilty of absenteeism. But women are more prone to take sick leave than men and to spend more time away from their jobs. Also, women are likely to spend longer between jobs when they do quit so that their average work experience is likely to be less. Finally, there is limited evidence of lower performance on the job by women, greater difficulty in meeting the demands placed upon them. Let us look at the evidence for these claims in greater detail.

Although levels of labour turnover in industry have attracted a good deal of attention from labour economists in the past decade or so, there are no official published statistics. Rather, information comes from a variety of academic and semi-official studies of the problem – often based on sample surveys of workers in particular plants, towns, or industries. Unfortunately many of these studies do not distinguish between male and female workers. But where such a distinction is made, the investigator usually reports that women exhibit somewhat lower rates of turnover than men. This was true in Kurman's study of metallurgical and metal-fabricating plants in the Ukraine (Kurman, 1971, p. 69); it was true in Antosenkov and Kuprianova's study of construction and engineering enterprises in Novosibirsk in both 1964 and 1970 (Antosenkov and Kuprianova, 1977, p. 164); it was also true in the NIIT's study of turnover in ten industries in the RSFSR for all sectors except sugar-refining (Danilov, 1973, p. 182; sugar-refining is a seasonal industry that employs a high proportion of temporary workers, presumably women, and a small permanent maintenance staff). On the other hand, Mikhailyuk claims that in her study of a number of enterprises in Odessa women left their jobs more often than men. She also claims that the average number of years employment record for women was only a half to two-thirds that of men (Mikhailyuk, 1970, p. 77). On balance, however, the evidence seems to suggest a lower rate of turnover for women, but all of the above authors also point out that the difference between the sexes in this respect is not large.

A number of the studies referred to above were undertaken to elucidate why such a high proportion of Soviet industrial workers left their jobs. (In the 1960s turnover in industry was running at an annual rate of 20 per cent and total separations at about 30 per cent. This meant that the average Soviet worker spent 3·3 years in one job; it has also been calculated that the average worker spends 3·2 years in the same occupation, 5·6 years in the same sector and moves from one town to another every twelve to fifteen years; Maslova, 1976, p. 34). The above-mentioned studies brought out significant differences in the reasons given by men and women for changing their jobs. In the Novosibirsk study, for example, more than a half of all women gave personal reasons (health, marriage, birth of a child, study) for quitting, while only a third of the men cited these factors (Antosenkov and Kuprianova, 1977, Table 3.1). A similar pattern is evident in an earlier Leningrad study, although differences between the sexes are not so pronounced (Blyakhman *et al.*, 1965, p. 58). Mikhailyuk also comments on the prevalence of domestic reasons among the women who left their jobs in her sample from Odessan enterprises (Mikhailyuk, 1970, p. 77).

On the other hand, it appears that in spite of the fact that women earn less than men, fewer women than men cite dissatisfaction over pay as a reason for leaving. In Novosibirsk in 1970, for example, almost a fifth of men gave this reason while only 5 per cent of women did so. Men were also more likely than women to quit because of dissatisfaction about the quality or quantity of accommodation offered by their enterprise; women, however, cited the absence of places in day-nurseries or kindergartens as a reason for leaving more often than men (Antosenkov and Kuprianova, 1977, Table 3.1). Similar differences were reported in the Leningrad study (Blyakhman *et al.*, 1965, p. 158).

Turning to factors more closely connected with the job: in both Leningrad and Novosibirsk men were more likely than women to cite occupational-qualificational reasons for leaving, that is, dissatisfaction with the job or with the absence of prospects for advancement. Women, on the other hand, more frequently referred to poor working conditions – claiming that their work was physically taxing, dirty, or harmful (Antosenkov and Kuprianova, 1977, Table 3.1; Blyakhman *et al*., 1965, p. 58).

The picture that emerges from these and other studies is that Soviet women, even when employed, are more concerned with domestic responsibilities than are men. (But it appears that it is still in general the man's responsibility to provide housing for the family.) Women still regard their occupations more as a job and less in terms of a career than do men; they are less responsive to questions of career advancement. They are also realistic about their relatively low wages; they do not feel themselves under such strong pressure to seek out opportunities for higher earnings. Finally, there is some suggestion that women (at least those employed in industry and construction) find their jobs physically demanding, that many of them are under some strain.

A number of investigators have also reported that women are less likely than men to be guilty of absenteeism. (Although official figures on absenteeism in industry are published, they are not differentiated by sex; for such information one is forced, once again, to rely upon sample-survey materials.) Since absenteeism is frequently associated with drinking in the Soviet Union, its greater prevalence among men is hardly surprising. Women's absences from work are more often foreseen and thus are classified as 'absent with the consent of management'. (For details see Shishkan, 1976, p. 114; for a counter-example, which should not, I think, be taken too seriously, see Klivets, 1978, p. 11).

The evidence so far suggests that in Soviet conditions women may well constitute a more stable and reliable, if less enthusiastic, workforce than men. But this may be misleading. There is evidence to suggest that they are off sick more frequently than men, both on their own account and in order to look after their children. This will be explored at greater length later in the chapter, but at this time it is worth noting that in the Novosibirsk study of turnover referred to above women cited ill-health as a reason for leaving twice as frequently as men (Antosenkov and Kuprianova, 1977, Table 3.1). Also, in an earlier study (also in Novosibirsk) of workers who had expressed a desire to quit their jobs, a fifth of women referred to the state of their health while only 7 per cent of men did so (Kalmyk, 1970, pp. 210–11).

There is other evidence that indicates that women constitute a less stable workforce than the turnover studies might suggest. A number of inquiries have reported that women much more frequently than men have breaks in their employment records. Most often, though not invariably, these are connected with childbirth or the need to look after sick children. In view of the fact that for the past twenty or twenty-five years women have been able to take up to a year's paid and unpaid leave when they have a baby without incurring a break in their employment record for social security purposes, the prevalence of interruptions must be largely attributable to an insufficiency of pre-school child care places.

Evidence about the prevalence of interruptions in employment for men and women is taken from a number of academic and semi-official studies based on sample surveys. (The Soviet social security authorities do not publish the relevant statistics.) The most comprehensive, and most recent, of these was undertaken by the RSFSR State Committee on the Utilisation of Labour Resources in the early 1970s. It reported that some 10 per cent of men in its sample had breaks in their employment record while 54 per cent of women did so. In more detail, the distribution of women by length of break was as follows (Kotlyar and Turchaninova, 1975, p. 127):

|  | % |
|---|---|
| No break | 46 |
| Up to 1 year | 31 |
| 1–3 years | 12 |
| More than 3 years | 11 |

These figures imply an average break of ten months (nineteen months for those women who in fact have an interruption in their employment record). A similar proportion of women with broken employment was reported in a Leningrad study for 1966, but a rather lower one was given for another in 1970, also in Leningrad (Pimenova, 1966, p. 36; Kharchev and Golod, 1971, p. 37). Of the women in the RSFSR study who had breaks in their employment record, three-quarters of them were attributable to the birth of a child or caring for it. In the two Leningrad samples the proportions were 70 per cent and 75 9 per cent. Finally, the RSFSR study revealed wide regional variations in the prevalence with which women were forced to leave work in order to care for their children: in the Far East almost 60 per cent of women in the sample had breaks for this reason, while in the Central Region the proportion was little more than a fifth. In Ivanovo - the heart of the RSFSR's textile region - it was under 10 per cent.

There is other scattered evidence that supports the contention that women's responsibilities for their families account for a substantial proportion of time lost in industry. One sociologist, for example, claims that half of all days lost due to turnover can be attributed to the lack of pre-school child care facilities (Aitov, 1972, p. 59; this study refers to plants in Ufa). And a number of investigators have reported that women on average spend longer than men out of work when they change jobs.[1] Again, it is claimed that about 70 per cent of women take more than a year off work when they have a baby (Mikhailyuk, 1970, p. 78). Further, some economists predict that as living standards rise, the amount of working time lost by women who prefer to stay home with their children will increase. (See, for example, Antosenkov and Kuprianova, 1977, p. 45.) The necessity to look after children due to the absence of child care facilities or a preference for this mode of activity - at least for a time - may explain the relatively high levels of educational attainment observed among non-employed women in the 1970 Census. (See Shishkan, 1976, p. 79, for details.)

There is another factor which tends to undermine the employability of women in the USSR - or at least to reduce their prospects of promotion in spite of investment in their education and training. By social convention, it is still the case that the husband's job determines the family's place of residence more frequently than the other way around. This sometimes results in women having difficulty in finding work that corresponds to their qualifications or training. Such problems are more common in small towns than in large ones and are more prevalent in the mining and metallurgical towns of the eastern half of the country than in the more densely populated central and western regions (Kalmyk and Silchenko, 1970, p. 132). This factor may contribute to the greater dissatisfaction that women feel about their work and their greater lack of interest in their jobs remarked on by several investigators (Antosenkov and Kalmyk, 1970, p. 69; Aitov, 1972, p. 96). Absence of suitable jobs for men in the textile towns of central Russia, on the other hand, leads to a different problem: the men leave and women find it difficult to find a husband. (On this, see Kotlyar and Turchaninova, 1975.)

Two conclusions emerge from this survey of recent Soviet work on sex differences in work attitudes and performance. First, although the rate of turnover among women is somewhat lower than among men, this may be misleading. Women spend longer between jobs than do men; they are also more likely to take time off through ill-health. They are probably responsible for more than half the time lost in Soviet industry. A major factor in this loss of time is the inadequacy of state support for women in their role as mothers. Absence of pre-school child care facilities forces many women to retire from the labour force when their children arrive. There is also some indication that a proportion of women prefer to stay at home with their children for longer than the official maternity-leave period. (But this may in part be due to the fact that they would otherwise be engaged on work that they do not find particularly satisfying. See below.) The analysis of Chapter 3, however, suggests that these latter effects cannot be very large.

Secondly, women are apparently less likely than men to think of their work as a career. They are often dissatisfied with working conditions. They are less willing to undertake further training. Again, this can be attributed in part to the burden of domestic responsibilities shouldered by the average woman and thus, indirectly, to the lack of development of the services sector and child care facilities. It may also be attributable to the effects of protective legislation and social prejudice in assigning certain jobs as 'women's work'. And, of course, the effects of these are cumulative. If women are confined to monotonous and low-paid work, their commitment to their jobs and their willingness to undertake further training will be low; rather, they will seek personal satisfaction in other areas of their lives. But if women are more pre-occupied by domestic than work concerns, enterprise managers may be unwilling to promote them to more worthwhile jobs, to invest in their training. Rather, they will be confined to monotonous, unskilled and low-paid work. And thus the vicious circle is complete.

Shortcomings in Soviet policy, a failure to invest sufficiently in pre-school child care facilities and, perhaps, an inappropriate approach to protective legislation, together with social prejudice, have combined to frustrate the attainment of sexual inequality in employment. They have also had adverse effects on women in their other social role – that of mothers and wives. These are discussed below.

## Work and Health

In several recent studies of women who work (for the most part, manual workers in industry) attention has been drawn to the physical strain that the interviewees claim is associated with their jobs. More generally, it is suggested that the difficulties of trying to cope with home and job result in women suffering greater ill-health than men. In addition, children in day-nurseries and kindergartens are exposed to greater risks of infection than are those brought up at home. These children's illnesses add to the burden borne by women, leading to absence from work that in turn reduces both family income and the readiness of managers to train women for more rewarding work. Thus, women continue to be employed in menial (but often physically exacting) tasks with adverse effects on their health.

In a recent sociological study women were asked what was the greatest difficulty they experienced in connection with their work. The results are illuminating: 60·6 per cent of those answering the question referred to the great physical strain, *bolshoi fizicheskoi nagruzki*, of their jobs, 15·2 per cent referred to indispositions and feeling unwell, *boleznenost*, and a further 8·5 per cent mentioned time lost through their own or their children's illness. Only 15 per cent of the sample mentioned things like the difficulty of the job, its monotony, the prevalence of overtime, and so on (Levin, 1974, p. 285). In another study almost three-quarters of the female lathe-operators questioned complained of feeling exhausted at the end of their shift while less than half the men questioned mentioned this (Kalmyk and Silchenko, 1970, p. 151). If these results are typical, somewhere between a fifth and a quarter of women working in industry are made physically unwell by the effort of coping with two jobs. Perhaps as many as another three-fifths suffer some degree of strain.

These feelings of overload result in a greater incidence of sick-leave among women than among men (Shishkan, 1976, p. 115; cf. Akademii Nauk UzSSR, 1970, p. 71). It should be pointed out, however, that the scattered Soviet statistics relating to days lost through sickness include those that result from the necessity of having to care for children – a chore that usually falls to the mother. This inequity provoked the following tart comment from one economist (Shishkan, 1976, p. 115):

> Not only the mother, but the father and society have a responsibility for looking after children. Under socialism one might have expected these responsibilities to impinge upon the effectiveness of male labour. However, since this is still better paid, it is usually the mother and not the father who applies for a medical certificate to look after their child.

In fact, I have been able to locate very few statistics on sex differences in morbidity rates among the working population (although there are a number of comments in the literature to the effect that women take more time off than men), but those that exist suggest a significant difference between men and women. From Lithuania in 1965 there is a report of 61·8 cases of illness per 100 workers per year for men and 106·1 cases for women. Since the men who reported sick spent slightly longer off work than the women who did so, this study implied a loss of 12·5 days per male worker per year compared with 19·9 days per woman worker (Velichkene, 1970, p. 96). These figures are somewhat higher than those reported for Novosibirsk in the late 1960s (9·4 days per worker, with women sick more frequently than men) but the incidence of sickness is substantially less; that is, presumably, more Siberian workers were off for a shorter time each (Cherkasov, 1970, p. 131). The sex difference in incidence is also greater than that reported by either Mikhailyuk (referring to 1965) or Belitskaya (referring to 1967) (Mikhailyuk, 1970, p. 89; Belitskaya, 1971, p. 160). But the first of these sets of figures refers to a single factory in Odessa, the second to a single shop in a Leningrad factory. More recently, figures were given that imply that in Latvia the time lost per female worker is a third greater than that lost per man (Tsitse, 1976, p. 9; this figure apparently refers to the Latvian economy as a whole and not just to manufacturing). Finally, it has been claimed that 'Lithuanian doctors have established that women fall sick twice as frequently as men, and women with children half as frequently again as those without' (Ryurikov, 1976, p. 4).

Unfortunately the most carefully presented of the statistics on morbidity refer to the Baltic states – and these show both the highest incidence of female illness and the greatest disparity between men and women. It may be that female morbidity rises with female participation (which is high in the Baltic area) or it may be that the statistics referring to populations in various Russian towns are based on unrepresentative samples. I believe that the latter explanation contains the greater degree of truth.

The Lithuanian studies referred to above go further than a mere constatation of morbidity rates. They attempt to identify statistically significant regularities. It is reported, for example, that the incidence of sickness increases with age for both sexes; that women are sick more frequently than men and that the difference is significant in every age-group except that from 15 to 24 years. But family circumstances are relevant: in one sample, some 47 per cent of single women and married women without children visited the doctor during the survey period while 63 per cent of women with children did so – apparently on their own account and not for their offspring. More generally, it is claimed that as the number of children in the family increases maternal health deteriorates while paternal health improves. In part this will be a reflection of the health indicator used – the number of medical certificates issued and the number of working days missed. But the authors claim that the greatest incidence of sickness is among bachelors under the age of 24 years. (All the statistics in this paragraph are taken from Velichkene, 1970, and Kharchev and Golod, 1971 – themselves quoting unpublished work by the first author.)

Further, a different study claimed to have established a significant difference in morbidity rates between women in manual occupations and white-collar jobs in the textile industry, and this difference remains significant even when the researchers controlled for age and number of children. The same study, however, could find no significant relationship between morbidity and either housing conditions or income (Dolge, 1975, p. 62). The Lithuanian study referred to above failed to establish a significant association between the incidence of sickness and the prevalence of multi-shift working among women; those on a single-shift schedule were indisposed as often as those on three-shift regimes (Velichkene, 1970, p. 96). Thus the widespread dissatisfaction with shiftwork among women in the USSR, commented on in numerous studies, does not always lead to a deterioration in worker health. Finally, modernisation and technological re-equipment does not always lead to an improvement in the health of the labour force. Another study referred to an increase in morbidity after the introduction of automatic looms in a number of plants. This may in part be explained by an increase in norms (and hence workload) for those working on the new equipment (Tolkunova, 1973, p. 444).

Although one would like to obtain more comprehensive statistics on morbidity patterns among men and women in the USSR, I believe that certain tentative conclusions can be drawn from the material presented here. It appears that women lose more days work through ill-health than men. In part, this is conventional sickness, that is, it results from women taking time off more frequently than men to care for sick children, but it appears that, even allowing for this fact, female morbidity rates are higher than male ones. Secondly, the greater incidence of ill-health among women can be attributed in part to the physical strain of their jobs, to unsatisfactory working conditions, and in part to the 'double burden', to the difficulty of combining a full-time job with responsibility for running a home. Soviet reliance on abortion as the primary method of birth control will also contribute to measured differences in the incidence of sick-leave between the sexes. Finally, there is a suggestion that, at least before the mid-1970s, social security provisions for coping with childhood illness were inadequate. That is, it appears that the average duration of a bout of sickness was in excess of three days (the period for which a medical certificate and sick pay were available) with the result that family income and living standards suffered from the loss of the mother's pay. (Since for most families sick pay is provided at two-thirds of previous average earnings, childhood illness is the source of some financial hardship even now that the period for which it is available has been raised to seven days.)

So far in this section attention has been focused on the impact of Soviet social arrangements on the health of men and women. But there is evidence to suggest that effects of these arrangements were felt more widely, that the widespread employment of women may have adversely affected the health of children. This, at least, is the conclusion that emerges from a study of this question undertaken in the 1960s. The empirical results are based on samples of women in the town of Gorkii (working women were probably employed at the Gorkii Automotive Plant) but other Soviet sociologists and economists accept that its conclusions have a wider validity.

The study was unable to identify any substantial ill-effects of maternal employment upon children *in utero*, with the exception of a tendency of babies born to women who worked in plating shops, *tsekhi pokrytia metallov*, to have a below-average birthweight (Slesarev, 1965, p. 130). Differences emerged at the post-natal stage. Working women were much more likely than those who stayed at home to switch to artificial feeding or to opt for early weaning. (Given working conditions at the plant, these women had difficulty in maintaining their milk supply.) And morbidity was higher among bottle-fed babies than among those who remained on the breast (Slesarev, 1965, p. 133; the author reports that about a third of the children in his sample suffered from rickets!). Although the author does not make this point explicitly, the problems experienced by both the babies who were bottle-fed and those who were weaned early are probably due at least as much to inadequacies in the Soviet supply system (quality and availability of formula, of baby-foods, of vitamin supplements, and so on) as to the fact that their mothers worked.

Increased morbidity among the children of working mothers cannot be attributed solely to the adverse effects of job stress and feeding habits, however. These children are also those most likely to be placed in day-nurseries and kindergartens and other research in the 1960s showed that children in pre-school child care facilities fell sick more frequently than those cared for at home. This was particularly marked among babies and toddlers under the age of 18 months or 2 years old. (Litvyakov, 1969, p. 96). In part this can be attributed to the greater exposure of such children to risks of infection at a stage in their lives when their immunity-systems are not fully developed (and this would apply with most force to bottle-fed babies); in part, since married women at least may have had the option of staying at home with their children, one suspects that a disproportionate number of babies in day-nurseries come from poor families living in inadequate housing, and so on. (There is no explicit reference to attempts to control for family circumstances in the studies that report differential morbidity rates for day-nursery and home care.) The higher incidence of illness among children in child care facilities has also been attributed to overcrowding and low standards of care in day-nurseries (Akademii Nauk UzSSR, 1969, p. 158; Litvyakov, 1969, p. 96).

It is difficult to derive a simple statistical measure of the quality of care provided in Soviet day-nurseries, but the evidence available would seem to support this claim. It is known that the wages of those employed in pre-school child care facilities are relatively low; presumably, therefore, such work does not attract the best-qualified women. Also, although the ratio of children to staff is lower now than it was in 1940, it has been rising more or less consistently throughout the postwar period (*NK SSSR*, 1975, p. 674):[2]

*No. of children in day-nurseries per staff-member*

|  | All | Urban | Rural |
|---|---|---|---|
| 1940 | 15·6 | 16·5 | 13·3 |
| 1950 | 12·7 | 12·9 | 11·7 |
| 1960 | 12·8 | 12·9 | 12·6 |
| 1965 | 13·7 | 13·8 | 13·3 |
| 1970 | 14·1 | 14·2 | 13·6 |
| 1975 | 14·3 | 14·4 | 13·9 |

Since these figures include administrators, and since, in recent years at least, some child care facilities have become quite large, implying that administration involves considerable work (in 1975, the average urban pre-school facility, i.e. day-nursery and kindergarten, contained 139 children), the load per supervisor seems quite heavy. One wonders how much care and attention the individual baby or toddler gets when each woman is responsible for looking after fourteen of them.

It is interesting, but may be fortuitous, that official concern about the impact of pre-school child care facilities on children's health in the Soviet Union first surfaced in the 1960s, that is, at the time when, according to the figures given in the last chapter, availability of places in these institutions first became widespread. It is possible that earlier advocacy of the collective care for very small children was based on abstract reasoning with little appreciation of the wider implications of such a policy. Actual experience may have forced a reappraisal. It is more plausible, however, to think that collective care for very young children in the Soviet Union has always had deleterious effects on their health but that the virtual absence of empirical social research under Stalin meant that the authorities remained ignorant of the problem. Official concern then can be attributed to the renaissance of empirical sociology under Khrushchev. All the same, expansion in the scale of provision of day care facilities during the 1960s will have increased the size of the problem.

There is some evidence, then, that high rates of female participation in Soviet conditions have had deleterious effects on the health of both mothers and children. Shortcomings in the development of consumer services, inadequacies in protective legislation, in the social security system and in the network of pre-school child care facilities have resulted in a situation in which women find it difficult to combine the roles of worker and mother. The burden of domestic responsibilities placed upon the working wife is increased by the apparent unwillingness of the husband to share the load. Lack of free time makes it difficult for women with children to invest in the acquisition of skills. As a result, women are to be found disproportionately in low-paid, monotonous and often physically exacting occupations. This situation of overload has contributed to the decline in birth rates that has been a feature of at least the European parts of the USSR in the past few decades. This is taken up below.

## Female Employment and the Birth Rate

In almost all countries urbanisation, modernisation and economic growth are associated with a decline in the birth rate. It is possible that much of the fall in the Soviet Union can be attributed to the influence of these general social changes and not specifically to the high rates of female participation achieved. But a number of Soviet studies in the past ten or twenty years have explored attitudinal changes among women and they seem to imply that one component in the declining rate of population growth in recent years is a conscious attempt by women to restrict family size as a means of reducing the strain that they experience in combining employment with motherhood. Such a reaction has wider economic and social consequences which have been the source of some official concern. Falling birth rates in the past have resulted in the expected stagnation of labour supply for the rest of the century and this may undermine planners' attempts to maintain acceptable rates of growth of output and personal incomes. It also affects the ethnic composition of the Soviet population. Conscious restriction in family size in Soviet conditions means reliance on abortion. Repeated abortions may adversely affect women's health and may have contributed indirectly to a recent increase in peri-natal mortality. Some of these issues are discussed here.

Over the period covered by this book, the Soviet birth rate has fallen by more than half. In 1938–9 there were 139·5 births per 1,000 women of child-bearing age; in 1974–5 there were only 67·8 births. The rate of decline was particularly rapid in the early 1960s: in 1958–9 there were 88·7 births per 1,000 women of childbearing age, while six years later, in 1965–6, there were only 70·8 births (*NK SSSR*, 1975, p. 42). In the last decade or so little of the decline can be attributed to changes in the age-composition of the female population. Between 1965–6 and 1974–5 age-specific birth rates fell for all age-groups except the youngest. A substantial part of this decline can be attributed to a reduction in the number of births per woman – and hence to completed family size. In 1950 some 36 per cent of all births were to women having their third or subsequent child; in 1940 the proportion in this category was presumably even higher. In 1975, in contrast, only 26 per cent of births were to women in this category (*NK SSSR*, 1975, p. 41). The decline in birth rates is much more marked in the RSFSR and other republics in the European part of the country than it is in Central Asia, Kazakhstan and the Transcaucasus. If the results of a study of the relationship between social status and family size in Moscow between 1945 and 1965 can be generalised to the rest of the country, the decline in birth rates can be attributed to the adoption by skilled and unskilled manual women of a family size previously associated with white-collar status. That is, even in the 1940s, educated women in the USSR appear to have practised some restriction in the number of children they gave birth to; in the 1960s their example has been followed by manual workers (Sysenko, 1974, p. 40; for some data on birth rates by social group and occupation see Lapidus, 1979).

There is some evidence to suggest that birth rates were higher among housewives than among working women at virtually all ages in the late 1950s; they were even higher among kolkhoznitsy (*Vestnik statistiki*, 1965, no. 1, p. 92). I have not managed to find more recent data.

A study of couples marrying in Kiev in 1970 revealed that the average desired number of children was 2·03 to 2·10 for men, depending upon income; for women it was lower – 1·98 to 2·05. Between 2 and 5 per cent of the couples questioned did not intend to have children (Chuiko, 1975, pp. 114–15). In so far as these figures can be applied to the population at large, they suggest that desired family size is just about sufficient to secure population replacement. But, of course, desired family size in Central Asia is considerably larger. On the other hand, a number of couples in European parts of the USSR do not have their 'desired' number of children. Several studies have attempted to identify the factors that women claim impede the attainment of their desired number of children. Results from two of these are given in Table 10.1.

In the Moldavian sample the two impediments most commonly mentioned were poor health and inadequate housing; together these accounted for almost two-thirds of the sample. Given the nature of the question asked in

Table 10.1    *Distribution of Reasons Given by Women for not Wanting Another Child (%)*

|  | Moldavia | | | | Okulovka | Mariinskii Posad |
|---|---|---|---|---|---|---|
|  |  | *Those with Children* | | | | |
|  | *All Women* | *1* | *2* | *3+* | | |
| Material circumstances | 12·6 | 4·5 | 12·4 | 16·1 | 23·5 | 29·1 |
| Health | 28·1 | 28·1 | 25·8 | 35·5 | n.a. | n.a. |
| Housing conditions | 35·7 | 42·3 | 35·7 | 29·1 | 12·7 | 12·2 |
| Family relations | 12·2 | 11·3 | 16·3 | 10·2 | n.a. | n.a. |
| Age | 11·4 | 8·0 | 9·0 | 32·2 | n.a. | n.a. |
| Other, including absence of child care facilities | 16·1 | 22·1 | 10·4 | 2·0 | 19·1 | 25·2 |

*Sources and Notes:* Cols (1) to (4) Shishkan, 1976, p. 100; Cols (5) and (6), Khorev, 1972, p. 53.

The entries in Cols (5) and (6) were taken from a table listing improvements that women would like to see if they were to have their desired number of children, this is why entries do not sum to 100 per cent.

Entries in last row of Cols (5) and (6) refer only to availability of pre-school child care facilities.

Mariinskii Posad is in the Chuvash ASSR.

the small RSFSR towns, health was not mentioned, but some women complained of poor housing. The women in Moldavia also indicated that Soviet families find it a financial strain to have more than one child; material circumstances were mentioned by a quarter of the women questioned in the two RSFSR towns. Between a sixth and a fifth of the women questioned expressed dissatisfaction with the availability of pre-school child care facilities. The fact that the number of women mentioning this problem falls with the number of existing children reflects, I think, an acceptance by the women concerned of the necessity to stay at home with their children rather than the existence of some policy giving priority in the allocation of places to mothers with two or more children.

The discussion of the previous section indicated that attempting to combine motherhood with paid employment has had deleterious effects on the health of many women in the Soviet Union. This is confirmed by the figures in Table 10.1; the table also emphasises the importance of women's wages to the family budget and the cost that giving up work to care for children would impose. This is brought out by answers to a question in another survey: women in Leningrad in the early 1960s were asked why they worked and 54 per cent of them said that it was because of the necessity for supplementing the family budget (Golod, 1969, p. 31). The same answer was given by more than 40 per cent of women workers in a number of Ivanovo textile mills in the early 1970s (Morozov and Kurnosova, 1975, p. 38). On the other hand, only 9 per cent of women in another Leningrad sample said that they would give up work altogether if material circumstances allowed (Pimenova, 1966, p. 38), and only 16 per cent of the brides in the Kiev sample referred to above said that they would like to devote themselves solely to the care of their baby on the birth of a first child (Chuiko, 1975, p. 124; but more than half said that they would prefer part-time work, ibid., pp. 122-3).

This material suggests that women's motives for working are mixed. It is not only financial necessity that drives Soviet women into the labour market; rather, they also derive other satisfaction from their work. But for many families the arrival of a second or subsequent child would impose some financial hardship, a hardship that would be accentuated if the wife were to stop working. At the same time, the burden of domestic responsibility increases as the number of children increase. Women are aware of this and would like to reduce their overall workload by finding a part-time job (or at least a substantial proportion of Soviet women would appear to find this an attractive option). But the Soviet economy provides relatively few opportunities for part-time work. Women are thus faced with a choice between staying at home and suffering financial hardship, staying in full-time employment and suffering from overwork, or not having a second or subsequent child. Some Soviet women have chosen the third option.

The inadequacy of the Soviet housing supply in terms of quality and, perhaps more important, in terms of quantity is well known and will not be elaborated upon here. The figures in Table 10.1 suggest that the housing shortage may have contributed to a decline in the birth rate; those in Table 10.2 indicate that the nature of the causal link is more complicated than might at first glance be supposed. The table contains two crude indicators of the adequacy of housing supply in the Soviet Union, both based on the amount of space per person. In terms of these indicators (and even the so-

Table 10.2   *Adequacy of Soviet Housing Supply: 1940-75*

|  | Actual Housing Stock as Percentage of Need | | | |
|  | Total | | Urban | |
|  | Minimum | Rational | Minimum | Rational |
| 1940 | 55 | 33 | 66 | 39 |
| 1950 | 60 | 35 | 75 | 44 |
| 1960 | 72 | 45 | 94 | 56 |
| 1970 | 95 | 56 | 111 | 65 |
| 1975 |  |  | 120 | 71 |

*Sources and Notes:* Cols (1) and (2) Revaikin, 1974, p. 112; Cols (3) and (4) derived by applying the space norms implicit in Revaikin's figures to the urban population and comparing with actual urban housing stock. Housing stock figures from *NK SSSR*, 1963, p. 515, and *NK SSSR*, 1975, p. 576.
The minimum need is based on a norm of $10 \cdot 1$ m$^2$ per person.
The rational need is based on a norm of $17 \cdot 2$ m$^2$ of total (useful) space per person.

called rational norm only allows a modest 12 feet by about 13, including hallways, kitchens, etc., per person) the adequacy of housing in the USSR has increased steadily since 1940. At the same time the birth rate has declined. Either individual expectations have increased more rapidly than the availability of space, or space alone does not capture subjective perceptions of adequacy at all well – after all, it makes no allowance for the availability of amenities.

In so far as Soviet women decide to restrict the size of their families, there is little choice among contraceptive techniques. The pill is not widely available, nor are intra-uterine devices. Other, less certain methods are used but there is heavy reliance on abortion. This operation was legalised soon after the revolution, prohibited in 1936 and made legal again in 1956. Statistics on the prevalence of abortions are not readily available but the following figures (from Sokolova, 1970, p. 39) give some idea of the frequency with which Soviet women have recourse to this operation:

*Outcomes of Pregnancies in Leningrad Oblast (% of total)*

|      | Live Birth | Still Birth | Abortion | Other | Total |
|------|------------|-------------|----------|-------|-------|
| 1963 | 21·11      | 0·32        | 77·88    | 0·69  | 100·0 |
| 1965 | 20·41      | 0·28        | 78·74    | 0·57  | 100·0 |
| 1966 | 20·00      | 0·26        | 78·97    | 0·77  | 100·0 |
| 1967 | 19·92      | 0·25        | 79·08    | 0·75  | 100·0 |

Again, on the basis of a sample of women aged 40–46 years in Tbilisi in 1960, it was reported that of the average of 11·9 conceptions per woman, 3·6 resulted in a live birth, 0·5 terminated in a spontaneous abortion and 7·8 were terminated by an induced abortion (Tsitsishvili, 1967, p. 44). Two comments are in order here: Georgia is an area with a relatively high birth rate and most of the reproductive lives of the women in this sample would have fallen in the period when abortion was illegal. It is to be expected that abortion rates in the RSFSR in more recent years would be higher.

Another inquiry, based on interviews with a sample of women having abortions in a number of towns in the RSFSR in 1958–9, reported an incidence of 10·55 abortions per 100 working women per year (and 4·15 abortions per 100 non-working women per year) (Sadvokasova, 1968, p. 212). On the basis of very crude calculations, these figures imply that the number of abortions and the number of live births per 1,000 women aged 15–49 years are approximately the same. Either there was an extremely rapid increase in the frequency with which women resorted to abortion in the 1960s, or the figures quoted for Leningrad oblast above are atypically high. It is true that the birth rate fell rapidly between 1959 and 1965, but I suspect that the latter conjecture is the more true. Although he does not give an explicit figure for the incidence of abortions, Kharchev also claims that working women are 2·5 times more likely than housewives to resort to the operation (Kharchev and Golod, 1971, p. 88). This does not appear to be implied by Ryabushkin's figures, however; but the form in which these are presented makes any direct calculation and comparison impossible (Ryabushkin, 1966, p. 139).

There is also some evidence to suggest that abortion is used as a means of avoiding increases in the burden of domestic responsibilities borne by Soviet women. Sadvokasova claims that married women are much more likely than single ones to resort to abortion (Sadvokasova, 1968, p. 211). Another study reported on the outcomes of unwanted pregnancies (the interviewees were female manual workers in a number of Moscow factories): if the woman had no child, some 22 per cent of unwanted pregnancies resulted in a birth, if she had one child, this dropped to 3 per cent and with two or more children none of the women in the sample went on to have a baby (Belova and Darskii, 1968, p. 33).

Sadvokasova also suggests that, on the basis of her investigations, some 4 to 6 per cent of women abort their first pregnancy, and perhaps as many as 15 per cent of women in urban areas have more than one abortion a year (Sadvokasova, 1968, p. 212).

Sadvokasova herself has expressed concern over the possible consequences to women's health of the frequency with which women resort to abortions (1968, p. 222):

This operation [abortion] frequently leads to serious immediate and distant complications, adversely affecting menstruation, the course of the next pregnancy, and sometimes leading to secondary infertility. Further, repeated abortions can serve as a cause of prematurity and foetal abnormalities in subsequent pregnancies.

I am not competent to pass judgement on the adequacy of the medical analysis underlying this assessment. But it may serve as a link to the recent rise in infant mortality in the USSR which two Western scholars have associated in part with an increase in the incidence of prematurity (Davies and Feshbach, 1980, p. 17).

The statistical material presented in this section has been less than authoritative, but in general terms it appears to support the following conclusion. Difficulties in combining the roles of mother and worker, poor housing, income barely adequate to satisfy rising expectations, shortages of pre-school child care facilities, and so forth, have contributed to a decline in the Soviet birth rate. This has been achieved by frequent resort to abortion. Not only has this decline in the birth rate led to an incipient shortage of labour and complicated the task facing economic planners for the rest of the century, but the method by which it has been achieved may have contributed to a rise in infant mortality.

The evidence produced in this chapter adds weight to the doubts that have recently been expressed by Soviet economists and sociologists about the viability of the strategy adopted by the authorities for attaining sexual equality. Participation rates have been high, but women's commitment to their jobs has been undermined by their preoccupation with domestic matters. Women are likely to have less work experience than men of the same age and educational qualifications, to spend more time away from work, to suffer from more ill-health. On the other hand, the widespread employment of women has, arguably, had an adverse effect on the birth rate, on infant mortality and, perhaps, on the general health of the population. The recognition (if not the emergence) of this complex of social and economic problems has resulted in calls for changes in the state's policy towards female employment. This issue is explored at greater length in the concluding chapter.

## Notes: Chapter 10

1 See, for example, Danilov, 1973, p. 205, or Antosenkov and Kuprianova, 1977, p. 191. This result can only partly be explained by the existence of a few women with very long periods of unemployment, since it is Soviet practice when calculating the average time spent between jobs to exclude all those who have been without work for more than 180 days on the grounds that they can be presumed to have left the labour force.

2 The table in the statistical handbook from which these figures were taken includes a note which states that, in 1975, in addition to the staff listed, some 144,000 medically qualified child supervisors, *meditsinskie sestry-vospitateli*, were employed in day-nurseries. What this means is unclear. If they were full-time employees, the child/supervisor ratio falls to 11·96; but in this case, why were they not included with the regular staff? If their responsibilities are limited to periodic health-checks on the children and general supervision of sanitary standards, the conclusion given above is probably still valid.

*Chapter 11*

# Conclusion

In previous chapters the position of women in the Soviet labour force has been described and an attempt has been made to explore how far the policies pursued by the Soviet government have contributed to the attainment of sexual equality in employment and, to a limited extent, in society at large. In this final chapter I summarise the earlier argument and offer brief suggestions about the likely directions of change in policy over the next ten years or so. I also comment on the reasons why I think the Soviet approach has been only partially successful.

### The Position of Women in the Soviet Labour Force

In so far as sexual inequality can be measured by disparities in earnings, Soviet policy must be adjudged to have failed. In the 1970s the gross earnings of women were some 60 to 65 per cent of those of men. This disparity is of the same order of magnitude as that observed in an industrial economy like Britain; it is somewhat greater than those found in Eastern Europe or in Scandinavia. Further, although available statistics leave much to be desired, there is little to suggest that differences in the earnings of men and women have diminished in the past two decades.

This disparity in earnings cannot be attributed to rate discrimination in any simple sense; to their credit, the Soviet authorities have prohibited this for more than half a century. And, since it is only rate discrimination that Soviet economists and sociologists term sex discrimination, they are able to deny the existence of this latter in the USSR in spite of substantial differences in the earnings of men and women. The disparity in the earnings of the two sexes cannot be ascribed in any large measure to differences in hours worked; part-time employment is very seldom met with in the state sector. On the other hand, women are more likely than men to suffer seasonal unemployment in agriculture and men are the more likely to work overtime or to have second jobs. Also, women are more likely than men to interrupt their employment for domestic reasons. Taken together, these findings suggest that some part of the observed disparity in earnings can be attributed to differential participation in a broader sense. But for the most part disparities must be the result of occupational segregation. A major part of this study has been devoted to an exploration of this phenomenon and of the reasons why Soviet policy has not brought about its diminution.

The policy of rapid industrialisation adopted in 1928 resulted in a substantial increase in the number of women in paid employment. In 1939 female participation rates were high by international standards and they have continued to increase in the past forty years. By the mid-1970s the USSR could claim to have achieved virtual full employment for women – at least in the more industrialised European part of the country. Rising participation rates have resulted in some expansion of occupational choice for women but they have not been accompanied by any reduction in the tendency for men and women to do different jobs. Or rather, while segregation may have fallen among white-collar workers, it appears to have increased among manual non-agricultural employees. Further, women still predominate in occupations that elsewhere are regarded as women's work – the textile trades, garment manufacture and services; they possess fewer industrial skills than men; they are less likely to work with machines. Among white-collar workers and in professional occupations, however, women have made notable gains; although such occupations as nursing or secretarial work are exclusively female in the USSR (as in most other countries), women have penetrated many male occupational preserves. But women are still under-represented in positions in which they might be called upon to exercise managerial authority.

The persistence of occupational segregation in the USSR has been attributed to the operation of the educational system, to the difficulties faced by women in reconciling the twin roles of mother and worker and to limitations on job choice that result from protective legislation. Soviet economists and sociologists have also alluded to the existence of prejudice and discrimination on the part of those in authority.

The educational attainments of both men and women have risen markedly in the past forty years and the gap between the sexes has more or less disappeared. Indeed, young women now have more formal education than their male contemporaries. These developments make it unlikely that persisting differences in earnings can be explained by simple differences in 'human capital'. But women are less likely than men to acquire market-relevant skills. In part this is a consequence of protective legislation which precludes the enrolment of women in courses that would train them for jobs in heavy industry. In part it reflects self-selection by girls and women themselves. That is, probably as a result of social attitudes and pressures, girls are more likely than boys to enrol in courses that provide training for jobs in the less well paid services sector or in light industry – or, finally, to go directly from school to work with no vocational training. In addition, domestic responsibilities make it difficult for women to combine work and study; as a result fewer women than men raise their qualifications in the first ten or fifteen years of their working lives.

Soviet labour law and social security regulations contain a number of provisions designed to make it easier for women to combine motherhood and employment. The authorities have also acknowledged that they have an obligation to provide working women with material assistance for domestic work and child care. For much of the Stalin period, however, the law was ignored and its provisions were eroded; its major impact seems to have been to exclude women from those training facilities that would have given them the qualifications necessary for the more skilled jobs. More recently, recodification may have reduced the number of industrial occupations open to women.

Similarly, for much of the period the assistance provided by the social welfare system has been meagre. Only limited resources have been devoted to child care facilities and this has resulted in interruptions in women's employment. The virtual absence of child allowances has meant that, in these circumstances, maternity has often been associated with poverty. For mothers who are employed,  shortcomings in the Soviet trade network and the non-availability of services have resulted in a substantial extra burden. This has been aggravated by the unwillingness of Soviet men to help with domestic chores or to take their share of the responsibility for child care.

The strain of attempting to be both mother and worker has had an adverse effect on the health of employed women in the USSR and this in turn has had an impact on female employment. First, ill-health and domestic pre-occupations reduce the commitment of women to work; they result in sick-leave and higher turnover; they lead some women to choose undemanding jobs. Secondly, they result in a lack of career-orientation, in an unwillingness or an inability to improve skills or seek promotion. The strain of the so-called double burden has also affected women's ability to discharge their second social role. It appears to have been implicated in the fall in birth rates and, possibly, in the recent rise in infant mortality.

The Soviet authorities are faced with a complex of social problems; doubt has been thrown on the viability of the strategy that they have adopted for achieving sexual equality in the labour market; even the high rates of female participation, upon which they have increasingly come to rely, have been called into question. The nature of the alternatives that have been suggested is discussed in the next section.

### A New Policy towards Women's Employment?

Declining birth rates, a rise in infant mortality, evidence that morbidity is higher among working women than men and among children in pre-school child care facilities than among those brought up at home, together with information about the position occupied by women in the economy have convinced specialists and, I believe, the political authorities that Soviet policies towards female employment are inadequate. The experience of the last twenty years has revealed a conflict between the social objectives of a satisfactory rate of population growth (and hence expansion in labour supply) and sexual equality, predicated upon the more or less permanent attachment of women to the labour force.

Essentially, this is the conflict between the two social roles of women and it has always been implicit in Soviet (and, indeed, socialist) strategy. But, previously, it may have been masked by the fact that fewer women were in full-time employment; or adverse effects arising from it may have been rendered socially acceptable by short-term emergencies like the Second World War. But developments in the 1960s and 1970s have resulted in a reassessment of the relative merits of motherhood and female employment and prompted a number of policy debates.

For the most part, academic discussion has focused on the changes in policy necessary to eliminate or alleviate the social problems described in the past two chapters. Lip-service is still paid to the desirability of reconciling the claims of job and family upon a woman's time, but the dominant trend among proposed solutions emphasises a woman's commitment to her children at the expense of her career prospects. This appears to be true, also, of recent innovations in policy. In this sense, then, the Soviet authorities and the Soviet academic community can be said to be pro-natalist.

A major topic of discussion among academic demographers in recent years has been the causes of the decline in the birth rate in European parts of the USSR and what policies the government can adopt to reverse the trend. Attention has centred on the economic factors that, women claim, deter them from having a second or a third child. These are housing, material circumstances and, possibly, the availability of pre-school child care facilities. Little is said about the first of these; the existence of a housing problem in the Soviet Union is widely acknowledged, it is admitted by planners and no new policy initiative seems to offer the promise of a speedy solution. Similarly, an increase in the availability of day-nursery places does not amount to a new policy and, in any case, raises the question of morbidity among young children. Consequently, the emphasis has been on the introduction of new financial incentives for motherhood.

Two alternative approaches to the question of additional financial incentives for motherhood have been canvassed: the reorganisation of child allowances and an increase in paid maternity-leave. The present Soviet system of child allowances provides cash payments effectively only for the fourth and subsequent children; the amounts provided have not been changed since the late 1940s and are thus out of proportion with current income levels and the cost of additional children to the family budget. Since most women who marry have one child, it is argued that child allowances should be paid for the second and third children. It is suggested that the prospect of a modest payment for the fourth child does not and cannot offset the deterrent effects of a real reduction in per capita family income occasioned by the arrival of the second. Further, it is pointed out that two or three children per family are sufficient to ensure population replacement or even a modest rate of growth.

The case for a reorganisation of the family allowance system has recently been argued by the eminent Soviet demographer Boris Urlanis (1976, pp. 68–71) but there has, as yet, been no sign that the authorities are ready to adopt such a policy. Urlanis claims that there is opposition to child allowances in some quarters on the grounds that they undermine work incentives[1] and this may partly explain why more attention has been paid to the second approach mentioned above.

In the past ten or twenty years labour economists, sociologists and demographers have raised the question of the length of time that it is desirable that a mother should spend with her child after its birth. Estimates vary, but most would agree with the following statement: 'in any case one can say that a year is the minimum period for which a mother should be with her child. It would be more correct to speak of two or even three years.'[2] Withdrawal from the labour force for this period will result in a fall in family income. It also has implications for a woman's career prospects and for the demand for places in day-nurseries.

In order to cushion the family against this decline in income – and thus encourage more women to stay at home with their children – a number of specialists have advocated the introduction of cash benefits for women payable after the expiry of their official maternity-leave (that is, the fifty-six days post-partum leave for which they now receive full pay). In this context the example of Hungary is cited with approval. But in the Soviet case it has been suggested that these payments would be more effective if they were made proportional to forgone earnings rather than as a fixed ruble amount (Urlanis, 1976, p. 72). Such a system would also accord more closely with the socialist principle of distribution. The introduction of these payments, it is argued, would contribute to an increase in the birth rate in two ways. First, it would reduce the immediate financial hardship associated with the birth of a child and thus induce more working women to contemplate the possibility of a second or subsequent child. Secondly, by enabling more women to spend more time as housewives, it is hoped that they might be induced to exhibit demographic behaviour characteristic of this social group.

There is some evidence in recent policy innovations that the authorities too favour a reduction in the permanence of women's attachment to the labour force although it is not clear whether they see this as contributing primarily to an increase in the birth rate or to a reduction in childhood morbidity. In 1968 women were given the right to retain their jobs as well as an unbroken employment record for social security purposes if they remained at home until their child's first birthday. In the early 1970s levels of maternity pay were raised, and the conditions on which sick pay was available to women who stayed at home to care for children were liberalised. Both of these measures will have improved the financial position of families with small children. The introduction of the family income supplement also has reduced the compulsion felt by women in some families to return to work as soon as possible after the birth of a child. The impact of all these measures has been indirect, so their intention is unclear. But a decision of the Twenty-Fifth Party Congress (1976) promised to introduce 'partially paid leave for working women who remain at home with their children for their first year' (cited from Urlanis, 1976, p. 68). More recently, it has been stated that these benefits will be introduced in the next (Eleventh) Five-Year Plan period (Rzhanitsyna, 1979, p. 64). Also, both the Twenty-Fifth Party Congress and the directives of the Tenth Five-Year Plan (1976–80) promised to increase the availability of part-time employment and putting-out work for women (Urlanis, 1976, p. 68; Rzhanitsyna, 1979, p. 66). These clearly indicate a desire to facilitate if not to encourage more women to stay at home with their children.

At the same time, economists have pointed out that the introduction of such payments for women would be less costly than a further expansion in the network of day-nurseries, and more effective in reducing the incidence of childhood diseases than attempts to improve the quality of existing facilities. (See, for example, Sakharova, 1973, p. 72; Litvyakov, 1969, p. 96.) All of this would seem to suggest that the Soviet authorities are in the process of adopting a policy in which a majority of women withdraw from the labour force for a year or more after the birth of a child. Indeed, Sergeeva and Litvyakov suggest that this is already the case (ibid., p. 97).

The recent emphasis on financial incentives for motherhood, both in the academic literature and in policy innovations, betokens, I believe, something of a revision in Soviet priorities. There is less weight attached to the desirability of ensuring proper career structures for women and more to the desirability of providing suitable conditions for women to discharge their reproductive functions. Or, rather, official policy is somewhat less committed than previously to securing equality of access to employment opportunities for both sexes. Recent changes in the ambit of protective legislation, in so far as they close off rewarding careers to women, should be seen as further evidence for this change.

I do not want to suggest that the changes in Soviet policy or priorities have been substantial. It is not a case of adoption of a substantially new scale of values, of a return to primacy for domestic virtues, but more of a (subtle) change in relative priorities. All the same, it has provoked opposition. Shishkan, for example, while recognising that conditions in day-nurseries at present lead to a higher incidence of sickness among the children of working mothers, does not draw the conclusion that these institutions should be phased out. Rather, she suggests, they should be reorganised; resources devoted to pre-school child care should be increased, if necessary by increasing the fees charged to parents. In this way, the health of children could be improved at the same time as women retained their attachment to the labour force. She has also objected to economists, sociologists and demographers who, directly or indirectly, advocate a reduction in female employment in the interests of raising the birth rate (Shishkan, 1976, pp. 84 and 88). Her views are shared by a number of other women. They are convinced of the over-riding importance of the fullest possible participation by women in paid employment as a precondition for sexual equality.[3]

### Sexual Inequality and Soviet Theory[4]

As a result of their analysis of the causes of sexual inequality, Soviet policy-makers have attached great importance to women's participation in paid employment as a means of overcoming it. This official emphasis on participation has been complemented by two further sets of policies: the law has been used to regulate the terms and conditions of female employment; and resources have been devoted to the education of women and to the provision of services designed to facilitate the reconciliation of employment and maternity.

But the Soviet experience with this approach suggests that, unless social conditions are suitable, legislation guaranteeing equality of opportunity for women will not in itself lead to a reduction in occupational segregation. Further, if it is the case that men and women do different jobs, legislation prohibiting rate discrimination will not result in the elimination of disparities in earnings. Rather, in so far as separate male and female labour markets exist, wage relativities in each will be determined independently of conditions in the other. In such circumstances a policy of increased female participation, by making the supply of female labour more elastic, may well result in increased earnings inequality. This effect is likely to be strengthened if, as a result of concern for women's reproductive functions or out of a possibly misplaced paternalism, women are precluded by law from undertaking certain jobs or working in certain conditions.

In fact, the Soviet record with regard to both protective legislation and the supply of services in the past half-century has been mixed. But shortcomings are likely to have been mutually offsetting to a certain degree. Thus, I do not think that one can attribute the failure of the Soviet authorities to achieve sexual equality only to the fact that the resources committed to this purpose have been insufficient. It is possible, even likely, that disparities in earnings would have persisted even if the labour law had been observed under Stalin and if planners had devoted more resources to the provision of welfare benefits and other services. That is, I believe that reasons for the failure of Soviet policy can be found at the level of Soviet theory.

As pointed out in Chapter 1, Marx and Engels believed that the family lay at the root of the problem of sexual inequality under capitalism. But they suggested that, with the abolition of private property in the means of production, the bourgeois family would lose its *raison d'être*; it would no longer need to function as a vehicle for the administration and inter-generational transmission of capital. However, neither Marx nor Engels was explicit about what would follow, about how the family would evolve under conditions of socialism. Some attempt was made by Soviet socialists in the 1920s to suggest that the nuclear family should be replaced by socialised child care and residential communes. Such suggestions received little popular support at the time and little further thought has been devoted to the problem in the past half-century. This, I think, is a crucial flaw. Unless this issue is thought out, it is unlikely that state policy will be able to resolve the conflict between employment and maternity that so many women face; indeed, policies of the Soviet type may well accentuate occupational segregation and its consequent inequality.

The Soviet authorities in the 1920s retreated from the idea of communal living and socialised child care partly on grounds of cost. But also, I believe, a majority of the population at that time found such a solution unattractive. (This is surely true of the rural population which made up four-fifths of the total and is probably true of a majority of workers. Residential communes exercised greatest appeal for intellectuals.) Further, in the 1920s, the Soviet government was faced with the problem of caring for a large number of orphan children, the flotsam of war, civil war and revolution, and despite the undoubted success of the methods advocated by Makarenko, the general opinion was that such (enforced) socialised upbringing was inferior to that provided by a 'real' family. Finally, the social conservatism of individual Soviet leaders should not be neglected; the idea of family life appealed to many of them – as it had, I believe, to Marx and Engels.

In any case, either consciously or by default, a decision was taken in the early 1930s (if not in 1926) to preserve and strengthen the nuclear family. This was to be the vehicle through which children would be raised, consumption organised and, often, the problems of the elderly resolved. And such a decision is consistent with the broad outlines of socialist theory.

It must be recognised, however, that unless there are changes in the intra-familial division of labour, unless men's attitudes to housework and domestic responsibility change, such a decision in conjunction with an emphasis on female participation is likely to produce symptoms of strain. It will result in a double burden on women as has in fact been observed in the USSR. Its consequences for social life may well be similar too.

Further, it implies a naive economic determinism to believe that male attitudes will change automatically, rapidly and painlessly as a consequence of the socialist revolution, the expropriation of private capital, as was recognised at the Third Comintern Congress in 1921 (see above p. 5). On the contrary, male attitudes towards the domestic sphere probably enjoy a certain autonomy; in the absence of an explicit programme of re-socialisation they may persist for a considerable period of time. No such re-socialisation campaign accompanied the Soviet decision to strengthen the family and, although individual sociologists have suggested recently that something might be done in this direction, I believe such a programme to be unlikely in the near future (if only because it would run counter to the embourgeoisification of Soviet values that took place under Stalin; on this latter see Dunham, 1979).

Any substantial change in the position of women in the Soviet economy and in Soviet society requires, I believe, a change in male attitudes as well as (or rather than) changes in resource allocation priorities. Such a new direction to policy is unlikely to occur in the absence of an autonomous women's movement. As Marx wrote more than a century ago, 'jeder, der etwas von der Geschichte weiss, weiss auch, dass grosse geselschaftliche Umwälzungen ohne das weibliche Ferment unmöglich sind' (*Werke*, 1965, p. 582).[5]

More general Soviet attitudes to the role of the Communist Party and the possibility of independent political organisation by interest groups within the society probably rule out such a development in the short term. But it is not only a question of repression or suppression. As I have pointed out at various times in the course of this book, there are academic economists and sociologists in the USSR who view the position of women in their country with concern, who are critical of the inadequacies of past and present Soviet policies in this area. Their writings have done something to bring home to policy-makers the nature and extent of these shortcomings. On the other hand, there is less ground for supposing that this recent academic work has had the effect of clarifying and articulating the inchoate dissatisfactions of ordinary women. Yet, even in the USSR, the articulation of discontent is probably a precondition for radical changes in policy. Judging from the outside, it seems that Soviet women have not yet achieved the state of self-awareness necessary for the active expression of dissatisfaction with their position in society. Until that happens, I fear that they will remain less equal than men.

## Notes: Chapter 11

1   Urlanis, 1976, p. 71; in fact he states that some people consider that child allowances conflict with the principle of distribution according to labour, *narushaet printsip oplaty po trudu*. The role of this principle in Soviet attitudes to distribution and redistribution is discussed at greater length in McAuley, 1980b. There is some evidence that fears about the impact of the availability of cash grants on work incentives delayed the introduction of the family income supplement. For details see McAuley, 1977.

2   Urlanis, 1976, p. 71; Kuprienko favours a year (1976, p. 36), Sergeeva opts for 1·5 to 2 years, as do Kotlyar and Turchaninova (Litvyakov, 1969, p. 98; Kotlyar and Turchaninova, 1975, p. 15).

3   On the other hand, Shishkan at least is in favour of an expansion in part-time employment for married women; she would also like to see a reduction in the number of women employed in physically exacting (but often relatively well paid) jobs in the construction industry.

4   Some of the ideas advanced in this section are discussed at greater length in Maxine Molyneux's paper 'Women's emancipation under socialism: a model for the Third World', and I am grateful to her for letting me read an early draft of this.

5   Anyone who knows anything about history also knows that great social progress is impossible without the active participation of women.

# Bibliography

N. A. Aitov, *Tekhnicheskii progress i dvizhenie rabochikh kadrov*, Moscow, 1972.
A. K., 'Demograficheskaya problema: zanyatost zhenshchin i rozhdaemost', *Voprosy Ekonomiki*, no. 5, 1969, pp. 157–9.
Akademii Nauk MSSR, *Sotsialno-ekonomicheskie problemy trudovykh resursov*, Kishinev, 1971.
Akademii Nauk TuSSR, *Raspredelenie i ispolzovanie trudovykh resursov Turkmenskoi SSR*, Ashkhabad, 1971.
Akademii Nauk UzSSR, *Trudovye resursy Uzbekistana: problemy raspredelenia i ispolzovania*, Tashkent, 1970.
Akademii Nauk UzSSR, *Regionalnye problemy vosproizvodstva rabochei sily v Uzbekistane*, Tashkent, 1976.
E. G. Antosenkov (ed.), *Opyt issledovania peremeny truda v promyshlennosti*, Novosibirsk, 1969.
E. G. Antosenkov and V. A. Kalmyk (eds), *Otnoshenie k trudu i tekuchest kadrov*, Novosibirsk, 1970.
E. G. Antosenkov and Z. V. Kuprianova, *Tendentsii v tekuchesti kadrov (dinamicheskii aspekt analiza)*, Novosibirsk, 1977.
E. G. Antosenkov and T. A. Silchenko, 'Ekonomiko-statisticheskii analiz professionalnogo sostava uvolivshikhsya rabochikh', in E. G. Antosenkov, 1969, pp. 88–114.
Y. V. Arutyunyan (ed.), *Sotsialnoe i natsionalnoe*, Moscow, 1973.
D. Atkinson, A. Dallin and G. W. Lapidus (eds), *Women in Russia*, Stanford, Calif., 1977.
G. Baldwin, *Projections of the Population of the USSR and Eight Subdivisions by Age and Sex: 1973 to 2000*, US Department of Commerce (Bureau of the Census), P-91, No. 24, Washington, DC, 1975.
G. Barker, 'La femme en Union soviétique', *Sociologie et Sociétés*, vol. IV, no. 2, pp. 159–91.
S. Bekhodzgaeva, *Zhenskii trud v promyshlennosti Kirgizii*, Frunze, 1965.
E. Ya. Belitskaya, 'K voprosu ob izuchenii zabolevaemosti promyshlennykh rabochikh (opyt mediko-sanitarnoi chasti Leningradskogo Metallurgicheskogo Zavoda im. XXII S'ezda KPSS)', in *Voprosy sanitarnoi i meditsinskoi statistiki* (Uchenie zapiski po statistiki No. S–3), Moscow, 1971, pp. 153–68.
V. S. Belova, *Reshenie zhenskogo voprosa v SSSR*, Moscow, 1975.
V. Belova and L. Darskii, 'Mnenia zhenshchin o formirovanii sem'i' *Vestnik Statistiki*, no. 8, 1968.
S. Benet (ed.), *The Village of Viriatino*, New York, 1970.
V. Bilshai, *Reshenie zhenskogo voprosa v SSSR*, Moscow, 1959.
L. S. Blyakhman, A. G. Zdravomyslov and O. I. Shkaratan, *Dvizhenie rabochei sily na promyshlennykh predpriatii*, Moscow, 1965.
E. Boserup, *Women's Role in Economic Development*, New York, 1970.
*Bulleten finansovogo i khozyaistvennogo zakonodatelsva*, 1933, no. 47.
*Bulleten Gosudarstvennogo Komiteta SSSR po trudu i sotsialnymi voprosami*, no. 12, 1978.

M. Butenschon, 'Frauenemanzipation in der UdSSR: Anspruch i Wirklichkeit', *Osteuropa*, vol. 27, nos 2 and 3, 1977.

J. G. Chapman' 'Equal pay for equal work?', in D. Atkinson *et al.*, 1977.

*Chelovek i ego rabota*, Moscow, 1967.

G. Cherkasov, *Sotsiologia truda i profsoyuzy*, Moscow, 1970.

G. Cherkasov, 'Sotsialnye problemy zhenskogo truda v SSSR v usloviakh razvitogo sotsializme', in *Vlianie . . .* , 1975.

B. Chiplin and P. Sloane, *Sex Discrimination in the Labour Market*, London, 1976.

P. M. Chirikov, *Reshenie zhenskogo voprosa v SSSR, 1917–1937gg*, Moscow, 1978.

L. V. Chuiko, *Braki i razvody*, Moscow, 1975.

V. Ya. Churakov, *Aktualnye problemy ispolzovania trudovykh resursov sela*, Moscow, 1972.

R. Conquest (ed.), *Industrial Workers in the USSR*, London, 1967.

L. M. Danilov, *Dvizhenie rabochikh kadrov v promyshlennosti*, Moscow, 1973.

E. Z. Danilova, *Sotsialnye problemy truda zhenshchiny-rabotnitsy*, Moscow, 1968.

E. Z. Danilova, 'Sotsialnaya rol zhenshchiny-materi', in *Dinamika . . .* , Moscow, 1972. pp. 41–7.

C. D. Davis and M. S. Feshbach, *Rising Infant Mortality in the USSR in the 1970s*, United States Department of Commerce, Bureau of the Census, P-95, No. 74, Washington, DC, 1980.

N. De Witt, *Education and Professional Employment in the USSR*, Washington, DC, 1961.

*Dinamika izmenenia polozhenia zhenshchiny i sem'ya*, 3 vols (Sovetskaya Sotsiologicheskaya Assosiatsia, Institut konkretnykh sotsialnykh issledovanii, Akademii Nauk, SSSR), Moscow, 1972.

N. T. Dodge, *Women in the Soviet Economy*, Baltimore, Md, 1966.

N. T. Dodge, 'Recruitment and the quality of the Soviet agricultural labor force', in J. Millar (ed.), *The Soviet Rural Community*, Urbana, Ill., 1971.

N. T. Dodge, 'The role of women in the Soviet economy', in NATO, *Economic Aspects of Life in the USSR*, Brussels, 1975.

N. T. Dodge, 'Women in the professions', in D. Atkinson *et al.*, 1977.

N. T. Dodge and M. Feshbach, 'The role of women in Soviet agriculture', in J. Karcz (ed.), *Soviet and East European Agriculture*, Berkeley, Calif., 1967, pp. 265–305.

N. V. Dolge, 'Sotsialno-gigienicheskie aspekty izuchenia professionalnykh i semeinobytovykh faktorov formirovania vremenoi netrudospsobnosti tkachikh i pryadilshchits', in *Vlianie . . .* , 1975.

V. Dunham, *In Stalin's Time*, Cambridge, England, 1979.

B. Farnsworth, 'Bolshevik alternatives and the Soviet family: the 1926 Marriage Law debate', in D. Atkinson *et al.*, 1977, pp. 139–66.

M. Fedorova, 'Ispolzovanie zhenskogo truda v selskom khozyaistve', *Voprosy Ekonomiki*, no. 12, 1975, pp. 55–64.

M. G. Field and K. I. Flynn, 'Worker, mother, housewife: Soviet women today', in G. H. Seward and R. C. Williamson (eds), *Sex Roles in Changing Society*, New York, 1970, pp. 257–84.

V. I. Filipov, K. M. Smirnov and D. A. Matelenok, 'Osnovnye napravlenia sovershenstvovania uslovii zhenskogo truda v mashinostroitelnoi i elektro-tekhnicheskoi otraslyakh promyshlennosti', in *Vlianie . . .* , 1975, pp. 74–8.

M. Fogarty, R. Rapoport and R. N. Rapoport, *Sex, Career and Family*, London, 1971.

S. F. Frolov, D. Ya. Dmiterko and V. B. Yuzhina, 'Sovershenstvovanie struktury trudovykh kollektivov v otraslyakh narodnogo khozyaistva s preimushchestvennym ispolzovaniem zhenskogo truda', in *Vlianie* ..., 1975.

V. R. Fuchs, 'A note on sex segregation in professional occupations', *Explorations in Economic Research*, vol. 2, 1975, pp. 105–11.

M. Galenson, *Women and Work: An International Comparison*, Ithaca, NY, 1973.

E. Ginsberg, 'The job problem', *Scientific American*, November 1977, pp. 43–51.

M. Power Goldberg, 'Women in the Soviet economy', *The Review of Radical Political Economics*, July 1972, pp. 60–74.

S. I. Golod, 'Zhenskii trud i sem'ya: rezultaty sotsiologicheskogo issledovania "dvoinoi" roli zhenshchiny v obshchestve', *Nauka i Tekhnika* (Riga), no. 11, 1969.

L. A. Gordon and E. V. Klopov, 'Nekotorye problemy sotsialnoi struktury Sovetskogo rabochego klassa', in O. Yanitskii (ed.), *Urbanizatsia i rabochii klass v usloviakh nauchno-tekhnicheskoi revolutsii* (Akademii Nauk, Institut Mezhdunarodnogo rabochego dvizhenia), Moscow, 1970, pp. 191–211.

L. A. Gordon, E. V. Klopov and L. A. Onikov, *Cherty sotsialisticheskogo obraza zhizni: byt gorodskikh rabochikh vchera, segodnya, zavtra*, Moscow, 1977.

E. S. Gorodetskii and P. V. Savchenko, *Sochetanie urovnya oplaty truda i obshchestvennye fondy potreblenia v kolkhozakh*, Moscow, 1974.

E. B. Gruzdeva, 'Osobennosti obraza zhizni intellegentnykh rabochikh' *Rabochii klass i sovremennyi mir*, no. 2, March–April 1975.

C. Hakim, 'Sexual divisions within the labour force: occupational segregation', *Department of Employment Gazette*, November 1978.

F. Halle, *Women in Soviet Russia*, London, 1934.

A. Heitlinger, *Women and State Socialism*, London, 1979.

S. Jacoby, *Inside Soviet Schools*, New York, 1975.

V. A. Kalmyk, 'K voprosu modelirovania tekuchesti rabochei sily', in E. G. Antosenkov, 1969, pp. 130–59.

V. A. Kalmyk and T. A. Silchenko, 'Sotsialno-ekonomicheskaya obuslovlennost otnoshenia k mestu raboty', in E. G. Antosenkov and V. A. Kalmyk, 1970.

L. G. Kamovich and O. V. Kozlovskaya, Sotsialnye razlichia sredi rabotnikov umstvennogo truda na promyshlennom predpriattii', in *Sotsialnye razlichia i ikh preodolenie*, Sverdlovsk, 1969.

E. I. Kapustin, 'Tarifnaya sistema i ee rol v organizatsii i regulirovanii zarabotnoi platy', in A. P. Volkov (ed.), *Trud i zarabotnaya plata*, 2nd edn, Moscow, 1974, pp. 247–73.

A. Kh. Karapetyan, 'Nekotorye voprosy statistiki dokhodov rabochikh i sluzhashchikh', in I. Yu. Pisarev (ed.), *Metodologicheskie voprosy izuchenia urovnya zhizni trudyashchikhsya*, Moscow, 1959, pp. 52–85.

E. V. Kasimovskii (ed.), *Trudovye resursy: formirovanie i ispolzovanie*, Moscow, 1975.

A. G. Kharchev, *Brak i sem'ya v SSSR*, Moscow, 1964.

A. G. Kharchev and S. I. Golod, *Professionalnaya rabota zhenshchin i sem'ya*,

Leningrad, 1971.

A. G. Kharchev and S. I. Golod, 'The two roles of Russian working women in an Urban area', in A. Michel (ed.), *Family Issues of Employed Women in Europe and America*, Leiden, 1971, pp. 32–42.

B. S. Khorev (ed.), *Malyi gorod: sotsialno-demograficheskoe issledovanie nebolshogo goroda*, Moscow, 1972.

J. E. King, *Women and Work: Sex Differences in Society* (Department of Employment Manpower Paper No. 10), London, 1974.

L. Kirsch, *Soviet Wages*, Cambridge, Mass., 1972.

P. Klivets, 'Kak my sebya vedem . . . ', *Literaturnaya Gazeta*, no. 31, 2 August 1978, p. 11.

*Kommentarii k zakonodatelstvu o trude*, Moscow, 1975.

*Kommunisticheskii internatsional v dokumentakh, 1919-1932gg*, Moscow, 1933.

D. L. Konstantinovskii, *Dinamika professionalnykh orientatsii molodezhi Sibiri*, Novosibirsk, 1977.

V. P. Korchagin, *Trudovye resursy v usloviakh nauchno-tekhnicheskoi revolutsii*, Moscow, 1974.

V. G. Kostakov and P. P. Litvyakov, *Balans truda (soderzhanie i metodika razrabotki)*, Moscow, 1965; 2nd edn 1970.

A. E. Kotlyar, 'Metodologicheskie voprosy izuchenia struktury zanyatosti po polu v territorialnom razreze', in A. Z. Maikov, 1973, pp. 400-34.

A. E. Kotlyar and I. Kirpa, 'Demograficheskie aspekty zanyatosti v gorodakh raznymi promyshlennymi strukturami, *Vestnik Statistiki*, no. 7, 1972, pp. 12-18.

A. E. Kotlyar and A. Shlemin, 'Problemy ratsionalnoi zanyatosti zhenshchin', *Sotsialisticheskii Trud*, no. 7, 1974, pp. 110-19.

A. E. Kotlyar and S. Ya. Turchaninova, *Zanyatost zhenshchin v proizvodstve*, Moscow, 1975.

A. E. Kotlyar, S. Ya. Turchaninova, T. N. Kudryavtseva, G. I. Savina and Yu. M. Lukashuk, 'Professionalno-otraslevaya struktura zanyatosti zhenshchin v promyshlennosti RSFSR', in A. Z. Maikov, 1973, pp. 379-99.

G. Kotov and V. Kvachev, 'Vyravnivanie ekonomicheskikh uslovii khozyaistvovanii', *Ekonomika selskogo khozyaistva*, no. 7, 1976, pp. 86-90.

V. I. Kozachenko, 'Iz opyta konkretnogo sotsialno-ekonomicheskogo izuchenia trudovykh resursov kolkhozov', in A. N. MSSR, 1971, pp. 3-31.

V. V. Ksenofonteva, 'Career plans of 8th and 9th grade students and their realisation', in M. N. Rutkevich, 1969, pp. 46-55.

V. S. Kulikov, *Rol finansov v povyshenii blagosostoyania Sovetskogo naroda*, Moscow, 1972.

K. Kulli, 'Ispolzovanie nerabochego vremeni trudyashchikhsya i problema raspredelenia obshchestvennogo truda', in *Vosproizvodstva rabochei sily i effektivnost truda pri sotsializme*, Tallin, 1975, pp. 73-82.

L. P. Kuprienko, *Vlianie urovnya zhizni na raspredelenie trudovykh resursov*, Moscow, 1976.

M. V. Kurman, *Dvizhenie rabochikh kadrov promyshlennogo predpriatia*, Moscow, 1971.

A. L. Labzin, 'Stroitelstvo kommunizma i ustranenie ostatkov neravenstva v polozhenii zhenshchiny', *Filosofskie Nauki*, no. 1, 1965, pp. 98-106.

G. W. Lapidus, 'USSR women at work: changing patterns', *Industrial Relations*, vol. 14, no. 2, 1975a, pp. 178-95.

G. W. Lapidus, 'Political mobilisation, participation and leadership: women in Soviet politics', *Comparative Politics*, vol. 8, no. 1, 1975b, pp. 90-118.

G. W. Lapidus, 'Occupational segregation and public policy: a comparative analysis of American and Soviet patterns', in B. Blaxall *et al.* (eds), *Women and the Workplace*, New York, 1976, pp. 119-36.

G. W. Lapidus, *Women in Soviet Society*, Berkeley, Calif., 1978.

G. W. Lapidus, 'The female industrial labor force', in A. Kahan and B. Ruble (eds), *Industrial Labor in the USSR*, New York, 1979.

L. Lennon, 'Women in the USSR', *Problems of Communism*, no. 20, July–August 1970.

B. M. Levin, *Sotsialno-ekonomicheskie potrebnosti: zakonomernosti formirovania i razvitia*, Moscow, 1974.

G. I. Litvinova and N. V. Popova, 'Istoricheskii opyt reshenia zhenskogo voprosa v SSSR', *Voprosy Istorii*, no. 11, 1975, pp. 3-18.

P. P. Litvyakov (ed.), *Demograficheskie problemy zanyatosti*, Moscow, 1969.

A. S. Lysakova, 'O zavershayushchim etape reshenia zhenskogo voprosa v SSSR', in *Chelovek, trud i byt* (Uchenye zapiski Svedlovskogo Pedagogicheskogo Instituta), Sverdlovsk, 1967, pp. 87-96.

A. McAuley, *Soviet anti-poverty policy, 1955-1975'*, Institute for Research on Poverty, University of Wisconsin, Madison, Wis., Discussion Paper 402-77 (mimeo.), 1977 (also issued as a University of Essex Economics Department Discussion Paper, 1978).

A. McAuley, *Economic Welfare in the Soviet Union*, London and Madison, Wis., 1979.

A. McAuley, 'Personal income in the USSR: republican variations in 1974', in NATO *Regional Development in the USSR: Trends and Prospects*, Newtonville, Mass., 1980a, pp. 41-59.

A. McAuley, 'Social welfare under socialism: a study of Soviet attitudes towards redistribution', in D. Collard, J. Lecomber and N. Slater (eds), *Income Distribution: The Limits to Redistribution*, Colston Research Symposium No. 31, Bristol, 1980b.

A. McAuley and A. Helgeson, 'Soviet labour supply and manpower utilisation, 1963-2000', University of Essex (mimeo.), 1978.

L. Mackie and P. Patullo, *Women at Work*, London, 1977.

V. F. Maier, *Dokhody naselenia i rost blagosostoyania naroda*, Moscow, 1968.

A. Z. Maikov, (ed.), *Problemy ratsionalnogo ispolzovania trudovykh resursov*, Moscow, 1973.

A. Z. Maikov and A. G. Novitskii, *Problemy nepolnogo rabochego vremeni i zanyatost naselenie*, Moscow, 1975.

G. A. Mailybaeva, *Zhenshchina i obshchestvennoe proizvodstvo (na materialakh Kazakhstana)*, Alma Ata, 1975.

T. I. Mamontova, 'Povyshenie roli obshchestvennykh fondov potrebleniia v reshenii sotsialnykh problem', in G. S. Sarkisyan (ed.), *Dokhody trudyashchikhsya i sotsialnye problemy urovnya zhizni naselenia SSSR*, Moscow, 1973, pp. 56-81.

W. Mandel, 'Soviet women and their self-image', *Science and Society*, Fall 1971.

W. Mandel, 'Soviet women in the work force and professions', *American Behavioural Scientist*, no. 14, November–December 1971, pp. 255-80.

W. Mandel, *Soviet Women*, New York, 1975.

E. Manevich, 'Ways of improving the utilisation of manpower', *Problems of Economics*, June 1974, pp. 3-23.

K. Marx, *The Communist Manifesto*, Moscow, 1955.

K. Marx, *The Critique of the Gotha Program*, New York, 1967.

K. Marx, *Werke*, Vol. 35, Berlin, 1965.

P. P. Maslov, 'Dopolnitelnye dokhody rabochikh', in I. Yu. Pisarev (ed.), *Voprosy povyshenia urovnya zhizni trudyashchikhsya*, Moscow, 1959.

I. S. Maslova, *Ekonomicheskie voprosy pereraspredelenia rabochei sily pri sotsializme*, Moscow, 1976.

G. Massel, *The Surrogate Proletariat*, Princeton, NJ, 1974.

J. Michal, 'An alternative approach to measuring income inequality in Eastern Europe', in Z. M. Fallenbuchl (ed.), *Economic Development in the Soviet Union and Eastern Europe*, Vol. I, New York, 1975, pp. 256–75.

V. B. Mikhailyuk, 'O meste zhenskogo truda v obshchestvennom proizvodstve', in *Upravlenie proizvodstvom i organizatsia truda*, Moscow, 1967.

V. B. Mikhailyuk, *Ispolzovanie zhenskogo truda v narodnom khozyaistve*, Moscow, 1970.

M. Molyneux, 'Women's emancipation under socialism: a model for the Third World' (mimeo.), 1980.

J. R. Moroney, 'Do women earn less under capitalism?', *Economic Journal*, vol. 89, no. 355, September 1979, pp. 601–13.

G. B. Morozov and I. L. Kurnosova, 'Trudovaya deatelnost zhenshchin i faktory vliayushchie na udovletverennost trudom v usloviakh sotsialisticheskogo obshchestva', in *Vlianie . . .*, 1975.

W. Moskoff, 'An estimate of the Soviet male–female income gap', *ACES Bulletin*, vol. XVI, no. 2, Fall 1974, pp. 21–31.

E. Nash, 'The status of women in the USSR', *Monthly Labor Review*, June 1970, pp. 39–44.

A. V. Netsenko, *Sotsialno-ekonomicheskie problemy svobodnogo vremeni pri sotsializme*, Leningrad, 1975.

J. Newth, 'Demographic developments', in A. H. Brown and M. Kaser (eds), *The Soviet Union since the Fall of Khrushchev*, London, 1975.

E. E. Novikova, V. S. Yazykova and Z. A. Yankova, *Zhenshchina, trud, semya*, Moscow, 1978.

V. M. Novozhenyuk, 'Nekotorye sotsialno-ekonomicheskie problemy zhenskogo truda v selskom khozyaistve', in A. N. Grzhegorzhevskii, L. N. Revin and G. Ya. Frolov (eds), *Proizvoditelnost truda: faktory i rezervy rosta*, Moscow, 1971, pp. 208–32.

G. Ofer, A. Vinokur and Y. Bar-Chaim, *Family Budget Survey of Soviet Emigrants in the Soviet Union* (Soviet and East European Research Center, Hebrew University, Research Paper No. 32), Jerusalem, 1979.

M. Pankin, 'L'goty zhenshchinam-rabotnitsam i sluzhashchim', *Sotsialisticheskii Trud*, no. 3, 1969, pp. 135–40.

Yu. P. Petrov, 'The formation of career plans in school', in M. N. Rutkevich, 1969, pp. 37–45.

A. L. Pimenova, 'Sem'ya i perspektivy razvitia obshchestvennogo truda zhenshchin pri sotsializme', *Filosofskie Nauki*, no. 3, 1966, pp. 35–43.

A. L. Pimenova, 'Novyi byt i stanovlenie vnutrisemeinogo ravenstva', *Sotsialnye Issledovania vyp.*, 7, 1971, pp. 34–46.

A. L. Pimenova, *Svobodnoe vremya v sotsialisticheskom obshchestve*, Moscow, 1974.

*Problemy trudovykh resursov Kabardino-Balkarskoi ASSR*, Nal'chik, 1975.

G. A. Prudenskii, *Vremya i trud*, Moscow, 1964.

N. E. Rabkina and N. M. Rimashevskaya, *Osnovy differentsiatsii zarabotnoi platy i dokhodov naselenia*, Moscow, 1972.

B. V. Rakitskii, *Obshchestvennye fondy potreblenia kak ekonomicheskaya kategoria*, Moscow, 1967.

A. Rashin, *Sostav fabrichno-zavodskogo proletariata*, Moscow, 1930.

F. N. Rekunov and N. A. Shlapak, 'The career plans of graduates of rural schools', in M. N. Rutkevich, 1969, pp. 104–15.

A. S. Revaikin, *Neobkhodimyi produkt, ego velichina i struktura pri sotsializme*, Petrozavodsk, 1974.

N. Rogovskii, 'Ratsionalno ispolzovat trudovye resursy', *Planovoe Khozyaistvo*, no. 11, 1973, pp. 16–23.

N. Rogovskii, 'Sovershenstvovat podgotovku rabochikh', *Kommunist*, no. 16, 1976, pp. 51–60.

M. Schwartz Rosenhan, 'Images of male and female in children's readers', in D. Atkinson, 1977, pp. 293–306.

E. S. Rusanov, *Raspredelenie i ispolzovanie trudovykh resursov SSSR*, Moscow, 1971.

M. N. Rutkevich (ed.), *The Career Plans of Youth*, White Plains, NY, 1969.

T. V. Ryabushkin, *Problemy demograficheskoi statistiki*, Moscow, 1966.

Yu. Ryurikov, 'Zolushki i koroli', *Trud*, 23 October 1976, p. 4.

Yu. Ryurikov, 'Deti i obshchestvo', *Voprosy Filosofii*, no. 4, 1977, pp. 111–21.

L. Rzhanitsyna, 'Aktualnye problemy zhenskogo truda v SSSR', *Sotsialisticheskii Trud*, no. 3, 1979, pp. 58–67.

M. P. Sacks, *Women's Work in Soviet Russia*, New York, 1976.

E. A. Sadvokasova, 'Rol aborta v osushchestvlenii soznatelnogo materinstva v SSSR', in T. V. Ryabushkin (ed.), *Izuchenie vosproizvodstva naselenia*, Moscow, 1968, pp. 207–24.

N. A. Sakharova, *Optimalnye vozmozhnosti ispolzovania zhenskogo truda v sfere obshchestvennogo proizvodstva*, Kiev, 1973.

O. K. Sazonova, *Perekhod k kommunizmu i problema obobshchestvlenia domashnego khozyaistva*, Moscow, 1965.

*Sbornik zakonodatelnykh aktov o trude*, Moscow, 1961.

S. Schwartz, *Labor in the Soviet Union*, London, 1953.

H. Scott, *Women and Socialism*, 2nd edn, London, 1976.

G. Sergeeva, 'Spetsifika zhenskogo truda i ego rol v ekonomike SSSR', *Ekonomicheskie Nauki*, no. 10, 1968, pp. 10–18.

G. Sergeeva, 'Trud zhenshchin v SSSR', *Planovoe Khozyaistvo*, no. 11, 1975, pp. 103–10.

J. P. Shapiro, 'The politicization of Soviet women: from passivity to protest', *Canadian Slavonic Papers*, vol. XVII, no. 4, Winter 1975, pp. 596–617.

N. M. Shishkan, *Sotsialno-ekonomicheskie problemy zhenskogo truda v gorodakh Moldavii*, Kishinev, 1969.

N. M. Shishkan, 'Nepolnyi rabochii den dlya zhenshchin v usloviakh sotsializma', *Ekonomicheskie Nauki*, no. 8, 1971.

N. M. Shishkan, *Trud zhenshchin v usloviakh razvitogo sotsializma*, Kishinev, 1976.

O. Shkaratan, *Problemy sotsialnoi struktury rabochego klassa SSSR*, Moscow, 1970.

Sh. Shlindman and P. Zvidrin'sh, *Izuchenie rozhdaemosti*, Moscow, 1973.

G. S. Slesarev, *Metodologia sotsiologicheskogo issledovania problem narodonaselenia SSSR*, Moscow, 1965.

G. S. Slesarev and Z. A. Yankova, 'Zhenshchina na promyshlennom predpriatii i v sem'e', in G. V. Osipov and Ya. Shchepanski (eds), *Sotsialnye problemy truda i proizvodstva: Sovetsko-Polskoe sravnitelnoe issledovanie*, Moscow, 1969.

J. Smith, *Women in Soviet Russia*, New York, 1927.

N. S. Sokolova, 'Statisticheskii analiz iskhodov beremennostei', *Zdravookhranenie Rossiiskoi Federatsii*, vol. 14, no. 3, 1970, pp. 38–40.

M. Ya. Sonin, 'Aktualnye sotsialno-ekonomicheskie problemy zanyatosti zhenshchin', in A. Z. Maikov, 1973, pp. 352–78.

V. I. Starodub, *Zhenshchina i obshchestvennyi trud*, Leningrad, 1975.

Ts. A. Stepanyan (ed.), *Rabochii klass SSSR i ego vedushchaya rol v stroitelstve kommunizma*, Moscow, 1975.

S. G. Strumilin, *Nash mir cherez 20 let*, Moscow, 1964, quoted in Urlanis, 1976.

I. A. Sukhachev, 'Tekhnicheskii progress v stroitelstve i problemy uluchshenia uslovia truda zhenshchin', in *Vlianie* . . . , 1975.

B. M. Sukharevskii, 'Zarabotnaya plata v SSSR', in A. P. Volkov (ed.), *Trud i zarabotnaya plata*, 2nd edn, Moscow, 1974, pp. 201–46.

M. Swafford, *Sex Differences in Soviet Earnings*, Vanderbilt University (mimeo.), 1977.

V. Sysenko, 'Differentsiatsia rozhdaemosti v krupnom gorode', in *Demograficheskii analiz rozhdaemosti*, Moscow, 1974, pp. 30–44.

N. G. Tarasov and V. V. Romashchenko, *Stimulirovanie truda i effektivnoe ispolzovanie tekhniki*, Moscow, 1974.

N. I. Tatarinova, *Stroitelstvo kommunizma i trud zhenshchin*, Moscow, 1964.

N. I. Tatarinova, 'Nauchno-tekhnicheskii progress i trud zhenshchin', *Voprosy Ekonomiki*, no. 11, 1973, pp. 57–64.

N. I. Tatarinova, 'Trud zhenshchin v SSSR', *Sotsialisticheskii Trud*, no. 9, 1975, pp. 7–16.

V. I. Tolkunova, *Pravo zhenshchin na trud i ego garantii*, Moscow, 1967.

V. I. Tolkunova, 'K voprosu o ravenstve zhenshchin v trude i bytu pri sotsializme', *Sovetskoe Gosudarstvo i Pravo*, no. 10, 1969.

V. I. Tolkunova, *Sotsialnaya pomoshch i trudovye l'goty zhenshchinam po materinstvu v SSSR*, Moscow, 1973a.

V. I. Tolkunova, 'Pravovye osnovy ispolzovania truda zhenshchin v SSSR', in A. Z. Maikov, 1973(b), pp. 435–52.

V. I. Tolkunova, *Trud zhenshchin*, Moscow, 1973.

A. Tsitse, 'Nasha rabochaya nedelya', *Nauka i Tekhnika* (Riga), no. 1, 1976, pp. 8–10.

D. R. Tsitsishvili, *Besplodnyi brak*, 3 vols, Tbilisi, 1967.

Z. V. Uchastkina, 'Vlianie nauchno-tekhnicheskogo progressa na soderzhanie i uslovia zhenskogo truda v tselyulozno-bumazhnoi promyshlennosti', in *Vlianie* . . . , 1975.

F. Kh. Umetova, 'Povyshenie kulturno-tekhnicheskogo urovnya kolkhoznits', in *Problemy* . . . , 1975, pp. 66–76.

B. Ts. Urlanis, *Narodonaselenie: issledovania, publitsistika*, Moscow, 1976.

I. Velichkene, 'Trud i zdorov'e zhenshchiny-rabotnitsy', in *Problemy byta, braka i sem'i*, Vilnyus, 1970, pp. 95–8.

*Vlianie nauchno-tekhnicheskogo progressa na izmenenia kharaktera zhenskogo truda v usloviakh sotsialisticheskogo obshchestva* (Tezisy dokladov vsesoyuznoi nauchno-prakticheskoi konferentsii), Ivanovo, 1975.

T. Volkova, *A Woman's Place in the USSR* (IMG Pamphlet), London, no date.

P. Wiles, *Economic Institutions Compared*, Oxford, 1977.

*Women in the Soviet Union*, Moscow, 1970.

Z. Yankova, 'O bytovykh rolyakh rabotayushchei zhenshchiny (k probleme osushchestvlenia fakticheskogo ravenstva zhenshchiny s mushchinoi), in

*Problemy byta, braka i sem'i*, Vilnyus, 1970, pp. 42–9.

Z. Yankova, 'Formirovanie lichnosti v bytu', *Sotsialnye Issledovania vyp.*, 7, 1971.

M. Yanowitch, *Social and Economic Inequality in the Soviet Union*, London, 1977.

Z. M. Yuk, *Trud zhenshchiny i sem'ya*, Minsk, 1975.

M. L. Zakharov and V. M. Piskov, *Sotsialnoe obespechenie i strakhovanie v SSSR*, Moscow, 1972.

Zh. A. Zayonchkovskaya, 'Obrazovanie i kvalifikatsia kak faktory podvizhnosti i adaptatsii novoselov', in *Urbanizatsia i rabochii klass v usloviyakh nauchno-tekhnicheskoi revolutsii*, Moscow, 1970, pp. 240–54.

J. Zuzanek, 'Time budget trends in the USSR, 1922–1970', *Soviet Studies*, vol. XXXI, no. 2, April 1979, pp. 188–213.

## Statistical Sources

*Gosudarstvennyi byudzhet SSSR i byudzhety soyuznykh respublik*, Moscow, 1966, 1972.

*Itogi vsesoyuznoi perepisi naselenia 1959g*, Moscow, 1962.

*Itogi vsesoyuznoi perepisi naselenia 1970g*, Moscow, 1973.

*Narodnoe khozyaistvo SSSR (statisticheskii ezhegodnik)*, Moscow, various years.

*Narodnoe obrazovanie, nauka i kultura v SSSR*, Moscow, 1971, 1977.

*Sel'skoe khozyaistvo SSSR*, Moscow, 1971.

*Trud v SSSR*, Moscow, 1968.

*Zhenshchiny v SSSR*, Moscow, 1960, 1975.

*Zhenshchiny i deti v SSSR*, Moscow, 1969.

# *Index*

## DATE DUE